Period Matters

Period Matters

Menstruation in South Asia

Edited by

FARAH AHAMED

MACMILLAN

First published in India 2022 by Macmillan
an imprint of Pan Macmillan Publishing India Private Limited
707 Kailash Building
26 K. G. Marg, New Delhi 110001
www.panmacmillan.co.in

Pan Macmillan, The Smithson, 6 Briset St, Farringdon, London EC1M 5NR
Associated companies throughout the world
www.panmacmillan.com

ISBN 978-93-89104-47-9

Typeset in Adobe Caslon Pro by R. Ajith Kumar, New Delhi
Printed and bound in India by Replika Press Pvt. Ltd.

Contents

1   Introduction: Panties with Purpose

FARAH AHAMED

10   I Carry My Uterus in a Small Suitcase

TISHANI DOSHI

11   Menstrual Matters

SHASHI DESHPANDE

18   'Hot Mango Chutney Sauce'

FARAH AHAMED

33   *Kotahalu Mangalya*: Menstruation Traditions and
Practices in Sri Lanka

ZINTHIYA GANESHPANCHAN

40   Raqs-e-Mahvaari: A Menstrual Dance

AMNA MAWAZ KHAN

45   The Christian Women Sweepers of Lahore

AYRA INDRIAS PATRAS

54   What If

FARAH AHAMED

56   *Menstrupedia*: India's Myth-busting Comic
Book Guide

65 An Activist's Fight for Dignified Menstruation
    in Nepal
    RADHA PAUDEL

72 Anandi: India's First and Only Certified
    Compostable and Biodegradable Pad

81 Periods Are Never Easy: Coping with Menstruation
    in Afghanistan
    MARIAM SIAR

87 Red Dye on a Pad: Two Transwomen on Their
    Experience of Menstruation

93 Plea for a Safe Haven
    VICTORIA PATRICK; TR. AMNA MAWAZ KHAN

95 Not Just a Piece of Cloth: A Goonj Initiative

107 My Menstrual Rights Bill: Awakening a Nation
    SHASHI THAROOR

130 Right to Bleed at the Workplace
    RADHIKA RADHAKRISHNAN

140 Blood on My Chair: The Need for Period-friendly
    Workplaces in Bangladesh

152 Behind the Braided Coconut Leaves
    K. MADAVANE, TR. SIBA BARKATAKI

165 Red Nectar of the Sacred Lotus: A Buddhist
    Perspective on Menstruation
    TASHI ZANGMO

175 Aadya Shakti, or Primal Energy
LYLA FREECHILD

179 Increased Period Poverty during Covid-19
in Lahore, Pakistan
AYRA INDRIAS PATRAS

184 The Worst Day of My Life: Menstruation and
Dysphoria

188 Advice for Pliny the Elder, Big Daddy of Mansplainers
TISHANI DOSHI

190 Menstruation in Fiction: The Authorial Gaze
FARAH AHAMED

201 A Caregiver's Perspective on Managing Menstrual
Hygiene
AYRA INDRIAS PATRAS

207 Digitizing Menstruation: Algorithms for
Cleansing Bodies
ALNOOR BHIMANI

216 Bleeding behind Bars: An Account of Menstruation
under Incarceration

221 What Has Dignity Got to Do with Menstrual Health?
MEERA TIWARI

231 Anguish of the Unveiled
VICTORIA PATRICK; TR. AMNA MAWAZ KHAN

235 Cloth, Ash and Blood: Conversations with Homeless
Women about Menstruation

243   Memory and Imagination: Reclaiming Menstruation
         SIBA BARKATAKI

251   Sowing the Seeds of a Menstrual Revolution:
         The First Menstrual Workshop in Balochistan
         GRANAZ BALOCH

260   *Hormo-baha*: Flower of the Body
         SRILEKHA CHAKRABORTY

271   *Homa Istrizia Azan Asan*: Our Women Are Free
         FARAH AHAMED

280   Hothousing: Embracing Menopause at Thirty-seven
         LISA RAY

286   *Biographical Notes*
294   *Copyright Acknowledgements*
296   *Photo and Illustration Credits*
297   *Notes*
317   *Acknowledgements*

Introduction

PANTIES WITH PURPOSE

FARAH AHAMED

MY INTEREST IN THE PROBLEMS FACED BY GIRLS DURING menstruation goes back twenty years, to the time when I was working in East Africa with the Aga Khan Foundation, overseeing their development projects. The Straight Talk Foundation in Uganda sponsored a newspaper supplement focused on raising awareness about HIV/AIDS, reproductive health and child rights, which was published every Friday. It was then that I read how underprivileged girls and women in Uganda managed their menstrual health. Even though I had been working at the grassroots level, that menstrual hygiene management was a problem had never occurred to me before. I had not heard of girls missing school because of a lack of access to menstrual products, poor sanitation and inadequate toilet facilities before this. I was shocked to realize that while the privileged enjoyed the luxury of choice in menstrual products, the poor had none. After that, it took ten years for the idea of taking action to ferment and develop into a concrete plan.

In 2011, my two sisters and I established an informal initiative called Panties with Purpose. Our objective was to promote menstrual health and raise awareness about the detrimental effects of girls in Kenya missing as many as sixty days of school a year because of a lack of access to menstrual products. This was damaging their chances for academic success and compromising their health and well-being. Through our first event, a one-day reproductive health workshop, we aimed to help 1,000 girls and give them underpants and pads.

Our strategy was simple: we would ask donors to give us new cotton underpants. Our reasoning was that if a donor bought a pair of underpants instead of donating cash, they would be more likely to talk about period poverty with their friends. Also, as we were not a registered NGO or a charity, this approach would make it easier for us to manage our operations.

What started as a discussion with family and friends soon spread farther, and we had strangers writing to tell us that they were hosting parties and asking their guests to contribute to our initiative. Organizations reached out saying they were including Panties with Purpose in their corporate social responsibility budget. Schools and colleges in Canada, Australia and the UK told us they were engaging their students in menstrual health debates, with one of them even hosting a menstruation awareness concert where the entry ticket was a packet of pads or underpants. Our target was 4,000 pairs of underpants. Each girl was to receive four pairs, but over the course of two months, we received over 40,000 pairs from sixty cities including Toronto, Mumbai, Sydney and Hong Kong. These were then transported to Kenya with the help of friends and a donation from Virgin Atlantic. Later, in a school in Kibera, Google sponsored our first-ever event on International Women's Day in 2011.

Since then, Panties with Purpose has reached over 16,000 girls and distributed more than 55,000 pairs of underpants and nearly as many pads. Through partnerships with community-based organizations, it has sponsored health education and skills-training workshops across 160 locations in Kenya. These include schools, hospitals, marketplaces, orphanages, prisons and shelters for the homeless and those living with HIV. Additionally, Panties with Purpose has engaged with organizations working in the area of menstrual health and developing environmentally friendly sanitary pad options using local materials such as sisal. We have lobbied for period-friendly schools and workplaces, the distribution of free sanitary pads in schools as well as the removal of the tampon tax. It became evident over these years that menstruation cut across every area of life.

It has been particularly encouraging to witness the gradual but perceptible difference in attitude throughout our network of organizations. For instance, the Kenya-based Ramgarhia Youth Sikh Association, after some initial ambivalence, has now included menstrual products as part of the care packages they send to help the poor around the country. Moreover, younger people are becoming increasingly involved in bringing about change. In Nairobi, my eleven-year-old-niece and her friends speak openly in assembly at their co-ed school about the challenges of period poverty in Kenya. They also regularly raise funds with the help of their peers, with the aim of providing a less fortunate school with a menstrual hygiene workshop, pads and underpants. For boys and girls in school to speak freely about periods and also take an active part in helping another school is a big step forward.

Between 2017 and 2019, while travelling through India and Pakistan, I spoke to girls and women about menstruation and learned about their local values and practices. While some stories were universal and similar to those I had encountered in East Africa, others were specific to their context. While living on the campus of a university in Lahore, I asked female faculty and students about pervasive cultural notions that periods were shameful. In 2019, with the help of a local arts organisation, SAMAAJ, we hosted the first period poverty conference in Pakistan titled 'Everybody's Business, Period'. The discussions ranged from menstruation and disability to period-friendly schools and workplaces, to entrepreneurship endeavours. After that, it took three years of persistent efforts to make the university 'period-friendly'. When I lobbied the senior administration to install vending machines with menstrual products in the women's hostels, the excuses I received included: 'Refilling the vending machines will require male staff to enter the hostels. We can't allow it;' 'The machines will have to be ordered from China and take many months to come, it's too complicated;' 'The washrooms don't have enough space and the women are coping, so what's the need for this?' and finally, 'The machines will be rarely used, it makes no commercial sense.' There was little understanding and compassion towards supporting women during menstruation.

My earliest memory relating to periods goes back to when I was eight years old, growing up in Nairobi, watching Kenyan television. After *Little House on the Prairie* came an advert for Stayfree Maxi Pads. It began with a blonde girl in white jeans riding a bicycle, talking about Stayfree being 'soft and fluffy', and promising girls could be 'free' to do anything they wanted. It showed blue ink from a dropper filling a sanitary pad and ended with the image of two blonde girls on horses galloping into the sunset. I was scared of horses, I didn't have a bike, I wasn't blonde and I had no idea what the blue ink blotting the pad was about. I thought it was some kind of magic potion which girls in other countries took to help them with their sporting activities. Later, I saw one of my older cousins with a packet of Stayfree, and I showed surprise. 'Yes,' she said, laughing as she hid it under her jumper and went to the toilet. I imagined her having a secret life, riding horses and doing all kinds of exciting things which no one in the family knew about. A few years after, my mother showed me a biology textbook and explained all the labelled body parts, preparing me for what lay ahead. But I still couldn't relate to it. Then in my teenage years in the 1980s, at a girls' convent school, my mother wrote a note for my swimming coach, Mr Ali: 'Please excuse Farah from swimming today, as she has female problems.' He read the note and said aloud, in front of everyone, 'Female problems?' And he sent me away to sit alone under a tree in the shade. Some of my friends had not yet started having their period, and they plied me with questions. I was mortified and refused to go to school the next day. This anthology has similar stories of how girls – and boys – learn about menstruation from their mothers, sisters and friends, and how some men only find out about it after marriage.

The idea for this book came to me one afternoon in the summer of 2019 while working on an essay on how menstruation had been portrayed in fiction, by female and male authors. It occurred to me that the diversity of the experience of menstruation could best be reflected in a book which included both fiction and non-fiction. I wrote a proposal with a prospective list of contributors, the well-known and others I had yet to discover, and identified what I would like them to write about and my vision for the book.

My decision to focus on South Asia was motivated by two events. The first is when I was stopped and asked if I was menstruating as I was about to enter a Jain temple in India. The second is when I picked up a packet of sanitary pads while shopping at a supermarket in Pakistan and a male shop attendant rushed over and told me to hide it in a brown bag to avoid being humiliated at the checkout counter. I found both incidents disturbing – being questioned about intimate details of my body by a stranger and having my behaviour in a public space controlled because menstruation was associated with shame. I realized once again how much I had taken for granted.

At the time the book was conceived, I knew only a few of the contributors on my list. But incredibly, every person I approached was willing to participate and share thoughts and ideas. Despite the remote geographies, from the tribal areas of Balochistan in Pakistan, to cities in Nepal, to the fields of India, to the nunneries in the mountains of Bhutan, and to the rough terrains of Afghanistan, the contributors have supported this project with enthusiasm.

Menstruation, despite being a natural, healthy occurrence, is a topic often buried in fear and shame, and its discussion is even taboo in many societies. Historically, in some cultures, men have refused to acknowledge it, in order to maintain a romantic image of women. In others, it is still linked to ritual impurity and lunar madness, while in some communities, it is seen as a sacred time associated with healing, psychic powers and female solidarity. However, over the past few years, there has been a shift towards bringing menstruation and menstrual health out into the open, making this an opportune time for the publication of this book.

This volume carries a breadth of perspectives: those of politicians and policymakers, entrepreneurs, artists, academics, students, nuns, activists, poets, prisoners and the homeless. It provides a glimpse into the way menstruation is viewed by people from different backgrounds, religions and classes. Alongside the well-known artistic and academic contributors are those who are usually missing from the mainstream discussion on the subject. Each essay, artwork, story or poem explores a different aspect of how menstruation is experienced in South Asia.

Tashi Zangmo's essay explores the context of the Buddhist nuns of Bhutan and recounts her ongoing efforts with the Buddhist Nuns Foundation to revolutionize menstrual health in the nunneries. Activist Granaz Baloch explains in her essay how she defied traditional notions of tribal honour, or Baloch mayar, and conducted the first-ever menstrual health workshop in Balochistan. Radha Paudel, who has been working in Nepal over the past thirty years, writes about her mission to have menstrual dignity acknowledged as a human right. Shashi Tharoor relays his radical Menstrual Rights Bill which was tabled in the Lok Sabha in the Indian parliament. Meera Tiwari's research on Uttar Pradesh and Bihar utilizes a 'menstrual dignity framework' to analyze data collected from street theatre performances. Radhika Radhakrishnan puts forward the case for period leave in the workplace, and women from Bangladesh share the difficulties of bleeding in the workplace and at school. Novelist Shashi Deshpande, whose fiction openly mentions menstruation, narrates her own story of menstruation and how she grew out of the shame and misconceptions associated with it.

We hear about the challenges of getting one's period when incarcerated in Pakistan from Erum. Farzana and Chandan relate how mimicking the rituals of menstruation helps them to feel more feminine as transwomen, and Javed, a transman, shares his trauma of dysphoria. In her poems, Victoria Patrick imagines the hardships of the women menstruating during the traumatic days of Partition and the homeless women who have to cope with menstruation without even the most basic of amenities. Srilekha Chakraborty offers her insights into working with India's indigenous Adivasi community. Tishani Doshi shares two poems, one about her relationship with her uterus and the other as a note for mansplainers. Zinthiya Ganeshpanchan looks at how women from the Sri Lankan diaspora practise menstruation rites and rituals. Prachi Jain and Anshu Gupta talk about the NGO Goonj's efforts to help women cope with their periods during natural disasters like cyclones and floods and in the aftermath of communal riots. Ayra Indrias Patras describes how a mother helps her daughter with a mental disability to manage her period and how poor women in Pakistan coped with their periods during the Covid-19 pandemic. She also underlines the case of the female Christian sweeper community of Lahore, who have no access to public washrooms. In a personal essay, Lisa Ray writes about how her illness and the consequent treatment affected her menstrual cycle and triggered an early onset of menopause. Mariam Siar highlights how different her understanding is from other women in Afghanistan, and through a Proustian lens, Siba Barkataki reflects on memory as loss, and how writing about menstruation can be about reclaiming a forgotten part of one's identity. From the Kalasha women in Chitral, Pakistan, we hear about Bashali where they go every month during their period, for solidarity and rest.

My essay on the male and female writer's gaze when writing about menstruation in fiction, reveals how authors either have compassion for their menstruating characters or objectify them. In the two short stories, authored by K. Madavane and myself, we illustrate the obsession and fascination with menstruation which exist simultaneously with feelings of revulsion and unfamiliarity. I was moved to write my story after interviewing homeless women living near a shrine in Multan, and when I watched Meesha Shafi's music video 'Hot Mango Chutney Sauce', after which the story is titled, it felt integral to the story. My poem, 'What If', is based on my observations of the sweeper women in Lahore.

Discussing innovation and entrepreneurship, Aditi Gupta reflects on promoting menstrual literacy among young children across India through Menstrupedia's comic books. Alnoor Bhimani expounds on how period-tracking apps construct the self, and Jaydeep Mandal recounts his journey to creating India's first compostable and biodegradable pad at Aakar Innovations. Apart from writing, menstrala (art inspired by menstruation) plays a powerful part in this anthology: Rupi Kaur's photo essay, reproductions of Anish Kapoor's oil paintings, Lyla FreeChild's menstrual blood art and Shahzia Sikander's neo-miniaturist art, photographs of the wall murals made by young people in Jharkhand and Sarah Naqvi's delicate needlework. And with graceful movements, Amna Mawaz Khan offers a perspective on menstruation through the choreography of her menstrual dance. Each artist, using his or her preferred medium, has shone a light on different aspects of menstruation.

To condense the plurality and complexity of menstruation in a single book is a daunting task, but the originality of *Period Matters* lies in how disparate genres and forms of art and writing in this collection illustrate both the variances and commonality of the experience.

I Carry My Uterus in a Small Suitcase

TISHANI DOSHI

I carry my uterus in a small suitcase
for the day I need to leave it
at the railway station.
Till then I hold on
to my hysteria
and take my
nettle tea
with
gin.

Menstrual Matters

SHASHI DESHPANDE

MY MOTHER NARRATED THIS STORY TO ME IN WHAT NOW seems such a distant past that I am surprised I remember it at all. Time has nibbled, of course, at the edges of the story, but the core of it remains intact. It is the story of the wedding of my mother's older sister. She, the bride, must have been about eleven. Certainly not more, since the rule was that a girl had to be married before her menarche. After the wedding, she continued to stay with her parents until she 'grew up' (one of the many euphemisms for menstruation). Only then was she sent to her husband's home with much éclat, her virginity intact. This wedding I am talking about was a five-day affair, and at some point, during the course of those five days, the bride, to everyone's astonishment and her family's horror, seemed to go wild, running about in a frenzy, not letting anyone get close to her. When she was finally captured, the mystery was solved. She had started her period and had been terrified by the sight of her own blood. Perhaps she thought she was dying and had panicked.

Fast forward some fifty years. Things had changed a great deal. Girls were no longer married so young, they went to school, even to college, if they were lucky and their parents liberal enough. The girl in my next anecdote discovered red in her underwear when she got home from school. She was scared into silence. She had a vague idea of what it might be, but surely it could not happen to her! She was only eleven. She hoped that it was some kind of an aberration and would stop. It didn't. She had no choice then but to tell her mother what had happened. My mother (yes, I was that girl) took my news in her stride and took care of the practical part of it. There were no sanitary pads then. If there were, people who lived in small towns did not know about them and most could not afford them. And therefore, my mother sat at her Singer sewing machine and stitched protective pads out of old, soft cotton saris. These 'pads' had to be washed every day. By me, of course. I hated this part of my five-day ordeal as much as I hated what had happened to me. A mixture of anger and resentment overwhelmed me as I scrubbed at the pads. And helplessness. This would now happen every month, and I would be burdened with the awfulness of it forever and ever. So it seemed to me.

At the time, I had just recovered from a bout of typhoid, and part of the treatment had been starvation. And I had to walk three miles to school and back every day. This was in addition to spending seven hours in a school which had no proper toilets with running water for girls; instead, there was only a kind of hole in the ground for our use. Apart from this lack of sanitation, I had to deal with pain, cramps, bleeding and the constant fear that I had perhaps stained my dress. Without eyes at the back of my head, I could not check for stains, nor could I ask any one of my friends because this blood was not to be talked about. I was surrounded by a halo of silence and shame.

The first time I got my period, I told my mother I would not go to school the next day. She agreed. 'Not go to school?' I heard my father say sharply. 'Is she going to miss school every month now?'

He spoke to my mother, not to me. It was as if a curtain had come down between us and he could not talk to me. Like I was no longer the same girl to whom he had spoken freely until then. In fact, I was no longer a girl. Menstruation is not a rite of passage to adulthood; it is a sharp knife that flashes down, separating the girl from the woman in a moment. But it is only the body that accepts womanhood; the mind remains a girl's mind. Hence the bewilderment, the confusion. There was no one to whom I could talk about this. I could have spoken to my sister, but, though older than me, she had not yet had her first period. None of the girls in school ever spoke of it, either. They seemed so untroubled that I wondered whether I was the only one who suffered this shameful thing. I soon realized then that this was the unspeakable, the unmentionable.

The first time this unspoken agreement of silence was broken was when we were studying a Sanskrit text in our last year of school. We were reading an extract from the Indian epic, the Mahabharata. It was from the dramatic episode in which the Pandava king, Yudhishthira, is tricked into gambling by his Kaurava cousins and loses his kingdom and his four brothers. The desperate king is provoked into staking the common wife of the five Pandava brothers, Draupadi. And he loses her as well. The Kauravas, who wanted the kingdom by hook or by crook, are elated. They send messengers to Draupadi, telling her that she is now their maid, ordering her to come to them. She refuses to go. Finally, one of the Kaurava brothers drags her to the court while Draupadi pleads, 'Don't do this, let me go, let me go, I am ...' The Sanskrit word for 'menstruating woman' used in the epic is *rajasvala*.

What, we asked our Sanskrit master, did it mean? A bashful man who never looked his girl students in the face, he hemmed and hawed and finally said, using a commonly used euphemism for periods, 'She was "sitting out".'

I'd heard this phrase before, at my mother's family home. Like in all orthodox families, women had to 'sit out' three days of their periods. This meant they sat on the ground, sometimes on a small mat, with some essentials including a plate, cup and glass in which they would be served food and water – from a distance, of course. Women were impure during their periods and would pollute anyone or anything they touched. So, they sat in isolation, doing absolutely nothing until the fourth morning when they would be given a bath. After this, they could return to their normal lives. Those who defend traditional practices said that this gave women some much-needed rest. What kind of rest was it, sitting on the ground, leaning against a wall, sleeping on a hard surface? This, while she suffered from cramps, backache, and heavy bleeding too. It was a punishment. It is not surprising that one of the names for menstruation is 'the curse'.

An aunt told me the story of how once, when she was only a girl and was 'sitting out' and needed to go to the toilet, she could not, because there were visitors in the room. She could not appear before strangers at such a time. One of her cousins, a boy, said, 'Come with me,' and, held a sheet in front of her so that she would not be visible to the guest and took her to the toilet. 'I almost died of shame,' she told me. The shame of having to appear before strange men. The shame of having people know what was wrong with her. The shame of having to make her bodily problems public. Girls were made to understand, almost without being told, that menstruation was a very private matter, you could not speak of it, not even to brothers and fathers. And yet it became public when they observed the 'sitting out' custom.

My sister and I were lucky, as our father did not believe in any of these rituals. We never had to seclude ourselves, we were never in the not-to-be-touched state. Yet the shame lingered. Which is why I was excited by the Draupadi story, fascinated by the thought that a woman of those times spoke openly of her period, and it had been recorded in what is almost a sacred book.

In time, the sense of shame receded. It helped that my sister became a student of medicine, and I heard her and her friends speak with candour of their own periods. The subject was no longer taboo. I also came to terms with the idea that there would be a few days each month of which I had to take note if I was planning anything. I kept an eye on the calendar with the same intense interest with which a weatherman watches the approach of a cyclone or a tornado. It certainly helped that sanitary pads came into India when I got older. And after marrying a doctor, I was able to look at menstruation more logically, see it as part of the reproductive process. I could admire the miraculous way in which it worked, the cyclical nature of women's fertility, the almost clockwork-like regularity of the cycle. Menstruation, for me, became the play of hormones in a woman's body, each performing its role, then bowing gracefully out, allowing another to take its place in the dance. Later I read Simone de Beauvoir's words in *The Second Sex*: '[A woman's body] is the prey of a stubborn and foreign life that each month constructs and then tears down a cradle within it ...' Constructing a cradle within a woman's body – what a wonderful idea. In my early writing years, I wrote a short story about a young girl's first experience of menstruation, and how it connected her to her mother to whom she had never felt close to until then. Was this wishful thinking, was I remembering my own severely practical mother who had done what was needed, but had not comforted or made me feel that what had happened to me was not a catastrophe?

Things have indeed changed greatly now. Sanitary pads are advertised with very overt messages of 'absorption' and 'comfort'.

Recently, young women started a campaign to 'demystify' menstruation, speaking openly about it on social media. Have we left the idea of the impurity of women during their periods behind us? Obviously we have not, for we found ourselves, to our surprise, confronted by the same old taboo surrounding menstruation.

In any conversation about menstruation in India, the story of Sabarimala is bound to come up. In 2018, this famous temple in Kerala in southern India was at the centre of the controversy. It is a place which attracts a large number of pilgrims, in spite of the harsh regimen they have to follow before setting out on the pilgrimage. The deity of the temple is a celibate god, one who is said to be unable to bear the presence of women of reproductive ages in his space. For this reason, women between the ages of ten and fifty were not allowed inside the temple. The arguments against allowing women inside the temple were both absurd and abominably sexist: that their presence would defile the temple (it had been purified after the few times women had sneaked in), that male pilgrims would be distracted, and so on. Two women went to the Supreme Court, questioning the ban, which clashed with their constitutional rights to equality and the freedom to worship. And suddenly a woman's menstruation was no longer a mysterious not-to-be-mentioned fact, but right there, out in the open, in the public domain. The Supreme Court held that the ban was illegal, and that treating women as impure because they menstruate was a kind of untouchability and thus untenable.

I remember the furore that followed. Two women decided to enter the temple, and they did it under the protection of a police escort. But when they reached the top (the temple is on a hill), a dense wall of male pilgrims was waiting for them. The opposition to women entering the temple was incredible. Even women had joined the protest. They marched in processions, carrying banners that said: 'Ready to Wait'. This was in reference to the rule that women between the ages of ten and fifty could not enter the temple. The photograph of a man chasing a woman who had managed to reach the top to attack her with pepper spray showed a kind of cruelty which should have no place in a temple. Now, at the time of writing, the matter has gone again to the Supreme Court and a nine-judge bench will soon hear the case. Religion, custom and tradition are invoked in favour of the ban. It is strange that they don't realize the absurdity of it, for religion, custom and tradition have been established by men, the rules of religion have been laid down by them. To use old injustices to perpetuate a new one makes no sense. I see here not a misogynist god, but men thrusting their misogyny on a god. I now realize that the idea of women being unclean because of their periods is one so deeply instilled in the minds of men and women that it will be hard for them to let it go. My mother often used to say, 'Boys are clean,' making me think of my own body as gross. It took me years to shake this feeling off, to understand that the human body, male or female, is a miracle of creation.

I turn once again to Simone de Beauvoir, who had the prescience all prophets have, and said in *The Second Sex* that 'the peculiarities that signify her [a woman] specifically as a woman ... can be surmounted in the near future.'

When I look at girls and young women today, when I see them leading active lives, joining the army, the police, climbing mountains, winning sports medals, it seems to me that they have indeed surmounted many of their problems. But how do we explain what is happening in the Sabarimala case? The country waits for the Supreme Court to decide whether faith (in the old sense of women's impurity because of menstruation) matters more than women's constitutional rights. In the meantime, however, women have forged ahead and taken this very natural phenomenon in their stride.

'Hot Mango Chutney Sauce'

FARAH AHAMED

IT WAS ONLY YESTERDAY WHEN THE LAST GIRL, MARYAM, TOOK her turn with paracetamols and cheap alcohol. A few weeks earlier, Zainab had done the same, but Laila, who had followed Hafsa, had slit her wrists. When the police took us in for questioning, we said we were ready to cooperate. We even offered to share our photographs. After all, who better than us could explain what happened to the girls? We sit in the row of kiosks on the left side of the car park as you face the front of the shrine. The *tasbih*s and Ajrak scarves hanging on the frames of our windows provide a curtain from behind which we observed the events as they unfolded in the shrine compound.

Maryam's tragedy occurred ten days before the Sufi festival of Urs, which, as you probably know, celebrates the union between the physical and spiritual. We'd decorated our kiosks with green flags, and the mausoleum was lit up with blue lights. It was in the evening at around seven o'clock, when we were in the middle of haggling with pilgrims over the price of prayer books and postcards, that we saw the two policemen striding through rows of cars towards the shrine. We quickly pulled down the kiosk shutters and followed the officers through the chanting devotees lighting clay lamps, the boys offering birdseed on plates, and the qawwals chanting under the mimosa tree. The shrine entrance was covered in a haze of smoke from the hundreds of diyas lit by pilgrims. To tell you the truth, the trouble started with Hafsa. She was thirteen, the youngest of the girls living in the shrine backyard. She cut her wrists and then slipped into the canal, just behind the shrine. None of us reported her as missing; there was no reason why we should have. It was the people in the chowk behind Baba Safra Road who alerted the authorities. They said they'd found a half-drowned girl lying on the banks of the river. Later, the policemen told us when they'd dragged Hafsa over the low slope, and laid her on the ground, she'd smelt of sewage, and her eyes had the wild look of someone possessed. Her shivering, wasted body was covered in muck and slime, and the skin around her eyes and mouth had turned a dark grey. Her wet hair was tangled with bits of debris, and around her neck she had a tasbih. The policemen said when they checked her body more carefully, they found hidden in her underclothes a knotted plastic bag with an expired, crumpled entry ticket to a Meesha Shafi concert. The policemen made enquiries, but no one could tell them who the girl was, until Imran (from kiosk number 28), hearing about the incident at the chowk, volunteered that it was likely she was one of the homeless shrine girls. After they'd made sure the girl was still alive, the policemen put her on a stretcher and brought her to Baba Rehman for identification. The gossiping whispers from the bazaar made us realize that, thanks to Hafsa, our peaceful neighbourhood, the sacred site of the mausoleum of Pir Z, in Multan, City of Saints, had overnight become the site of a scandal.

This had happened around the middle of June, the start of the monsoon season, when the mosquitoes came in hordes, breeding by the dozens, in the stagnating pools of water in the potholes in the alleys and in the crevices of dilapidated buildings surrounding the shrine.

At that time, Erum Bibi was in charge of looking after the girls and living with them in the backyard. She told us she'd found Hafsa, the day she'd attempted suicide, sitting on the pavement by the shrine entrance. She was wearing her usual dirty white salawar kameez with the red hem, and stirring a mosquito-infested puddle with her bare hands. Erum Bibi told us she'd warned Hafsa, if she got dengue fever, there was no money for medication, so she'd die. And Hafsa had replied, 'I don't care, I'm already dead,' and held up her arm covered in welts and bites. Erum Bibi shouted at her to stop being stupid, but Hafsa stuck her hand back into the murky pool and carried on sifting the sludge.

To help the police understand what had really happened between June and August, we've pooled together the photos we had taken individually on our mobile phones and tried to arrange them chronologically; a few are blurry, but all are nonetheless revealing.

Photo #1 shows the shrine compound shortly before Hafsa's suicide attempt. Aftab, from kiosk no. 27 had taken the snap. He sells tasbihs with beads made from sheesham, walnut and mulberry wood. The policemen discovered that the tasbih around Hafsa's neck was one of these and asked who'd given it to her. We pointed out that it was possible for anyone who visited the shrine to have bought the beads and presented them to Hafsa. The police conceded this was true. Which put an end to this line of enquiry. Photo #1 is evidence of the heavy rainfall we had that day. The green flag on the mausoleum minaret is limp, the windows of the mosque which are usually open are bolted and the carpets from the Pir's dargah are hanging to dry on the branches of the old walnut tree. The lower-right corner of the image shows a silhouetted figure sitting on the steps near an empty flowerpot filled with rainwater. Aftab confirmed to the policemen that the girl they had found was Maryam. He said he was sure it was her because Maryam never tied her hair and was always scratching her scalp. If you look more closely at the photograph, you'll see that against the backdrop of the dense, grey clouds and the shadow of the mosque, Maryam is captured in the act of combing her hair.

But let us return to Hafsa. After she'd been rescued from the canal, she was carried on a stretcher by two paramedics and accompanied by two policemen to the shrine. As soon as we saw them, we immediately closed our kiosks, rushed to offer our help, and directed them to Baba Rehman's office. Baba Rehman's family have been the official caretakers of the shrine for the past many decades. Legend has it that Pir Z's spirit visited Baba's ancestor in his dreams and commanded him to dedicate himself and the future generations of his family to the service of the shrine. Since then, Baba's family has lived on the compound in the two rooms behind the mosque. His office, which is the front room, has a wooden desk and two chairs. The other room has a double-size Master Molty Foam mattress, with a plastic cover, leaning against the wall. Near it, on a small shelf, is a pile of religious books, a skull cap, a folded prayer rug, a copy of the Quran and a mirror. On a washing line suspended from one end of the room to the other, are six starched and ironed white *kanzu*s on hangers. Baba is in his mid-fifties, only ten years older than us, but because he's thin and bent, you'd think he was more elderly. He has thick black hair, a long beard and wears a pair of round wire-rimmed reading glasses. You will never spot him without his white skull cap. When he saw us outside his window – a small crowd with policemen and a stretcher in the courtyard – Baba burst out trailing the green cloth used to cover Pir Z's tomb. He let out a long wail, and at that very moment, when we raised our hands and looked up at the minaret, the limp flag and the sky covered in thick clouds, Hafsa hauled herself up on her elbows. She looked straight at us, gave an unearthly smile, and collapsed again on the stretcher.

The policemen asked Baba if he could identify her, and Baba let out a cry, 'Allah, have mercy, she's a daughter of the shrine.' They asked Baba if he knew what had happened, and he replied, 'Nothing's in our hands; it's all Allah's will.' The policemen said that that was all very well, but they needed proper answers. Meanwhile the paramedics kept pointing to Hafsa, saying the police should hurry up because it was obvious the girl was suffering. Baba became distraught. 'Who am I?' he said. 'Who am I to understand what tortures a girl's mind?' He turned to us and asked what he ought to do. Moved by the difficulty of his situation, we offered to help get a truck to transport Hafsa to the nearest hospital and arrange auto-rickshaws for Baba and ourselves to follow her. At that time, there was no sign of the other shrine girls. We wondered where they were, as they were usually together, and concluded that they were keeping their distance because they were afraid of the police.

There are four shrine girls: Hafsa, aged thirteen, Laila, fifteen, Maryam, sixteen, and Zainab, seventeen. We can confirm their mothers must have been like them, destitute and homeless – why else would they have abandoned their babies at the shrine? But as we told the police, their fathers could've been anyone. Baba had put Erum Bibi in charge of looking after the girls.

It was while Hafsa was being hoisted into the back of the truck, that we spied the other three girls, crouching behind an abandoned fruit and vegetable cart. We saw that their faces registered the same shock we'd had when we'd seen a seemingly dead Hafsa in her dirty white salwar kameez, lying on the stretcher, her wet hair in clumps around her head. When the truck driver honked, we shouted at the crowd which had gathered from the chowk to move out of the way.

We followed the truck with Hafsa, the paramedics and policemen to a nearby public hospital. In the emergency room, we observed Hafsa on the stretcher watching with unnerving disinterest the efforts being made to save her life. She did not quail when Dr Arshad stuck a needle in her arm for a blood transfusion nor when he stitched up her wrist wounds. Dr Arshad asked Hafsa if she knew suicide was a cardinal sin in Islam. Hafsa did not reply but turned her head and looked at us. Dr Arshad said he couldn't understand why she would do such a thing, and Hafsa replied, 'I missed Meesha Shafi's concert.' We could not believe our ears – was this really because of Meesha Shafi? Baba threw up his hands crying for Allah's mercy from the *besharam* Meesha Shafi. This justification from Hafsa, the only explanation we ever got from her, was a type of a suicide note because Hafsa, like the other girls, was illiterate.

The girls held a certain fascination for us. Even though their palms were rough and covered in calluses, they were thin as sticks, and their hair was matted with dust and sweat – they were like a flash of lightning in a dark monsoon sky. We'd seen them growing, running around the car park playing hide-and-seek, and we knew when they entered adolescence, because they stopped their childish games and began covering their heads with scarves. After that, only when their scarves slipped were we able to catch a glimpse of their sullen teenage faces. The expression in their dark, shining eyes was teasing and mistrusting at the same time.

On Baba's orders, the girls sat at the shrine entrance, reciting poetry in praise of Pir Z and begging. Whatever they collected, they gave to Baba. We often discussed whether Baba had sired one, if not all, the girls. However, we never came to any conclusion, although we agreed that Zainab was the one most likely to be his, because she was as stubborn as him and when he'd learnt that Zainab was pregnant – she didn't know with whose child – he had cried for hours before lashing out at all the girls with shrewish screams.

Although the girls were nothing to us, it pained us to see them sulking in the car park and calling out to strangers saying they were hungry, begging and pleading for a few rupees. Sometimes we'd offer to buy them ice creams or sweets but only if they came to our kiosks and talked to us. As they grew older, we even promised to buy them new dresses. However, the girls always kept their distance, although, even in their reserve, there was familiarity. Once when we saw Hafsa showing off a new pair of shoes, and Maryam distributing bright-coloured glass bangles to her friends, it crossed our minds that one of us must have been secretly generous. But the girls gave no indication who it might've been. And no matter what season it was, just before daybreak, when the *azaan* rang out from the mosque, the girls would appear on the steps, in the same rags except in the winter when they had thick shawls given to them by some or other well-wisher, draped around their thin bodies. It was impossible for us to tell what they really thought of us.

But they had one male in their circle, Yunnus, the *maalangi*. This young, mad dervish lived with them in the backyard. He could've been brother to any of the girls, but we have no way of knowing for sure. It was Baba's policy to send away to an orphanage any young boys abandoned at the shrine steps, but because Yunnus was mentally disabled and incapable of harming anyone, let alone fending for himself, Baba relented when Erum Bibi pleaded she'd look after him. Yunnus is now probably in his early or late teens, and he has separate sleeping quarters, just outside the male public washroom, a few metres away from the girls. You'd recognize him if you saw him by the wild, unbalanced look in his eyes and his floppy, long hair. He always wears a brown kurta–pyjama tied too high at the waist, and the trousers flap around his ankles. During the day, he played with the girls and with grunts and half-words he'd tell us how they offered him sweets, showering them on him in such a hurry that he didn't know who'd been the first to give. We were amazed to see that it was true; the girls trusted him even though he was an idiot, laughing at his silly antics and showing him their uneven yellow teeth. Because Yunnus did not own any shoes, his feet were always infested with jiggers, and when he'd come to sit with us, he'd listen to us banter, cheerfully removing them. When we'd tease him, he'd protest with rapid gestures and swear he didn't know the girls' secrets, and when we'd taunt him about which girl he was sleeping with, he'd cry and mumble, with tears rolling down his face, that they were his sisters.

Let's return to the day they found Hafsa in the canal. The policeman who had searched Hafsa and found the ticket to Meesha Shafi's 'Hot Mango Chutney Sauce' concert, pocketed the ticket. And it was only at the hospital, after Hafsa mentioned Meesha Shafi to Dr Arshad, that the policeman remembered he had it and gave it to Baba. After staring at it, Baba crumpled the ticket and threw it at us, swearing. 'Who am I?' he said. 'What am I to do about this whore?' This was the first time we had heard him swear. Photo #2 is the front of the ticket, and you can see why Baba was so upset by it. It has a picture of Meesha Shafi with a mocking smile, red painted lips, dark glasses and a big nose ring. Photo #3 is the back of the ticket.

After a week, Baba referred to the event as 'Hafsa's accident', as though she'd cut herself in a minor fall. But then Erum Bibi let it slip that she'd found a stash of paracetamols and a bottle of liquor wrapped in a newspaper hidden under a pile of rags in the backyard. This led us to debate why Hafsa had opted for the razor, instead of pills and liquor, and why drowning herself in the canal had failed. We came to the conclusion that Hafsa had not really known what she was doing. However, Aftab, from kiosk no. 27, claimed he understood Hafsa best, and said it was obvious that she did it to embarrass us. When we questioned him further, he replied it was 'self-evident'. That led us to discus whether it was obvious or not, and we concluded that it wasn't, and there was no reason why it should be.

Hafsa was kept under observation for a week. The hospital records showed that the artery in her left wrist was split, but because she was right-handed, the gash in her right wrist was not as deep and the lower part of the artery was intact. Dr Arshad used dissolving sutures to stitch up both arteries. Each of her wrists had twelve stitches. We do not have photographs of her wrists.

The evening Hafsa returned from the hospital, we were standing under the awning of Imran's kiosk discussing the IPL scores. We saw an auto-rickshaw drive up. Baba alighted, holding a newspaper over his head as an umbrella, followed by Hafsa. She was wearing her old white salwar kameez with the red hem, and her arms, which were both in slings, were raised above her head, as she tried to protect herself from the shower. Baba dragged her through the car park, up the steps and into the shrine.

The weather cleared in the coming days, and one morning when the sky was an intense deep blue and the sun was shining, we saw Hafsa and the other girls sitting on the steps at the entrance, just as they used to. A flower seller from the bazaar had brought them a basket of dead roses and the girls were plucking the petals and gathering them in small heaps to sell to pilgrims. We were relieved that things were back to normal.

Imran was not the only one who had a theory about Hafsa's suicide attempt. His father looked at each one of us straight in the face and asked, 'Who's the mother? Who's the father?' even though he knew full well none of us could possibly know. Salim, from kiosk no. 29, who isn't given to saying much, was convinced it was just because Hafsa had simply wanted to die. But Aftab kept insisting Hafsa was evil and cursed.

The week after Hafsa returned from hospital, we visited Baba with a box of his favourite sohan halwa. Baba took the *mithai* from Aftab, covered it with a newspaper and laid it to one side. Then he began swearing at the besharam Meesha Shafi, saying the whole *tamasha* was her fault. 'Who am I?' he said. 'Am I to blame? It is Allah's will.' He gave each of us a dozen of his new business card, saying we should distribute them. The front had the image of Baba in a white kanzu and skull cap, holding a tasbih; the back read: *For shrine donations contact Baba Rehman, Mobile: 031-911-786. Allah rewards those who give.* Photos #4 and #5 are shots of the front and reverse of Baba's card. Later, however, some of us remembered it differently. Imran recalled that Baba invited us to his office, passed around the halwa, and we had sat in silence wondering about the truth.

One incident stands out in our memory. It was when Salim told us he'd found, in the rubbish heap behind the shrine, rags soaked in blood which he said belonged to the girls. We mocked Salim for sniffing around the girls like a dog in heat and jeered at him for following the smell of fresh blood like a *churail*. Shortly after that, when we threatened to beat him if he didn't show us, Yunnus took us to see some bricks drying in the sun which he said the girls had made from the ash they'd collected from the clay lamps. He demonstrated, with jerking movements, how the girls wrapped each brick in a rag and used it to absorb the blood that dripped down their legs every month. Repulsed, we called Yunnus a pervert. But even as we joked, we'd never been more aware that the girls were no longer children, but young women. We noticed their budding breasts, the swagger of their hips and a new listlessness about them. And by and by, we came to realize that if one of them was on her cycle, all of the girls would disappear because they were forbidden from entering the shrine, begging at the steps, or eating free food from the langar. This was a relief, for the very idea of female blood was repugnant to us.

However, we all admitted that what really infuriated us was Meesha Shafi and the 'Hot Mango Chutney Sauce' concert. According to Imran, pop concerts were immoral. Salim said Hafsa was a thief as it was obvious that she'd stolen Baba's money to buy the ticket, while Aftab insisted, irrespective of the concert, that Hafsa was going to hell for attempting suicide. We interrogated Erum Bibi about the ticket. She clarified that although Hafsa had shown it to her, the girl had refused to tell her from where she'd got it and who'd promised to take her, only to be let down on the day of the concert. These questions left us at a dead end, as none of us wanted to ask Hafsa for answers.

If you look at the hospital records, you'll see that Dr Arshad's assessment of Hafsa's mental health is quite detailed. He diagnosed her attempted suicide as 'an act of aggression provoked by extreme poverty and the degradation of her life'. Dr Arshad's reports were shared with us by Erum Bibi, who'd removed and returned the file from Baba's office at our request. Photos #6, #7 and #8 are images of the relevant pages. Dr Arshad also warned Baba that any further such incidents could lead to negative publicity and closure of the shrine by the Multan City Council. This frightened Baba and led him to make some changes. After Hafsa returned from hospital, the girls no longer begged at the entrance steps, the roof of the backyard was repaired, and a lockable toilet and washing area with a tap with clean running water was allocated to the girls. However, the biggest difference we noticed was not in Baba, but in the girls' attitude.

One Sunday evening, about a month after the incident, we heard loud music coming from the shrine compound. The track sounded suspiciously like Meesha Shafi's 'Hot Mango Chutney Sauce', so we rushed to check what was going on. Imagine our disgust and horror when we found the sounds emerging from a radio in Baba's office, the door was wide open and the girls were dancing and belting out the lyrics, 'Why are you so jealous?' Hafsa was standing on Baba's desk swinging her hips; Maryam was prancing around, her hair wild around her face; Zainab, with her swollen belly, was waving her hands in the air; and Laila was jumping up and down doing *bhangra*. Aftab called them besharam whores, Salim covered his ears and asked for Allah's mercy, and Imran said the bitches belonged in hell. We could not believe our eyes, and when Hafsa jumped off the table and slammed the door in our faces, we knew then – there was no hope for them.

We asked Erum Bibi whether Baba was responsible for this new, foolish leniency, and she said Baba was ignorant and away visiting a neighbourhood mosque, and she no longer cared if he found out. 'Haven't I been young myself?' she said. 'Is this what life is about? Men with skull caps, long beards, paunches and roving eyes paying a few rupees to sleep with you?' She confessed that the girls' youth and beauty had begun to annoy her. 'Now I'm just like one of those bloody pigeons circling the minaret – they eat, shit and die. No one cares.' She also admitted after Hafsa's suicide attempt that she'd threatened Baba with blackmail unless he agreed to the renovation in the backyard.

But of all the events that transpired, what surprised us the most was the *qawwali mehfil*. Baba came to our kiosks to invite us to the musical event, where he said the girls would also be present, saying it was to give thanks to Allah for Hafsa's recovery. Our astonishment, however, soon changed to disapproval, as we concluded it was all just a further reflection of Baba's hypocrisy. Nevertheless, we were keen to go.

On the afternoon of the mehfil, the tattered flag on the minaret was replaced, and Baba received a delivery of dried fruits, sohan halwa, and two dozen quarter-pint-size cartons of chocolate milk. Photo #9 shows the new flag on the minaret. That evening, we locked up our kiosks early and went to Baba's office. For the occasion, Baba had put on a clean white kurta–pyjama, and a black velvet waistcoat.

We trailed after him to the mosque, up the stairs, bumping against each other as we passed through the narrow stairwell to the eighth floor. As we climbed higher, the light coming through the windows on the ground floor faded, and by the time we reached the sixth floor, it was pitch dark. We kept going, our fingers feeling the walls for support, until Baba opened a small wooden door and led us into a room. The setting sun filtered in through arched windows, and diyas burned bright. The musicians were already there, seated on a carpet in the middle of the room, and Baba asked us to make ourselves comfortable next to them.

As our eyes adjusted to the light, for the first few minutes, we saw sitting across from us shapeless, unidentifiable figures. Because they were all in black and their heads were covered in white scarves, we could not tell who was who, but we knew it was the girls. And as we kept looking, we were able to make out which of them was Hafsa. She was sitting at the end of the row, staring at her hands in her lap. Then suddenly, as though she could feel our eyes on her, she looked up and her scarf slipped from her head. She quickly pulled it over her head again and we noticed that her bandages were gone. To cover the scars on her wrists, she had wrapped tasbihs around them, and to stop the wooden beads from sliding, she'd stuck them to her skin with pieces of Elastoplast. You can find similar tasbihs in Aftab's shop.

Baba told the musicians to begin, and accompanied by tablas and a harmonium, the men began singing a qawwali. We all joined in clapping to the beat, except for Hafsa, who sat without moving. Then Baba shouted out, 'Oi, malaangi,' and Yunnus came in dancing and smiling like the idiot he was. We nudged each other, grinning. Even though it's difficult to say exactly how old Yunnus is, that evening he danced with the innocence of a twelve-year-old. Over the years, we'd watched him growing and expected he'd be dead by the time the girls were adolescents. But now they were young women, and he was still a child. We've known all along that Baba made Yunnus do things which no one should agree to, which explained his crazed look, his silly, lopsided grin, and his fear of Baba.

Yunnus began turning, his arms slightly raised in a smooth dervish whirl. The musicians began chanting and as the refrain became louder, Baba shouted for Yunnus to spin faster. It was at that point, when the mehfil reached its peak, that Hafsa stood up and made her way to Baba. Shocked, Baba raised his hand, and the musicians stopped. Pulling at the beads on her wrist, Hafsa asked if she could be excused. The sound of her exhausted voice sent a tremor through us. After a momentary pause, Baba replied that it was up to her. Hafsa tugged at the beads, the Elastoplast came unstuck snapping the thread, and the beads scattered on the floor. 'Go then,' Baba said, as Hafsa crossed over to the door. We did not hear her climbing the stairs, but we heard the sound of her feet running above us and about twenty seconds later, we heard the heavy, wet sound of her body falling and landing on the concrete ground. First, there was a long sigh, then there was a loud, sharp crash, like the sound of a coconut breaking open. We sat immobile, as though waiting for the strains of a mehfil from someplace else to fill the air, expectant that its tempo would pick up any moment with rapid tabla beats. Baba rushed to the door, and we followed him down the stairs, until we were pushed to the side by the screaming girls

We found Erum Bibi holding Hafsa with her hand under the girl's neck, stroking her hair. Hafsa must have hit her head on the cement but there was no blood anywhere. She seemed to be peacefully asleep, and her white scarf fluttering in the wind added to this effect. Erum Bibi picked up Hafsa's head and gently laid it on her lap. Baba raised his hands, Yunnus banged his fists on his chest, and the girls collapsed in a heap next to Hafsa.

Photo #10 shows the spot marked X, where Hafsa's body had landed near the cone-shaped monument where the diyas are lit on Thursday evenings. Photo #11 is of the beam in the ceiling in the men's washroom and the rope Yunnus used. Photo #12, taken just before Maryam's body was discovered, shows a flock of pigeons circling the minaret. Photo #13 shows the wall in the backyard where the poster, before we ripped it off, advertised Meesha Shafi's concert, 'Hot Mango Chutney Sauce'.

Kotahalu Mangalya: Menstruation Traditions and Practices in Sri Lanka

ZINTHIYA GANESHPANCHAN

ONE SATURDAY AFTERNOON, WHEN I WAS TWELVE YEARS OLD and playing in the garden, I noticed some brown stains on my underpants. This was the end of my childhood as I'd known it. My mother immediately locked me up in a room so that I would not interact with any male family members and also to protect me from the evil spirits menstruating girls were thought to be vulnerable to. She also gave me a *giraya* (betel nut cutter) to place under my pillow to ward off the evil spirits.

That evening, I was asked to change into clothes provided by a *redi nenda*, or a washerwoman. Sri Lanka has a deep-rooted caste system, and a washerwoman is considered to be of the lowest caste. So asking a menstruating girl to wear a washerwoman's clothes is to tell her and the family that she is symbolically impure and unclean. Over the next six days, I wore the clothes brought by the redi nanda, and was only allowed a diet of vegetables, boiled eggs and rice with no spices or oil. While I was quarantined in my room, my mother and an aunt visited the village astrologer, the *rathna weda mahattaya*, to read my horoscope. This is a common practice. My mother told him that I had started my period, and he asked her for the exact place and time, as well as the colour of the clothes I'd been wearing when I began bleeding. Based on this information, he calculated the date on which it would be auspicious to end my isolation, a forecast of my future including details of my marriage, when the pubertal bathing ritual ought to take place and the colour I should wear after completing it. To this day, I still carry a copy of his prescriptions and predictions.

On the date suggested by the astrologer, I was escorted out of my isolation with a towel covering my face and taken to the outdoor bathing place through the back door. The male members of my family were kept away from me, just in case I polluted them and brought them bad luck.

During the ritual, I sat on a wooden bench placed on a mat sprinkled with unhusked rice, facing the direction prescribed by the astrologer. A branch of an araliya tree (temple tree) was also placed in the same direction, with its white milky sap leaking onto the floor. The oozing tree and paddy are symbols of fertility. Thereafter, water from a new clay pot or *kalaya* was filled with water and flowers petals, which was poured over me several times to purify me from the *kili* of evil, a contaminant that is said to surround menstruating women. The bathing ritual is concluded with the redi nenda smashing the kalaya. At the end of the ritual, she is given a gift.

After the bathing ritual, I put on my new blood-red dress with white flowers made of Indonesian batik fabric, specially tailored by my aunt for the occassion. I entered the house from the front door, to signify my entry into womanhood. At the door, a coconut was placed at my feet, which I had to break open with the blunt edge of a knife. The manner in which the coconut splits (first hit, equal halves or unequal halves, more water in one half than the other and so on) is taken as a sign of what is to come. My family then presented me with gifts of jewellery, perfumes and cash. My mother gave me a pair of gold earrings and my father, a watch and necklace. Later that evening, the *kotahalu mangalya* – a celebration held to mark the occasion – was organized. A scrumptious traditional feast was laid out for family and friends, who brought gifts to congratulate me. This was not unique to me but a common practice in my village.

The initiation rituals practised in Sri Lanka around puberty are exciting, but very soon one realizes that it is a monthly occurrence which has to be dealt with on one's own, while following a strict code. There was no information available, nor were we taught what was to be done or how to manage our period. Most mothers and aunts were reluctant to discuss the subject even with their own daughters and nieces, and even though I had attended a convent school for girls, no teacher talked to us about puberty.

While growing up, I had little access to period products and like many women and girls, I used rags made from discarded old clothes such as used towels, sarees and sarongs. We reused these cloths, washing and drying them after use. However, the shame around menstruation meant that I was unable to wash my rags openly or let them dry outside on the washing line in the sun. Instead, this had to be done secretly at the back of the house and the rags were left to dry in bedrooms, under the bed or mattress, always out of sight. Often, the cloths did not dry, and I had to use damp rags. It was not uncommon for women from the same household to share rags and I often shared mine with my sisters and mother. I remember, much later when pads were available in shops, my mother whispering to the shopkeeper, asking him for a packet of pads. He would wrap it in a newspaper or a brown bag, and tie it with a string, and put it together with the rest of our groceries. With the arrival of supermarkets and pharmacies, the practice of wrapping pads in a brown bag has become less common, but it is still done in many places. In some cases, women specifically ask for it.

◆

Over the last thirty years, Sri Lankan society has undergone a transition. These were brought about due to a range of factors including but not limited to the growth and liberalization of the economy in the mid-seventies, the prolonged Sinhalese-Tamil ethnic conflict in the northern and eastern parts of the county the youth unrest in the south as well as urbanization, which have led to large-scale migration internally as well as across the borders. Moreover, urbanization has resulted in the breakdown of rural economies centred around agriculture and caused overcrowding in urban slums.

These changes have also influenced the rituals and traditional practices around puberty and menstruation. Today in Sri Lanka, the ancient rite of isolating women during menstruation is not widely practised, and wherever they are carried out, they have been modified due to ideological and practical reasons, but the stigma and shame around menstruation continues to persist. For example, while I was working with Tamil and Muslim women living in refugee camps displaced by ethnic conflict, I learnt of the obstacles they faced when trying to preserve traditional menstruation rituals. This was due to the cramped conditions in the camps where girls could not be isolated (as I was when I got my first period), financial hardship (so traditional gifts were not an option) as well as difficulties in accessing a trusted astrologer. I found the same to be true for impoverished families working and living in urban plantations and slums.

With the liberalization of the economy after 1978, the situation in Sri Lanka, particularly in the urban areas, improved in relation to access to period products such as commercially made sanitary pads. The availability of such products, even though limited, made life more comfortable for those who could afford them. However, for women living on the margins, refugees, plantation workers, slum-dwellers, the incarcerated, the homeless, appropriate menstruation management and access to menstrual products continues to be a challenge. Many have no choice, but to use rags made out of discarded cloth, newspapers or leaves.

Forty-three-year-old Pushpam lives in a camp for internally displaced people. She had this to say when asked how she managed her period:

'Here in the camp, even getting sufficient food is a problem, let alone pads. If we are lucky, we will have a pack of pads among the food rations we get each week, if not, we have to buy them from the shop. Since we don't have the money for them, I and my daughters use rags which we share among us.'

Ranjini, a twenty-four-year-old young woman who works on a tea plantation, said:

'I have never used a pad and since we don't even have rags at home other than the clothes we wear, when I have my period, I lie all day on a mat in the living room. If there are newspapers or other papers available, I use them as pads. During those days, because I miss work, I don't get paid, so money is always short.'

When Rita, a forty-nine-year-old, was released from prison, she shared with me her experience of having her period in jail.

'I was incarcerated for three years for smuggling drugs. While I was there, I was given three or four pads a month. This was never enough. During the last few months my period was very heavy, and there were times when I needed to use three pads a day. However, I only had one, so I was forced to use it for over twelve hours. At times, I could smell the bad odour coming from the soiled pad, which was unbearable.'

Affordability is only one part of the problem. Other challenges include washing and disposal of used products. A majority of the women in the villages wash and dry the soiled rags at home, and when they are no longer reusable burn or bury them in their back gardens. Some also throw them into open-pit lavatories which are common around the villages. However, waste disposal is more difficult for women like Pushpam and Ranjini, who live in refugee camps. And for those living in urban slums, where the only source of running water is a public tap, washing and bathing is difficult because of a lack of privacy. Thirty-six-year-old Saku, who lives in one such slum, explained:

'It is really uncomfortable when we wash clothes together as not only other women but also the men who hang around the tap can see us washing our rags. So, I now wash my rags in an old saucepan and dry them in the room.'

The lack of education and information means that there is very little knowledge about menstrual hygiene among a majority of women and girls in Sri Lanka. They are unaware of the risks associated with unhealthy practices such as sharing rags or using the same pad or tampon for prolonged periods. There is also a lack of understanding about the damage caused by commercial pads to the environment. While non-governmental agencies have taken some initiatives to improve health education and menstrual hygiene awareness, this has not been enough, and a majority of the disadvantaged women continue to suffer in silence. Much work remains to be done.

Raqs-e-Mahvaari: A Menstrual Dance

AMNA MAWAZ KHAN

MY PRACTICE OF INDIAN CLASSICAL DANCE IS ROOTED IN twenty years of learning and linked to an age-old tradition of communicating a particular story to an audience or community through spatial and dynamic movements. For me, the dance is a vehicle for a story which is conveyed through specific movements. Dance is both self-expression and self-exploration. As a dancer I take responsibility for telling a story. The essence of the idea behind the story is inherent not only in how the body moves, but in an awareness of where you are in space, an awareness of your entire being. This is done through rhythmic motions and movements in the form of *nrittya* (expressive) and *nritta* (technical) dance.

From deep dance immersion over many years, I have discovered a certain consciousness, an inner strength which envelop both the *yoni* and the *lingam* energies. These manifest for me in the vision of the riverine goddess of the Indus. The earliest evidence of dance in South Asia is the figurine of the Dancing Girl of Mohenjo-Daro, which is interestingly translated as the mound of the dead. The small bronze sculpture, excavated from the Indus Valley ruins in 1926, was created over 4,500 years ago and is considered to be a rare and unique masterpiece. The statue reflects the aesthetics of a young female body as conceptualized during that historical period. It was named Dancing Girl based on an assumption about her profession. This image came to my mind as I started thinking about the idea of the menstrual dance. Women dancing is an ancient South Asian tradition almost as primordial as menstruation itself.

When I was commissioned to choreograph a menstrual dance, I browsed some of the art, poetry and interviews in this collection, *Period Matters*, to try and understand the diversity of stories and the vision for the book. I also reflected on my relationship with menstruation and how it had evolved over the years. From shame and embarrassment, to confusion and anger, and even disappointment when it marked the end of an unsuccessful fertility window, I have come to accept it now sometimes as a phase of creativity and power. I say sometimes because the cyclical tumult is not constant; the experience varies from month to month. Like dance, the menstrual cycle is always in flux in my body, shifting, moving and changing me. I thought particularly about shame and power and how these could be conveyed in a two-minute-long dance piece, with each second of each minute depicting the transition through the month.

I developed the idea of 'Raqs-e-Mahvaari', a menstrual dance, drawing on the symbolism of the lunar cycle, relying on my own experiences of menstruation, childbirth and dance. I imagined the piece as a musical rhythm composed of a pattern of seven beats, repeated four times to signify a full menstrual cycle. I wanted to express through dance and music, movement and stillness, the association between the blood moon and my own period. One a mystery suspended in the sky, proudly shining for all the world to see, and the other, a terrible secret of shame and trauma suppressed behind closed doors. And yet the two are intimately connected, whether it be the mood swings during different times of the month, lunar madness affecting those who are particularly sensitive, synchronized periods between close friends, or the unpredictability and variability of the menstrual cycle affecting us like tidal waves. I would convey, through music, dance and movement my interpretation of menstruation using *rawaangi* (flow), *mudra*s (hand gestures) and feet movements. With the moon as backdrop, I saw myself moving across the stage with an egg (relying on a small ball as a prop), dropping it, letting it flow freely, to show the bodily transition through the month and the bleeding. I would use red paint on my feet and make a circle as I danced. While at first the red paint would make strong markings on the floor, this would fade through the dance. Each step, stamp or tap would depict the ebb and flow of the bleed, the ascension and collapse as the month passed. The *bhramari* (whirl) would echo the cyclical nature of both the menstrual cycle and of life.

When thinking about the ideal music for the story I wanted to tell, I went through various ragas. I considered adapting the dance to the *rupak taal* to create the seven-beats-in-four-cycles movement. However, this did not work. I decided on *raga megh*, the monsoon raga, or cloud raga, because its melodic pattern captured the build-up of expectations and pent-up emotions before the coming of the rain beautifully. I asked a friend, a student of the Patiala *gharana*, to sing an *alaap* which would capture what I had conceptualized. Once I received her voice recording, I experimented with different alaaps. I eventually found a mood which illustrated the duality of the public and private nature of menstruation: indignity and creativity.

For the performance, I was undecided about what to wear, but eventually settled on my mother's forty-year-old Bhopali deep green kurta and dupatta. As I searched though my wardrobe, its dark colour and shine, two complementary elements, drew me to it. I instinctively felt that it was appropriate for my 'Raqs-e-Mahvaari' because it also honoured my biological and spiritual connection to my mother. The shooting took place over one day. I did the dance thirty times at a friend's workspace. I had not planned for thirty rehearsals of the dance, but it chimed with the cycle of a full month. I was pleasantly surprised at how different aspects of this dance were unconsciously resonating with each other. It also happened to be the second day of my period.

It struck me, while I was performing, after we'd moved aside the paraphernalia, how work and being in a *chaar dewaari* (four-walled space) is where often women have to be hyper-aware of all outward elements of their gender (while simultaneously hiding anything seen as too real) and deal with the many challenges of menstruation, from inadequate toilets, to cramps and headaches, to trying to access menstrual products. Period blood on the floor of a chaar dewari is the height of shame and embarrassment, and this would be shown by the blood red paint on my feet. My dance would be one in defiance of socio-cultural beliefs.

The dance begins with the depiction of the release of an unfertilized egg, and thus, the onset of menstruation. The literal interpretation is then followed by the figurative, as the theme of repression is illustrated through an overpowering shadow falling over my silhouette. I resist this through the dance, pushing it away in a slow yet sure gesture with my hands. The movement continues, with a steady beat and flow in steps, and then I raise my arms and turn on my feet to mirror the cyclical nature of menstruation. All the while, the backdrop of the lunar cycle endures. The whirling, or *bhramari chakkar*, the circle I draw with my feet covered in paint, my hand gestures, the raga and taal, all come together to illustrate the permanence of feminine power.

I'd like to end just by saying that for me, the process of creating and choreographing the menstrual dance, 'Raqs-e-Mahvaari', was a means of strengthening my self-affirmation – a type of human creative encounter with myself, and at a deeper level with others as well.

◆

'Raqs-e-Mahvaari' is the result of the author's collaboration with her friends. Amna Mawaz Khan would like to thank Wajahat Malik, Tania Husain, Zeejah Fazli and her teacher, Sai Krippa Prasanna, for inspiring her. The dance can be viewed on Youtube at https://bit.ly/3t0JqVe or by scanning the QR code below.

The Christian Women Sweepers of Lahore

AYRA INDRIAS PATRAS

THIS ESSAY FOCUSES ON THE CHALLENGES AROUND menstruation and menstrual health management faced by the Christian female sweepers of Lahore. The study is drawn from nine in-depth interviews and two focus group discussions, one with the sweeper women and another with the employees of Aahung, a non-governmental organization working in the area of sexual and reproductive health.

In Pakistan, Christians are a minority sect. They currently constitute 1.5 per cent of the total population[1] and an overwhelming percentage of them are sanitation workers, sewage cleaners and sweepers. In Lahore, Christians form 4 per cent of the city's population. Christians constitute 71 per cent of the employees of the Water and Sanitation Agency and 100 per cent of those working with the Lahore Waste Management Company.[2] In April 2018, an advertisement for sweepers, published by the Pakistan Rangers Headquarters in Sindh, stated only non-Muslims should apply for the job.[3] Discrimination on the basis of religion, occupation and one's background is common in Pakistan.

The story of Lahore's women sweepers is rooted in their historical and ancestral occupation of cleaning. In the Indian

subcontinent, between 1870 and 1920, people from the lower caste
or 'untouchables' from the Chamar and Chandala communities
were converted to Christianity by Western missionaries.[4] Such
religious conversion was supposed to encourage social mobility and
offer an escape from prejudice and discrimination. However, this
did not happen, and the curse of being an 'untouchable' continues
to hang over the Christian sweepers in Pakistan.[5] The Christian
female sweepers face intersectional challenges and marginalization
on account of their class, caste, religion and gender.

From as early as 5 o'clock in the morning, be it the scorching
summer or the bitterly cold winter, these women are out on the
streets of Lahore, cleaning with a broom in their hand. They can
be seen in Anarkali Bazaar, around the main roundabouts and
near the Lahore Fort. Unnoticed and 'invisible', one can find them
squatting on their haunches on the roadside, gathering dust and
rubbish in small heaps on the pavement to be collected by the
waste trucks. Their working environment is toxic, polluted and
unhygienic, but they are not given any protective clothing by their
employees nor offered any medical insurance or health benefits.
As a result, most of them suffer from chronic health problems
related to their occupation. Aside from the difficulties they face
working with dirt, they also have to deal with the lack of access to
washrooms during working hours.

A forty-seven-year-old woman who has been working as a
sweeper for the past fifteen years, explained how difficult it was to
find a public washroom for women.

'It has always been very easy for men to go by the roadside or
anywhere to relieve themselves. But for women it is impossible;
we always have to control our bladders. As I've grown older,
I've found it harder to do this. I'm forced to look for secluded

places around bushes or thick trees. Sometimes, I've had to stop working and run home just to use the toilet. As Christians and sanitation workers, we cannot use the toilets in private shops because the owners believe we will contaminate and pollute them.'

Getting through the day becomes that much harder for a female sweeper during menstruation. One of the interviewees explained:

'Every month, the period brings additional difficulty and stress. This is because it is not easy to find a public toilet where we can change our pads or relieve ourselves while at work. This leads to other complications because when the cloth pad is soaked with dried blood, it scrapes against our skin and causes bruises. I often apply oil to the affected area.'

Still another said:

'Public toilets are only used by men. Because we don't have access to any toilets, we have to keep using the same pad for eight or nine hours. This causes irritation, pain and itching.'

It was no surprise that many of the women who were interviewed said that they preferred to stay at home during their period. However, when they did, their wages were deducted. One woman reported that when she took two or three days off during her period, her employer adjusted her salary.

She added that trying to assert their rights as employees turned out to be a pointless exercise:

'We have tried many times, but our supervisor is a man; he does not understand our problems. Men do not want to listen to us; all we want is a toilet. Our supervisor told us to use public toilets, go on the roads or find a government school and ask for permission. Our company just wants us to work; they are not bothered about our issues, and we feel ashamed and embarrassed to raise and discuss such matters again and again.'

Most major cities in Pakistan like Karachi, Lahore and Peshawar do not have adequate clean public toilet facilities and the ones available are in a poor condition because no regular maintenance work is carried out.[6] They lack running water and are mostly used by men, which makes them inaccessible for women. According to one survey, a single public toilet in Lahore services one million residents.[7] While the absence of public toilets makes coping with the challenges of menstruation impossible for female sweepers, unfortunately, the situation at home is not much better.

The sweeper community in Lahore lives in closely knit Christian settlements in slums situated near the peripheries of the city or on the outskirts of affluent housing complexes. These ghettoized slums usually comprise small one-room houses occupied by large families, often with as many as eight members. Toilet and bathing facilities are found in a common area and shared by two or three families. Consequently, even at home, a woman sweeper does not have access to privacy, a clean toilet or running water. A thirty-eight-year-old mother told me about the challenges of finding privacy:

'I, and my two young girls, face problems during our periods. We cannot change our pads in our bathroom at home because it is shared by twenty-nine people, including six members of my own family, three brothers-in-law, their wives and children. There is no privacy because we all live in one room. When my daughters tell my sons to leave the house because they need to change their pads, my sons don't understand, and the children fight. I've asked my husband several times to build a separate toilet for us on the rooftop, but he does not understand or listen.'

Generally speaking, women in Pakistan are embarrassed to talk openly about periods. During the course of the interviews conducted for this essay, it was observed that most of the participants were hesitant to share their concerns. One woman commented, 'It is shameful and dishonourable to talk about periods; good women ought to keep menstruation a secret.'

Many of them also believe that during menstruation they are dirty and polluted and consequently, observe rituals and rites such as not taking a bath, drinking cold water, eating spicy or iron-enriched foods, or attending religious or cultural events.[8] A female sweeper has very few opportunities to socialize and have fun, and during her period her participation in religious and cultural events is further curtailed. But because of their understanding that they are contaminated at this time, they do not oppose the restrictions. One of the interviewees, a woman in her late sixties, had a very clear opinion about the status of menstruating women: 'Women are not clean during their period, and so it is right that we do not go to sacred places, touch the Bible, or take Holy Communion during the Sunday service.'

A widespread lack of awareness amongst women in the sweeper community about their reproductive health further contributes towards the perpetuation of myth and stigma around menstruation. The Pakistan school curriculum offers very little information about sexual and reproductive health.[9] A study conducted with 230 female patients, aged between fourteen and forty-five years, at the gynaecological department of a hospital in Peshawar, found that more than 50 per cent of them had no knowledge of the biological implications of menstruation before their menarche.[10] Similarly, in the interviews conducted for this study, it was found that even middle-aged women in the sweeper community did not understand the biological connection between menstruation and pregnancy.

This absence of knowledge compounds their fear and sense of shame at the onset of menstruation as well as their inability to manage it, often leading to mental stress and other emotional problems. During the focus group discussion, many women spoke about their young daughters having irregular periods and period cramps. However, despite knowing there might be more serious underlying medical issues, the women said they did not feel comfortable going to the hospital or clinic to see the doctor. A forty-three-year-old woman with three daughters, only one of whom was married, shared the plight of her unmarried daughters: 'If single girls go to the hospital for their menstrual problems, it is a bad omen and trouble for her parents because only married women can seek medical help with the permission of their husbands.'

Another challenge the women in this occupation face during menstruation is the unaffordable cost of sanitary products. They are forced to use cloth pads made from rags, old clothes or cheap second-hand scarves which they buy from the bazaar.[11] A woman with four daughters shared how burdened she felt by the heavy costs of providing for five menstruating females: 'I cannot afford to buy pads from the market every month for myself and my daughters. Commercial pads are very expensive, and my daughters do not like to use homemade cloth pads, but we have no choice. I've taught them how to wash, dry and reuse them.'

In Pakistan – aside from the prevalence of a dominant conservative social culture and patriarchy – the government, through media and advertising censorship around menstruation, reproductive health and feminine hygiene, also makes it difficult, if not impossible, to discuss the subject openly.'[12]

Aahung is an organization that has been working to improve the sexual and reproductive health education of men and women in Pakistan for the past twenty years. It was the first to research and develop a culturally sensitive reproductive health manual. One of its key objectives has been to advocate for the inclusion of life-skills-based education to support the Pakistani youth who are particularly vulnerable to forced early marriages, poor menstrual hygiene management, sexual violence, HIV and other sexually transmitted infections.

In an interview, a senior officer working in the area of reproductive health at Aahung noted:

'There exists in Pakistan a great deal of stigma and shame around menstruation, largely due to people's conservative mindset and gender-based stereotyping which has a severe impact on all aspects of women's and girls' rights, including their human rights to equality, health, housing, water, sanitation, education, work, freedom of religion or belief, safe and healthy working conditions, and the right to take part in cultural and public life without discrimination. In this day and age, no one can deny the great power of television and mass media. Despite the cyber revolution, television and cinema remain powerful media through which one can inform, educate, entertain and create awareness. These media can serve to advocate, whether subtly or forcefully, and such advocacy definitely affects how the audience thinks about or relates to certain subjects. It is also undeniable that Pakistani culture is steeped in patriarchy, which is perpetuated through various media. The lack of conversation around topics that relate to women's health and rights is a direct result of this gender discrimination and thus there exist strict controls over what is aired on television and allowed in cinema. Hence it is no surprise that films like *Padman* are censored by local authorities. We still have a long way to go to before we discuss and bring focus to women's reproductive health and rights publicly, specifically menstrual hygiene management.'[13]

The Aahung official also highlighted the hurdles they faced while working on menstrual hygiene management among adolescents. Religious teachings, stigmas and taboos with regards to menstruation and one's body and private parts hinder open conversations. Moreover, the lack of government support and misinformation on social media also hamper menstrual health management.

However, despite these challenges, there has been some movement towards change. A group of university students in Lahore demonstrated against the silence around menstruation by creating artwork made of sanitary napkins on the walls of their campus buildings, with slogans demanding the normalization of conversations about menstruation.[14] A few women's networks and groups have started organizing talks on menstrual hygiene awareness for poor communities, and in 2019, the first-ever period poverty conference in Pakistan was held at LUMS (Lahore University of Management Sciences). Young entrepreneurs have come up with innovative solutions through new apps, social enterprise startups and social media such as Aurat Raaj, Girly Things and Her Ground. 'Sweepers are superheroes' is an advocacy campaign to raise awareness about the horrific working conditions of sweepers and sewage workers, and lobby for their dignity, safety and social protection. Although supporting women's menstrual hygiene is not a specific aim of this campaign as of yet, improved working conditions including access to proper toilet facilities are indeed part of their objectives.

I was particularly encouraged when a student asked me to connect her with a sweeper community living on the outskirts of Lahore. Together with a group of volunteers, under the banner of Aurat March 2021 (a women's movement in Pakistan), she conducted a discussion with women on menstruation and taught them how to make low-cost, reusable cotton pads.[15] Such steps, small as they are, can bring about a slow but steady change.

What If

FARAH AHAMED

What if
Not even begun
Your life was already over?
And what if each day was only
Bending, crouching, brushing, sweeping, clearing, swishing, swashing
Pavements, roads, streets, alleyways and gullies?
And what if at thirteen you told your mother, I have cramps,
I'm bleeding, I'm dying,
And she said, use this cloth, don't touch this food, don't take a bath,
don't meet your friends, don't smile at boys.
It's time to find you a husband.
At fifteen a mother, what if when you whispered to your husband,
Will the future be different for us?
He said, be grateful for what you have.
And when you complained to your boss, and asked for a female toilet
He said, sleep with me here and now, and I'll make it better for you later.
And what if at thirty a grandmother, and at forty widowed,
You never had a moment of pleasure?
And what if there was
No writing or reading, no singing or dancing, or brightly coloured dresses
Only coughing, spluttering, shaking, drooling, vomiting, shouting,

bleeding, crying, and being screamed at, jeered, and taunted
With no time for thinking, feeling, or dreaming?
And when you knock, knock, knocked on the doors of the church,
Pleading, let me in, I'm one of yours,
There was no answer.
And centuries later you are still squatting on the ground
Sweeping litter and leaves,
Bleeding on a rag.
And what if no one came forward to offer hope
Nor raised a hand to help?
And the years passed by like a flowing river
And you drifted and floated, and were lugged along
Sometimes almost drowning,
And the river continued its course, never changing across time,
Always dragging you with it, and tossing you up on a bank now and then,
Like the debris and rubble you swept from the streets.
What then?

Menstrupedia: India's Myth-busting Comic Book Guide

INTERVIEW | FARAH AHAMED

MENSTRUPEDIA IS A COMIC BOOK GUIDE TO MENSTRUATION created by Aditi Gupta and her husband Tuhin Paul in India in 2014. Since its launch, the book has been used to educate more than 13 million children. The comic aims to explain and normalize the biological process of puberty and menstruation. Through the use of relatable characters and a straightforward story, bright images and dialogue, *Menstrupedia* illustrates what menstruation is, in a way that is fun and engaging for children. The story goes like this: Priya Didi, a doctor, explains puberty to her younger cousin Pinki and her friends Jiya and Mira. When Jiya gets her first period during Pinki's birthday party, Priya Didi uses the opportunity to talk to the girls about menstrual health, hygiene and puberty. When the girls ask her questions, she offers them reassuring answers.

I learnt about *Menstrupedia* through Aditi's Ted Talk which has been viewed over 497K times on YouTube, at the time of writing this piece. I contacted her to understand what set her and Tuhin on the journey to creating the comic book and convert it into a social enterprise.

MENSTRUPEDIA 57

What is *Menstrupedia*?

Menstrupedia is a comic book that was created to inform and educate young people in India about menstruation. The objective of the book is to destroy myths and taboos around menstruation and normalize it as a biological process. Our aim is to help girls overcome silence, shame and taboos through a fictional story. The target readers are girls who are expecting to or have recently started their periods. We also wish to reach those women and girls who are already menstruating but do not have access to accurate information or know how to deal with their periods and the constraints around menstruation.

Menstruation in India is widely a taboo subject. Broadly speaking, women and girls are neither encouraged nor allowed nor expected to talk about it. In some cases, the shame that accompanies the subject prevents them from asking for sanitary napkins which means they would rather use coarse, unhygienic rags rather than ask for better alternatives and face embarrassment. It is not because they cannot afford it but because they are too embarrassed to ask for money to buy menstrual products.

Our goal was to not only tackle a social issue but also, equally importantly, find a business model that would allow us to do so while making profits. The core idea was to sell a comic book, as part of a business, which would help alleviate period poverty. The book is available in seventeen languages as a printed book, and there is an audiovisual edition as well. We have taken it one step further by organizing workshops and masterclasses for menstrual hygiene management educators, and supplemented the book with a blog, videos and other types of multimedia. We believe that a profit-making model like this is necessary to allow us to reinvest the proceeds in the business and scale it, and thereby increase the scope of our impact.

What motivated you to launch Menstrupedia?

My personal experience was the greatest instigator. When Tuhin saw me suffer the inconvenience of periods every month, he asked me several health-related questions which I could not answer satisfactorily. It came as a surprise to us that despite being well educated, neither of us really understood the basic biology behind menstruation. It made us think if this was true for us, then how much more unaware were underprivileged, uneducated girls and women? And how much more vulnerable to unhygienic menstruation practices were they? And how was it adversely affecting their well-being?

We recognized there was a problem that was affecting Indians and realized that we were capable of helping. We resolved to try and make a difference. Millions around the world continue to face the same challenges around menstruation – ignorance, taboos, myths and so on – and we believed our book could assist anyone anywhere.

In 2012, Tuhin and I quit our jobs and started working full-time on the comic book. We started by investing all our savings in it and the following year we launched a very successful crowdfunding campaign. We convinced our investors to let us launch the idea on a pamphlet instead of a book, and we studied its impact on fifty young girls and their parents. This pamphlet was designed in such a way that it explained menstruation with sensitivity and in a manner that most people would find culturally acceptable. In March 2013, we moved on to the next step which was developing the comic book. Eighteen months later, in September 2014, we had the first draft ready.

After the initial success of the book, both of us began a year-long research project in urban and semi-urban areas of India to try and establish the status of girls and women in relation to menstrual health. We discovered that most girls were ill-informed or entirely ignorant about the biological process of menstruation. Out of every ten girls we interviewed, at least three (30 per cent), had no idea what was happening to them when they first got their period. Interestingly, taboos and myths around menstruation existed both in urban and rural areas. While parents and educators agreed that girls should be taught about menstruation, they did not have the proper material and tools, and therefore were hesitant to discuss it. The ignorance and silence around menstruation were being passed on from one generation to the next.

What has been the impact of *Menstrupedia*?

The influence of *Menstrupedia* has been far-reaching. Before we published the guide, there was absolutely nothing available in the Indian market that could teach or inform young people about menstruation in a way that was clear and simple, without paying heed to the taboos. There was no curriculum in schools on reproductive health or menstruation and the chapter on reproduction which explained the menstrual cycle was often glossed over without a second glance.

Currently, with the endorsement of the Indian government, our book is being used in 7,500 schools in eleven states. Aside from India, *Menstrupedia* is also being published in Uruguay, China, Nepal, Hungary and Bangladesh. It has been translated into seventeen languages and is in circulation in more than twenty countries. Our comic book is being used by 270 NGOs and has reached 1.2 million girls globally. Our YouTube reach is eight million and growing. I think it would be safe to say that we have influenced, in some way, at least 5 million lives through our online and offline efforts. But the most significant outcome is the book's contribution to making the period conversation more open and informed. In other words, *Menstrupedia* has made the subject of periods 'cool'.

When *Menstrupedia* was first launched online in 2014, the articles on our blog were shared nearly 35,000 times. This helped mainstream both the comic book and the menstruation conversation. Every day we receive at least one testimonial on our website or a review on Amazon telling us how helpful the book has been. Readers have shared how it has helped bust myths and opened channels for an informed conversation about menstruation.

Of course, there are many others working in the area of menstrual health, and their efforts must be recognized. It is thanks to combined efforts by all stakeholders that taboos have been challenged and disproved, frank discussions are being held on various platforms and the rationale of banning women from entering certain sacred places during their cycle has been questioned. Everyone advocating for better menstrual health and hygiene has helped ensure that menstruation is an acceptable part of everyday conversation.

One of the things that we wished for when we first started out in 2013 was that girls should be able to support and educate each other about menstruation. In the past five or six years, we have seen this dream become a reality. Older girls, after having read *Menstrupedia*, have started teaching younger girls in their schools about menstruation. The shame and silence which came from ignorance and fear no longer holds the same power over them. And this is the future that we have envisioned for menstrual hygiene management and menstrual education: 'Each one to teach one.' We want to replace the lack of information and myths being passed on to young children with correct and factual information.

Our next project is *Boys Be Working*, which is a book for boys and includes a chapter on periods. This is because we believe boys should be educated about menstruation and included in the discussions. Without their inclusion, change is impossible.

Why do you think something like this had not been done before?

Several other books on menstruation had been available in the market before we published *Menstrupedia*; so our idea was not a new one. However, no one had developed the concept as we have. Our book projects menstruation as entirely a positive experience. This made it new and unique. Previous books on the subject have been very uninspiring, but we benefited from their experience, and it helped us refine our work.

Secondly, most of the organizations that promote menstrual awareness and health are, generally speaking, NGOs, whereas we are a business with a social angle. We needed a product that would not only be competitive but would also fill a gap in the market and meet the needs of parents, teachers, women and girls. And the product needed to be of excellent quality, so much so that people would be prepared to pay for it. That's exactly what we did. We created a competitive product that addressed a social issue which, in reality, concerned not just menstruators but also society at large.

We believe there is still a lot of work that needs to be done on menstrual education and reproductive health. It needs to be carried out in a culturally sensitive way to enable people to talk about it and empower them to break taboos. Only a sustainable business, and not a charity, can make this possible. Our biggest hurdle was initially the lack of funds, which we were able to overcome through crowdfunding.

What would you consider to be the ideal outcome in ten years?

When it comes to gender and sociocultural norms and practices as well as changing attitudes, ten years is a short time. However, if we look back to five or six years ago, nobody could have imagined that periods would be discussed as openly as it is now in everyday conversations in India.

We thought it would be a dream come true if girls taught and supported each other at school with correct information about menstruation without relying on an external educator, and that too has happened.

But for real change to occur, we need a generation of girls who are free from the burden of menstrual taboos, myths and ignorance. These girls will grow up to raise their children with proper menstrual education and awareness. So, our long-term goal is to educate and change a single generation. And that's how long it will take to bring about radical change in the prevailing environment – the time it takes to raise one generation. So far we have educated thirteen million children, and we look forward to doing the same for more.

What governmental regulations or legal frameworks have facilitated or impeded your venture?

The government has several adolescent health programmes – Rashtriya Kishor Swasthya Karyakram (RKSK), Swachh Bharat Abhiyan and Beti Bachao Beti Padhao Abhiyan – which focus on sanitation and girl child education. Such programmes have encouraged a number of projects focused on menstruation as well. Menstruation has been linked to sanitation and the need for proper toilets because many girls were found to be missing classes and dropping out of school altogether after they entered puberty.

It was against this backdrop that *Menstrupedia* was created, and I can safely say the government framework helped our project a great deal. I was also on the Technical Advisory Board of the Union Government, and my specific portfolio was menstrual hygiene management. In fact, our most important partnerships have been with the various governments, organizations and individuals who were inspired by the book and wanted to take it to the next level.

What has been the influence or contribution of foreign players in the space of menstrual healthcare in India?

I think it is true that when you are tackling a cultural issue or challenge in a culture that you belong to, it is difficult to look at the bigger picture. So I think foreign agencies in India have played a critical role in helping us see the adverse effects of restrictive cultural practices. For instance, by asking what these outdated cultural norms were doing to the economy or the gender dynamic and how they have affected girls' education.

Indeed, the very first research was actually done by private research agencies. Child in Need Institute or CINI (founded 1974) and Chetna (founded 1984), were some of the pioneering NGOs which addressed menstrual health under reproductive health (RH), using the 'Life Cycle Approach' to include every stage in a woman's reproductive life.[1] They helped in establishing some baseline data, which motivated local organizations to reflect on prevalent norms and practices. They also funded some of the earliest programmes for menstrual awareness and health in India.

These contributions were enormously helpful. Whatever is happening at a global level helps us reflect on things at a local level and think about how such and such problems are affecting our economy. For instance, you might not think that girls dropping

out of school affects the economy, but the truth is that there is a
direct connection between the two. If you were to ask why, you'd
realize the entire workforce pipeline is leaking. Then you discover
the source of the leakage is girls dropping out of school because
of lack of access to menstrual products. And it becomes evident
that many a girl's life comes to a halt at puberty, and it widens
the gender gap in education and the workforce. So yes, definitely,
when you look at global conversations, it helps you reflect and
delve deeper into local problems and question your own self-
limiting beliefs.

An Activist's Fight for Dignified Menstruation in Nepal

RADHA PAUDEL

MENSTRUATION IS A COMPLEX AND MULTIFACETED phenomenon. It is not simply about the average five days of bleeding which totals about seven years in an average woman's lifetime. Neither is it only about reproductive health. It is about the whole human experience which accompanies this biological process. Menstruation is referred to by various names in Nepal: monthlies, *par sareko*, *bahir sareko*, *pudo sareko*, *pakha lageko*, *panditni baneko*, 'she's gone to her maternal house', and so on. In west Nepal, menstruation and the rituals associated with it, are both referred to as *chhaupadi*, *chhui* or *chhui pratha*. The word 'chhaupadi' is composed of two words; 'chhau' (blood) and 'padi' (the state of bleeding). And in Kathmandu, it is referred to as the state of queenhood, of 'majhu' (Newari). But the restrictions on women remain the same, be it east Nepal, west Nepal or Kathmandu.

There are over forty types of restrictions related to food, touch, mobility and participation in day-to-day activities which are imposed across the country regardless of the menstruator's class, caste, education, geographical location and religion. The differences lie in the name, form and magnitude. Menstruators are not allowed to go out, attend cultural gatherings or even go to school for about five to seven days every month. Considered to be untouchable and impure during this period, they are also not permitted to participate in sacred rituals. Bathing is forbidden and the menstrual clothes are washed and dried privately and separately. They are also restricted from touching plants that bear fruits and vegetables for fear of contamination and kept out of the kitchen, temples and gardens. There are also dietary constraints, and sour foods and milk products are out of bounds during one's menstrual cycle.

Menstruators in Nepal, as in many other parts of the world, suffer because of fear, ignorance and lack of resources. Menstrual blood is considered impure and dirty, and in order to preserve the cleanliness of the entire family, menstruators are isolated and banished to the 'chhaupadi' (which could be a hut, a shed or a separate room, bed or corner of a room) with their separate or old clothes. In some parts of west Nepal, the sheds are usually made of mud, stone or grass, depending on the economic status of the family, and this indicator also determines the interior hygiene of the huts.

Chhaupadi, broadly speaking, conjures up the image of poor, uneducated people from west Nepal who practise this ritual out of ignorance. This is not always true as in many cases, it is because of a lack of resources and they have no choice. The citizens of Kathmandu or west Nepal have few options when it comes to maintaining sanitary conditions within their homes. Many middle-class and lower-middle-class families do not bathe every day due to scarcity of water. In the winter months, this becomes more difficult because even if there is water, there are no provisions to heat it.

It is my conviction that the notion of what chhaupadi is and how it is practised needs to be redefined by the Nepalese government as a policy. Their definition ought to be broader, along these lines: 'Chhaupadi is a practice of the Nepalese people wherein menstruators are isolated and restricted from participating in societal activities during their menstrual cycle. It varies in its forms, visibility and severity.' In the absence of such a redefinition, chhaupadi will continue to be understood as just the practice of exiling women to huts while the stigma, taboo and other types of discrimination will continue to exist under the guise of tradition, not just in Nepal but also in other parts of the world. In fact, when I met Nepalese people living abroad, I was shocked to discover that they practised chhaupadi in the name of preserving and upholding their culture and traditional values. Indeed, many forms of menstrual discrimination have endured into the twenty-first century because of unfounded notions about menstruation. I witnessed my sisters and mother undergo similar difficulties when I was only seven years old.

I have come to realize that the only way to overcome this form of discrimination is through three E's: education, empowerment and emancipation. The Radha Paudel Foundation's initiative – Dignified Menstruation – takes a holistic human rights approach and calls for a paradigm shift in thinking about menstruation, from hygiene to dignity. I have spoken along these lines at more than three dozen universities and conferences internationally.

Through a 'from womb to tomb' framework, which takes into consideration the social, cultural, economic, technological, political and environmental aspects of menstruation, I seek to mitigate the immediate, as well as the long-term, negative consequences of ill-informed menstrual discrimination, both in Nepal and beyond. My aim is to ensure that all individuals who menstruate, including transgender men, enjoy equal dignity and should suffer no violence, discrimination, abuse, stigma, shame, restrictions or harm on account of their menstruation.

I have travelled across Nepal and visited more than sixty of the seventy-seven districts to research the restrictions imposed on menstruating women. The restrictions are related to contact, food, mobility and participation in everyday activities and can be categorized as visible or invisible, and private or public. From the data I gathered, I concluded that over 95 per cent of families enforce these restrictions regardless of caste, class, region, education or religion because they consider menstrual blood to be impure, and that women's bodies and their belongings are contaminated during menstruation.

Since the declaration of the Millennium Development Goals by the United Nations and more so because of social media, the chhaupadi tradition has received much global attention and made its eradication a Nepal government priority. Thanks to the Safe Motherhood Program launched by the Government of Nepal, chhaupadi after childbirth has been banned, but it is still widely observed during menstruation. In 2005, the Supreme Court of Nepal asked the government to formulate legal guidelines to address this discriminatory practice. In 2008, the Ministry of Women, Children and Senior Citizens composed the beginnings of a draft document, the provisions of which were quite vague.

Nearly ten years later, in 2017, there was still no visible progress. In the same year, a group of activists including myself filed a report at the District Police Office in Dailekh Province, asking them to note the case of a woman who had died a few months earlier while in chhaupadi, due to neglect. We also asked them to recognize the fact that the local police had refused to acknowledge the true cause of her death. As a result of our lobbying and the efforts of other activists, a bill which proposed the criminalization of chhaupadi was passed later that year and became a law in August 2017. It decreed that a person could face up to three months in jail or a fine of $30 for bail or both for any kind of discrimination based on menstruation. In December 2019, under the provisions of this law, the police arrested the brother-in-law of a woman who died during chhaupadi.

There are other villages in west Nepal where communities have committed themselves to abolishing this tradition. In 2020, the Ministry of Women stepped into the picture by taking a lead role in bringing together the federal, provincial and local governments for a programme called 'Understanding Dignified Menstruation during the COVID-19 Pandemic'. Events under this programme took place in Kathmandu, Doti, Mangalsen Achham, Dullu and Narayan Municipality, Dailekh and Birendranagar in Surkhet where I was a key speaker. Both the fear of arrest and the promise of incentives have been utilized to bring about change but neither offers long-term solutions because they do not include interventions to address the ignorance and fear surrounding menstruation.

Dignified menstruation, according to the Radha Paudel Foundation and the Global South Coalition for Dignified Menstruation of which I am the founder, demands the active involvement of all stakeholders, women and men, girls and boys, faith and political leaders, civil society, private sector, government and media. Everyone must be held accountable for their contribution to the creation of an environment that ensures dignity during menstruation. Dignified menstruation can be defined by three P's:

- Principally, menstruation must be considered through a human rights lens.

- Practically, menstruation must be approached holistically by adopting WASH (water, sanitation and hygiene), education, health, empowerment and environmental impact.
- Psychologically, the menstruation dialogue must help deconstruct, reconstruct and reshape the unequal distribution of power due to menstrual discrimination, and it should cultivate a culture of equality, agency and confidence for individuals and groups, from childhood to grave, through collective efforts.

Currently the Radha Paudel Foundation–Global South Coalition for Dignified Menstruation is expanding its global network of people working towards the same vision. In 2014, we started making reusable sanitary pads and in 2018, we launched the first biodegradable pads in Nepal. In December 2019, the Radha Paudel Foundation and its partners marked, for the first time, Dignified Menstruation Day as part of 16 Days of Activism. This was a global campaign for the prevention of sexual and gender-based violence. Our rallying cry was: Dignified Menstruation for Ending Gender-based Violence and Ensuring Human Rights.

Mr Parbat Gurung, Nepal's former Minister of Women, Children and Senior Citizens, recognized the day and promised to endorse the draft policy on dignified menstruation, which we had put forward in 2017. This draft policy and report was also submitted to the UN in 2020 by the Ministry of Women and was an important step towards raising awareness and helping girls and women in Nepal struggling with the challenges of menstruation.

In 2020, the Ministry of Women in Nepal, in collaboration with the National Human Rights Commission and seventy other organisations from across the globe, marked the second International Dignified Menstruation Day under the theme of 'Menstrual Talk, Dignity First'. The three-day workshop concluded with a twelve-point declaration calling for immediate action. In 2021, the National Women Commission hosted a third edition of the workshop with the theme 'Dignified Menopause is a Human Right not Privilege'. Also in 2021, the Radha Paudel Foundation hosted a global summit on Dignified Menopause in Scotland. In 2022, the fourth International Dignified Menstruation Day will be celebrated in Nepal and twenty five other countries. Our efforts to amplify voices around dignified menstruation, education, research and advocacy work are gaining considerable ground, despite having zero funding from any government.

It is my conviction that with the aid of committed and collaborative stakeholders, the Radha Paudel Foundation will continue to positively impact the long-term goal of unconditional dignity for menstruators in Nepal and beyond, and also position our organization as a collective of important leaders and activists from the global south at the forefront of real and meaningful change.

Anandi: India's First and Only Certified Compostable and Biodegradable Pad

INTERVIEW | FARAH AHAMED

I SPOKE TO THE CEO AND FOUNDER OF AAKAR INNOVATIONS Jaydeep Mandal, who is based in Mumbai, to learn more about his journey to developing his unique product – Anandi, India's first fully compostable and biodegradable pad. His persistence and determination to help menstruators has led him to setting global industry standards and winning international awards for innovation.

What is Aakar?

Aakar is a social enterprise within the menstrual hygiene sector and the only certified manufacturer of compostable sanitary pads in India. It has two arms: hardware and software. The hardware arm is Aakar Innovation Private Limited, which sells patented compostable sanitary pads, develops machines for making sanitary pads and its raw materials. The machines produced include manual, semi-automated and automated ones.

The software arm is Aakar Social Ventures. Through this initiative, Aakar aims firstly to raise awareness about menstrual hygiene and the range of menstrual products available in the market. We do this through talks and showcases to discuss cloth, reusable cloth pads, normal pads, compostable pads, tampons and menstrual cups to help people make an informed choice. Instead of focusing on a brand, we work on the principle that people should be encouraged and given the freedom to choose one or a combined set of products as it suits them. Secondly, Aakar educates women about the science behind menstrual hygiene and reproductive health as there is a lack of awareness about the relationship between menstruation and childbirth. Men tend to be more interested and ready to support their wife, daughters and sisters when this aspect is highlighted. And we believe it is critical to include men and boys in the conversation.

What is innovative about Aakar's sanitary pads?

Aakar's Anandi pads are fully compostable and biodegradable. We are the first company to develop a biodegradable, compostable and completely safe version of SAP made of natural materials, called Bio-SAP. The generally and widely available commercial SAP is a chemical known as sodium polyacrylate which is harmful because it can cause rashes and dryness and other complications. For instance, in the past, tampons containing SAP have led to fatalities. It has been banned by the USFDA for use in tampons but not in sanitary pads and diapers, which is one of the key reasons for infections and skin irritations in women and nappy rash in babies.

Through Anandi pads, we offer a safe bio-alternative: a sanitary pad that relies on bio-based Bio-SAP. In fact, we believe Anandi is currently the safest sanitary pad in the world, not only because it contains no harmful chemicals, but also because it is the first and only pad in India to have obtained a Government of India lab certificate under ISO standard 17088, equivalent to the American standard and European standard for compostability. Many enterprises are attempting to develop new sanitary products, some of which are unsafe or non-compostable/non-biodegradable even though they claim to not be so. So, at a national policy level, Aakar worked with the Bureau of Indian Standards (BIS) as part of their advisory team to help develop new national standards for sanitary pads in India. Anandi pads' compostability standard has been used by the BIS as a reference to come up with the first compostable/ biodegradable pads testing standard for sanitary napkins in India – IS 5405:2019.

What is the difference between compostable and biodegradable sanitary pads?

By biodegradable, we mean anything which degrades naturally with time. It could take days, weeks, months or even years. The terms oxo-degradable and compostable are sub-categories of biodegradable. Oxo-degradable materials are those which, through heat, UV rays and sunlight, quickly disintegrate into microplastics. These are more harmful than normal plastics because they become part of the ecosystem as micro particles of plastics. For instance, if animals were to ingest them, they could die, or they could pass to humans through the food chain. For this reason, oxo-degradable plastics are banned in Europe and are in the process of being banned in the US.

Compostable materials disintegrate to become manure via a certain process within 90–180 days under suitable composting conditions without any negative impact on the ecosystem or the environment. The process and definition of what is compostable has been debated internationally and standards have been set by Americans, Europeans, and now we can say, Indians as well. For

a material to be environmentally safe, it must be compostable and
not just biodegradable.

What are the implications of this for sanitary pad manufacturers and the public?

Unfortunately, in India and other developing countries, many
companies, including menstrual pad startups often manufacture/
import products that they claim are biodegradable but in reality,
the products take more than 500 years to degrade or equally bad,
become microplastics post degradation. Both cause havoc to the
environment.

Another term, which companies have been using to mislead
the public, is 'organic'. Some companies purporting to sell organic
sanitary pads make this claim based on the fact that their pad
consists of a single top layer of organic cotton while neglecting
to mention that the underlying layers contain non-organic and
non-compostable materials. It is almost impossible that the entire
sanitary pad could be solely made of organic materials. I should
mention there are a few companies that have experimented with
alternatives such as organic cotton pulp pads, but they have very
poor absorbency.

What inspired Aakar to make compostable pads?

In 2012, I had the opportunity to work with the Aga Khan
Foundation on a menstrual hygiene project in Baghlan Province
in Afghanistan for a month. There, I carried out some research
to explore the possibility of setting up a production unit that
could make sanitary pads. I conducted focus group discussions
and interviews with women where they spoke openly about
their challenges with respect to menstruation. I discovered that

disposable sanitary pads were not freely available in the market because of the stigma and shame around menstruation but were sold instead in beauty parlours and other discreet 'women only' places. The other discovery I made was that there was no unobtrusive or hygienic way to dispose of the used pads and they would be disposed with the household garbage. Often these bags would be ripped open by stray dogs, and one could find soiled pads lying on the street. This was shameful, unhygienic and stressful for the women.

My research on girls and women living in villages revealed that they also threw used sanitary pads onto rubbish heaps or small pits behind their homes. Sometimes they would have to walk quite a distance to do this because they did not want their neighbours to know they were menstruating. However, these used pads sometimes found their way back into the village streets carried by stray animals, which was again both humiliating and unhygienic. These discussions made me realize that while access to safe menstrual products was one problem, disposal was yet another and provoked me to think about the environmental impact of the current disposal methods and possibility of a completely 'green' sanitary pad.

Tell us how the first unit was developed.

We first introduced [Arunachalam] Muruganantham's (Padman's) machine into a rural enterprise model. Our endeavour failed because the women complained that the pads were too thick, and the machines were difficult to operate. We shut down the unit and began exploring other options. I travelled across India to try and understand what others were doing and whether they had been successful and met various organizations and individuals, including a group of Ivy League students. I also investigated the products manufactured by multinational companies and came to the conclusion that no small machines were making sanitary pads that ticked all the boxes for the basic requirements of a pad: good absorption, retention, comfort, feel, fit, hygiene and design. I also discovered that the BIS had a benchmark for the quality of sanitary pads.

This prompted me to start designing a machine that could produce sanitary pads which met the basic needs of period management. After almost one and a half years, Aakar came up with the design for a manual machine that could produce pads according to international standards.

In 2013, I developed a fully compostable sanitary pad at Aakar. However, the napkin was very thick, and it did not use SAP. At the time, I was working on using locally available materials which would allow my product to be manufactured at a low cost. I experimented with various fibres like banana stem, water hyacinth, bagasse, jute and bamboo. I needed a material which was not only absorbent but also comfortable, soft and would not cause infections or rashes. I found that no single material fulfilled all these criteria, but a combination of them did, and this discovery paved the way for Anandi pads.

We tested and experimented with each of our new products and modified our design as needed. Initially, the sanitary pads were made without wings because we thought this was not a priority for village women. However, we soon realized that they preferred the wings for the security and comfort they provided. Accordingly, Aakar changed its machine design and developed a product with wings. From manual machines, we moved on to semi-automatic machines to make the pads. Today, Aakar uses an automatic machine for making Anandi pads.

What is Aakar's business strategy and model?

Aakar currently operates thirty manufacturing units across India, Kenya, Tanzania, South Africa, Zambia, Zimbabwe, Ghana, Cameroon and Nepal. Our aim is to reach every village in India because the majority of the female population lives in rural villages where girls and women do not have access to safe and hygienic menstrual products. All the pads manufactured and distributed in village markets are produced locally at the village level. This model involves women in the manufacturing, marketing and distribution processes, thus uplifting their standard of living through income generation. I am proud to say that Anandi pads by Aakar are by women, of women and for women.

For the past eight years Aakar's focus has been on villages, but over the last two years, we have been branching out to urban consumers. Based on the feedback we received, we realized that Anandi was not suitable for this demographic. Urban consumers had their own specifications as to what they consider to be an ideal pad, which, aside from anything else, had to be ultra-thin. Accordingly, Aakar developed an ultra-thin pad which was the first in the industry to use a bio-superabsorbent, as good as any multinational product available, but safe and entirely compostable.

Aakar has also set up village units funded by grants and support from donors, corporates and the Indian government. With these funds, Aakar supplies villages with the machinery and raw materials, as well as provides training to women on how to make the pads and market them. Our lab regularly tests these pads to ensure they comply with BIS sanitary pads standards set by the government. If they have any issues, Aakar provides further training to ensure the quality is improved to a satisfactory standard.

One of the women, Sajida, aged twenty-four, who works at the Anandi manufacturing plant in Dharavi (Asia's largest slum), said this: 'I now earn my livelihood from making these pads, and I can also help other women. Before this, I used to use rags, and it was very difficult. Now I use Anandi pads. Initially, I was embarrassed, but now after two and a half years I feel very comfortable and happy.'

How has Aakar's reputation and reach grown internationally?

In 2017, the Miss World Organisation contacted Aakar to promote its compostable pads and mini-factory model in India, and across the globe. In 2018, on Nelson Mendala's 100th birthday, we set up a manufacturing unit in Mandela's village which was inaugurated by the President of South Africa. In the same year, Anandi pads also received the Global Bioplastics Award in Germany at the 13th European Bioplastics & Bio-based Materials Conference. In 2019, Anandi received the prestigious 12th International Conference Award on Bio-based Materials. These awards are considered to be the Oscars of the bio-industry.

Also in 2019, the Miss World from Mexico, Vanessa Ponce de León, launched Aakar's new ultra-thin pads in India. As our international reach has expanded, we are committed to assigning a certain percentage of the profits earned from the urban consumer to help needy women and girls from rural areas. We hope to do this through the provision of free Anandi pads and menstrual hygiene education.

And I would like to add that Aakar would not have been able to have the impact and reach that it has had, without the support and partnership of a dedicated team, investors, advisors, mentors and vendor-partners, including of course our clients, consumers and beneficiaries.

Do you have any advice for anyone wishing to enter the area of startups in menstrual product innovation or partner with you?

Currently, there is a lot of misinformation around menstrual health and hygiene management in the market. This is fuelling the proliferation of shady manufacturers of pad-making machines which in turn are misleading startup investors and consumers alike. My advice would be to make sure that in-depth research is carried out before you invest, so that you are not deceived. We are already burdened by so much menstrual toxic waste, it would be preposterous to add to it, so look for an informed and sustainable solution.

Has the Covid-19 Pandemic influenced your future business strategy?

The pandemic has emphasized the need to really focus on healthy and environmentally sustainable solutions. Our strategy is to continue thinking about how we can share Anandi with the rest of the world, improve our current product, indigenize it further and lower its cost.

Periods Are Never Easy: Coping with Menstruation in Afghanistan

MARIAM SIAR

I WAS BORN IN AFGHANISTAN IN 1999 AND MOVED TO Australia in 2016, when I was seventeen. I am the second child in a family of six. Before I started my periods, my mother, who is a doctor, explained to me why I would get it and what it would be like. She reassured me and told me not to be frightened because this was a natural process which all girls go through at puberty. She encouraged me to take it in my stride and continue with life as usual, while taking extra care about my personal hygiene. 'Periods are never easy,' she said. If I had a headache or cramps, she said she would prescribe something for the pain. I got my first period when I was eleven years old. I was at my grandparents' house in Kabul with my family, and it happened right after we had had lunch. I went to the toilet and on discovering the blood, told my mother about it and she gave me a pad. She told my aunt, and later told my dad. No one made a big deal about it and my first period went by just like an ordinary occurrence.

I realize how lucky I am because both my parents are doctors. This has meant that frank discussions about the body and biological processes are common at our dinner table. For many girls in Afghanistan the situation is very different. UNICEF's 2016 Formative Research on Menstrual Hygiene Management (MHM) in Afghanistan, carried out in Kabul and the nearby Parwan Province, found that both a lack of knowledge and facilities are responsible for girls often missing school, and even dropping out, when they start menstruating.[1] The study, which was conducted jointly by UNICEF and Afghanistan's Ministry of Education, also found that 70 per cent of girls did not take a bath or shower during their period out of fear that it would make them infertile. Over 50 per cent had no knowledge of menstruation before getting their first period, which left them shocked and frightened. Moreover, less than 50 per cent of girls from urban areas received any menstrual hygiene education at school and majority of adolescent girls did not discuss menstruation with their mothers, teachers and classmates.[2] If this is the situation in the cities, one can only imagine how much worse it is in the rural areas.

In many traditional Afghan families, when a girl, either in or out of school, reaches menarche, she is thought to be ready for marriage and childbearing. Therefore, girls often hide the fact that they have started their period out of the fear that their families will stop them from going to school or marry them off. While most girls start their periods without any knowledge of what is happening to them, masculinity is celebrated with great pomp and show. In fact, male circumcision is a matter of pride for the family, and parties are organized to mark the occasion.[3] On the other hand, in some traditional Afghan families, menstruation is a shameful secret that is never discussed, not even between mothers and daughters.

Afghan women's transition into puberty is not acknowledged partly because the subject of female sexuality remains off limits.

Most teenage girls are terrified of the changes occurring in their bodies, and ignorant and confused about how to cope. To discuss it with male members of the family is unthinkable but because my father is a doctor and has an open-minded approach, I have been able to have frank discussions with him about my period and puberty. My mother too spoke very freely to her children, and I have never been treated differently from my brother. If, for instance, I am having a bad day because of my period, it is not a big deal for me to say to my brother, 'Please leave me alone, I've got my period.' He doesn't feel embarrassed, and I don't feel awkward saying it. It was my father who usually bought my pads when I was younger, and he did this without even asking. Periods have been completely normalized in my family.

However, misinformation about menstruation is widespread across Afghanistan, and young girls are encultured into traditional and often unhealthy rituals and practices. These include avoiding spicy and cold food, snacks, not bathing for the duration of their period (a purported hedge against infertility) and skipping social gatherings. For me it was quite different; I recall one time when my grandfather said to me as we were having lunch, 'Because you have your period, you should eat red meat. You need the iron.' I grew up being able to discuss periods very easily with all male members of my family. The fact that my grandfather told me to eat a certain food is also unusual, because it's the opposite for many girls. Growing up with this sense of empowerment and confidence has no doubt helped me cope better with my period.

The myths that Afghan girls grow up with, coupled with poor access to affordable hygiene products, has resulted in their poor physical and mental health, and had an adverse impact on their education. Many girls drop out of school soon after they begin to menstruate.[4] The lack of awareness surrounding menstrual hygiene management continues to have devastating consequences for Afghan girls and women. According to the 2016 UNICEF study, 29 per cent of girls miss school due to menstruation, and half were unaware of what it was before it started.[5] The report noted, 'Menstruating girls [are] unable to adequately manage their monthly menses with safety, dignity and privacy.' Ignorance has led girls and women to use dirty cloths, which gives them infections. Many were unable to find respite from pain as they felt too ashamed to ask for medication for cramps.

When I got my period, while it was a life-changing experience, I did not undergo any psychological trauma as such. But many Afghan girls are haunted by unarticulated expectations after they get their period; they are no longer children, but young women and they are expected to act with decorum and behave like adults. Some are not allowed to attend social events during their period and others are subjected to child marriages when they start menstruating.[6] For them, it means forgetting their childhood, becoming submissive, accommodating and acting with humility, especially towards men. Menstruation brings with it major bodily changes and humiliation for these girls.[7] The result is that many Afghan girls end up hating their transition to womanhood. Moreover, menstruation has a significant impact on their lives, especially their ability to attend and concentrate at school. Most girls don't have the money or the support from their families to buy menstrual products. While sanitary pads can be found in all supermarkets in major Afghan cities, depending on the city and area, pads are displayed on shelves along with other items, or kept hidden in a private section.[8]

In the past, small but significant efforts to change conservative attitudes and practices have been made but with the recent political changes and the Taliban takeover, it is difficult to determine the current situation on the ground. Most prominent among the initiatives carried out was a campaign by the Ministry of Education with support from the United Nations to train teachers to help female students better understand and prepare for their periods.[9] The first-ever National Guidelines on Menstrual Hygiene in Afghanistan were also published in 2018.[10] It included a training kit for teachers, as well as a comic book for adolescent girls. But whether these are in practice at present is debatable. The challenges in Afghanistan are many, and strong political will is necessary for any significant change. A 2021 report[11] published by WaterAid and UNICEF identified the progress made as well as the existing gaps with respect to achieving sustainable and inclusive menstrual hygiene services in schools and the opportunities for promoting and mainstreaming them. The report particularly focused on the need to ensure menstrual hygiene during the Covid-19 pandemic. The key achievements in this respect mentioned in the report include the School Health Policy (2019), the production of the menstrual health management teachers' guide, talking points for teachers, a comic book, UNICEF's Gender Unit and WASH training for government officials and the involvement of celebrities, local influencers, school and community leaders in various awareness campaigns.

However, there have also been some leaders, including women, who felt that discussing menstruation openly was a step too far. 'It's too early for Afghans to understand such issues,' said Mujib Mehradad, a spokesman for the Ministry of Education, adding that there were no future plans to introduce 'taboo' elements in the school curriculum.[12] This kind of attitude has hindered progress. There are other crucial challenges recorded in the 2021 report. About 29 per cent girls stayed absent during menstruation because schools did not have facilities for handwashing or changing and disposing used cloths/pads. As of 2019, 94 per cent schools lack basic handwashing with soap and water, which translated to almost 5.6 million children being denied handwashing facilities in schools in Afghanistan. With 65 per cent schools having limited water supply and 35 per cent with no water supply at all, hygiene management has been severely impacted. While 38 per cent schools had improved sanitation, 12 per cent had unimproved sanitation/non-functional latrines and up to 50 per cent did not have any latrine facility.

As can be seen from these statistics, there is much that needs to be done, both in terms of infrastructural support as well as education and awareness. These are numbers from before the fall of the Afghan government. With the Taliban at the helm of affairs, one can assume that the numbers will not remain the same.

After the fall of the Afghanistan Islamic Republic on 15 August 2021, life has become more challenging for common Afghans, and menstrual health is likely to have become even less of a priority than it was before. In an effort to play a small part in contributing to improving the plight of women, I registered an NGO – the Afghan Women's Support Group (AWSG) – in 2021. AWSG aims to help Afghan women access and uphold their rights, while assisting them in every aspect of their lives. And whenever an opportunity arises, the NGO will also carry out menstrual education workshops for both boys and girls. It is one of my dreams to help girls enjoy a smoother transition to puberty, the way I did. Periods are never easy, but armed with information, knowledge and support, a girl can cope better with this very natural phenomenon.

Red Dye on a Pad: Two Transwomen on Their Experience of Menstruation

INTERVIEW | FARAH AHAMED

IN INDIA, THE HIJRA COMMUNITY BROADLY INCLUDES transsexuals, eunuchs and transgender people and in Pakistan, they are also known as the *khwaja sira* in Urdu and *khusra* in Punjabi. They have an ancient history in South Asia. Pakistan's transgender population is estimated at about 500,000, but according to the 2017 census, there are only 10,418 people who identify themselves as transgender, because many do not register themselves as transgender to avoid being discriminated against.[1] The trans community survive in a precarious social niche as wedding dancers, providers of blessings in exchange for cash or beggars at traffic lights.

In a society that is often extremely hostile to transgender people, being recognized and accepted for who they are means the world to them. Transwomen, who have claimed femininity for themselves, have a complicated relationship with menstruation. Farzana and Chandan are two transwomen in their mid-fifties from Lahore who spoke to me about their relationship with menstruation. Originally from Okara, they had moved to Lahore as teenagers in hopes of finding work and a supportive community.

They live together in a small flat which has an attached bathroom and no kitchen, and rely on commercially prepared food. This is Farzana and Chandan's story.

'Every person has a deep-rooted desire; and for us, we long to be a "complete" woman. We want to feel more feminine, and so we imitate the experience of menstruation by wearing a sanitary pad for a week every month,' Farzana said.

'Of course we do not menstruate,' Chandan explained, 'but we try to mimic what it could be like to be a "real" woman and have the period. Some of us even complain about having backaches, cramps and headaches and other common menstrual symptoms, but in reality, there is nothing. Some khusra use red food dye or paint their pads to give the impression of blood and wear it all day.'

It is common practice in Pakistan for women to have dietary and socializing restrictions imposed on them while they are menstruating, and these too were followed by Farzana and Chandan.

'Just like women who are really on their period, we even abstain from certain foods and rituals as if we are really on our period,' Farzana said. 'We don't eat too hot or too cold or sour foods, and we don't take baths. We also keep away from holy places.'

But the practice of wearing sanitary pads had another purpose.

'The pads are also a form of security,' Chandan said. 'When we are out on the street walking or begging, or at parties we are often taunted, harassed, groped and subjected to unwanted advances. We wear a pad to protect ourselves from such treatment.'

Alongside the many difficulties trans people face, access to medical assistance is an important one, especially when it concerns their sexual health. They find it daunting to approach doctors because their concerns are sidelined and they are often abused or harassed by doctors, if not by other patients.

'Sometimes, the doctors and nurses don't know which ward to send us to, male or female,' Farzana said. 'They make fun of us while we suffer.'

Private medical care is costly.

'We can only afford to go to government hospitals because they provide free medical check-ups there,' Farzana said. 'Private medical treatment is unaffordable. However, at government hospitals we are subjected to humiliating experiences and doctors are reluctant to treat us.'

Chandan explained, 'One time I had an infection which I contracted from sharing a dirty toilet. When I went to the hospital the doctors insulted me, and I was forced to leave the hospital without receiving any treatment. However, luckily, I managed to raise some money from my friends and was able to obtain private but expensive medical treatment.'

Trans people in Pakistan are often disowned by their families and left to fend for themselves. 'I'm fortunate,' Farzana said, 'because my family and relatives always support and encourage me. I know they do this because I send them money. Recently, I even contributed to my sister's wedding.'

Many are less fortunate and end up joining a community with people who have faced similar discrimination and where they feel more accepted. Such communities are often led by a guru who is the leader and takes them under their wing. Gurus keep the community together and help its members find jobs, teach them to beg and give them a sense of belonging and solidarity. Some lobby for better rights, however, others have been known to exploit their members sexually.[2]

Farzana had run away from home when she was fifteen. She said, 'I learnt how to survive by watching others in my community. My guru gave me my name. I observed how they defended and protected themselves.'

Because of their unsettled lives or discrimination, many drop out of school and this exclusion from education means that 42 per cent of the trans community is illiterate.[3] 'When I was very young and at school,' Chandan said, 'a boy poked me with a pencil in my left eye and impaired my vision. Because of that I left school, so I can't read or write.'

Punjab is believed to have the highest number of transgender people, followed by Sindh, Khyber Pakhtunkhwa and Balochistan.[4] Pakistan has laws that protect trans rights and is one of only twelve countries that recognizes transgender identity on national ID cards.

In 2009, Pakistan's Supreme Court ruled that provincial governments should protect the rights of the khwaja sira, and in 2012, transgender people were granted the same rights as their cis counterparts, including the right to vote and to inherit property. In 2017, 'transgender' was included as a category in the national census, and the Transgender Rights Protection Act was passed the following year. The new law includes a provision which allows people to self-declare their gender.[5] Despite the laws, the khwaja sira meet with violent opposition when they discuss their needs, whether it is to do with their personal or professional aspirations. They find it difficult to get jobs and are often treated with suspicion and contempt.

As transwomen in Lahore, Farzana and Chandan are often ostracized. 'It's been like this for me my whole life,' Chandan said. 'We are used to people passing derogatory comments on our bodies.'

'Even now, on the streets, not a single day goes by when I am not jeered at,' Farzana said. 'While waiting at the gate, before coming in to speak to you, we were asked how much we were getting paid for our sexual favours.'

When and if they do manage to get domestic cleaning work, it is not an easy journey. If anything goes wrong, or if something goes missing, everyone is quick to accuse, blame, sack them. Their existence is precarious, and many are forced to rely on sex work and many others find it easier to beg. According to a 2016 survey, 51 per cent of trans people's overall income comes from dancing (including *toli*, ceremonial dances at weddings and births), 15 per cent from sex work and 12 per cent from begging.[6]

'Begging is like a job for us,' Farzana said. 'We dress up and go out to the streets to plead for money. What choice do we have? But there is no honour in begging. People help us with cash because they understand it is difficult for us. Another problem is that our reputation has been tainted by fake khusras. These are young men who dress up like us and pretend to be khusras. They often offer sexual favours too. All of this makes our lives complicated.'

However, religious and government sanctions often take away these limited sources of income from them. 'You can't imagine how difficult it is to survive,' Chandan said. 'Sex work and begging are illegal, while dancing is seen by religious authorities as un-Islamic. Many of our community have to resort to underground sex work and are targeted by the police.'

There are some NGOs in Pakistan like Wajood and Gender Guardian which support transgender people with basic supplies such as soap, shampoo and condoms. They even provide counselling services or facilitate work, but trans people in Pakistan are often disowned by their families and left to fend for themselves.

We don't believe we have any rights to anything,' Farzana said. 'We are completely marginalized. No one likes us.'

'Though our lives have no dignity, we support each other and keep ourselves happy,' Chandan said. 'Farzana has me and I have her, and we rely on each other.'

Plea for a Safe Haven

VICTORIA PATRICK

TRANSLATED FROM URDU BY AMNA MAWAZ KHAN

Desperation all around, bloodcurdling shrieks calling for help
Rivers of blood flowing in all directions
Intermingled with this rushing blood is another kind of blood
The immaculate blood of maidens
The hidden blood of the veiled
Shamed with the flow, they hide.
In the middle of fields, under canopies and in shelters
Each one for herself in this strange world.
No home, no possessions, only the clothes on her back
How does one thwart this unrelenting blood?
Hear my plea, my Protector!

الاماں الحفیظ

المناک منظر چیخیں پکاریں

خون کی ندیاں ہر طرف بہ رہی ہیں

اسی خوں میں شامل ایک اور خون بھی ہے

دوشیزاؤں کی عصمت کا خون

پردہ نشینوں کا پوشیدہ خون

جو سمٹی سمٹائی شرم سے زمین میں گڑی جارہی ہیں

سائبانوں اور پناہ گاہوں میں ،میدانوں

عجب نفسا نفسی کا عالم ہوا ہے

وہی تین کپڑے بے گھری بے سامانی

سمیٹیں بھی تو اس کو کیسے سمیٹیں

روکیں بھی تو اس کو کیسے روکیں

الاماں الحفیظ ، الاماں الحفیظ

Not Just a Piece of Cloth:
A Goonj Initiative

INTERVIEW | FARAH AHAMED

GOONJ, SET UP IN 1999 BY MEENAKSHI AND ANSHU GUPTA, is an organization in India which works with women in rural tribal communities and women in disasters to empower them and promote better menstrual health practices. Their efforts are significantly directed at including voices usually ignored in the mainstream debate on menstruation – menstruators living through natural disasters, those living with disabilities, migrant workers and tribal communities in remote areas.

I interviewed the founders, Anshu and Meenakshi, and Goonj's program analyst, Prachi Jain, to learn more about their work. Meenakshi, who remained behind the scenes until 2005, is especially passionate about including forgotten and unheard voices and building a pan-India civic engagement through Goonj. Prachi works with an initiative called Not Just a Piece of Cloth (NJPC), and her areas of interest are gender and sexuality.

How did the NJPC project start and what does it do?

Goonj's involvement in menstruation emerged from its core work of highlighting the basic, but ignored, need for clothing. While talking to women in rural India, Goonj discovered that the majority of them also struggled for cloth to manage their menstrual cycle every month. Instead of cloth, they were using sand, jute ash, rags, plastic or, indeed, anything they could find. Goonj realized that millions of menstruators in India (women, girls, transmen and non-binary folks) had little awareness about menstrual health and hygiene. In addition to this, the prevailing culture of shame and silence around women's bodies prevented them from asking questions or speaking up about the health-related menstrual challenges they face.

After the 2004 tsunami in Tamil Nadu, Goonj was given 100 trucks of cloth by the Indian government. In an effort to make optimal use of this cloth, the Guptas, together with forty women from the slums of Chennai, began working on turning the surplus cotton into menstrual cloth pads. As the project progressed, they realized that aside from menstrual pads, many women did not have access to adequate undergarments, and they began to make these as well.

Goonj views menstruation challenges at three levels:

1. Transactional: When women do not have access to clean and safe menstrual products including undergarments and/ or pads.
2. Infrastructural: When women have no private or secure bathing and toilet area, nor a proper waste disposal facility, or access to adequate medical infrastructure or institutional support to help them prioritize their health.

3. Mindset: When women are ignorant about their bodies and how to protect themselves (including dealing with the taboos and myths of shame which society imposes upon them during menstruation).

All of these contribute to compromising a woman's quality of life, making her vulnerable and exposing her to indignity and poor health. Goonj's work is aimed at addressing these challenges, and also changing misguided notions about menstruation and increasing menstrual literacy. For the organization, menstruation is not just a women's rights issue but a human rights issue, and its efforts have been directed towards building a wider ecosystem that normalizes, supports and nurtures menstrual health access, affordability and awareness in communities of women across India.

With this goal in mind, Goonj has reached out not only to women living in urban slums and rural villages, but also to those living in remote tribal areas, migrant and landless labourers, women with disabilities and those affected by disasters, amongst others. From the beginning, Goonj's aim has been to bridge the growing gap between those who live in the cities and those in the villages of India with regard to resources and opportunities.

Goonj's pan-India forum is called Menstruation Dialogues; Missing Voices, Missed Out Issues. The forum has highlighted the need for a more nuanced multi-sectoral and multi-faceted approach to supporting women across the cities and villages of India. While working on menstrual hygiene Goonj realized that menstruators faced three key challenges – the three A's: access, affordability and awareness. In the cities, the lack of awareness and affordability is a problem, while in the villages, women have to deal with all three. But both cities and villages are entrenched in the larger ecosystem of shame and silence around menstruation equally. Goonj found that many women live with the constraints of taboos and myths of impurity and untouchability during menstruation. In Tamil Nadu, when a girl from the Banagudi tribe starts her period, she is exiled to a small hut outside the village for five days. She is not allowed to bathe or be in contact with anyone and may only return to the main house when her period is over. When we asked a Banagudi man why he did not provide his wife with pads, he said he couldn't because the nearest market was fifteen kilometres away.

How has Goonj evolved since its establishment in 1999?

In 2004, when Goonj launched NJPC, there was no major research available on menstruation. With the NJPC – A Million Voices campaign, Goonj set out to ask people from both rural and urban areas to share their thoughts on menstruation. More than 12,000 Indians from across the country responded, sharing their experiences. Some of the responses were as follows:

'I saw how my aunt was prevented from paying her last respects to her mother's body before cremation, just because she had her period. It seemed very odd and awkward to me.'

'After the birth of my child, I wasn't prepared for my period, and it happened unexpectedly while I was at the office. My dress and chair became soiled. It was very embarrassing because everyone around me made me feel uncomfortable. In spite of being an educated, modern working woman, illogically, I felt as if I had committed a crime. I was shaken for the next few days and felt as if this incident was being talked about in every corner of the office.'

What has been Goonj's experience of working in disaster situations, remote areas and with migrant workers?

In 2019, Goonj conducted a survey in Bhatapda village in Odisha's Puri district after Cyclone Fani caused a landfall, to find out how women coped with menstruation after the cyclone. In the absence of adequate resources, women were forced to make do with whatever was available.

'I borrowed an undergarment from my daughter in the relief camp when I got my period. I was not prepared for it.'

'I had only one undergarment. If I needed another during my period, I borrowed it from my daughter. In fact, we all borrowed. But during Fani, none of us were prepared even with the basics. I should have been, but I didn't have the resources.'

In Assam in 2019, after a season of heavy floods, the women faced a complete lack of access to toilets and proper bathing areas. Clean water was unavailable for washing menstrual cloth, and there was no sunlight to dry them either. This led to infections and discomfort. Situations like these are a real challenge for Goonj. In regions where cyclones and storms are common occurrences, menstruators have no choice but to use wet cloths during their period. The question was how it can be ensured that there are enough dry cloths for them.

Goonj recognizes that poor women especially bear the brunt of any disaster. They are expected to be responsible for children, aged family members as well as contribute economically to keeping the family stable when the men migrate to other parts of the country in search of work. For communities living in remote geographical areas, the challenges are manifold. For instance, in the higher altitude regions of Guptkashi in Uttarakhand, where there are no gynaecologists on site for deliveries or other emergencies, the question of what women do when they have menstrual cramps or a urinary tract infection is rhetorical. Most women interviewed by Goonj agreed that due to ignorance about menstruation, young girls failed to pay attention to issues like irregular periods or infection, unaware that these problems could have fatal consequences if not treated on time. Education about general and reproductive health, as well as menstrual hygiene, is the need of the hour.

Ms Dinabandhu, the head of Kandhamal Zilla Sabuja Vaidya Sangathan (KZSVS), an Odisha-based partner organization of Goonj, explained the dire situation to the Goonj team: 'The local ANM [auxiliary nurse midwife] comes once a week to give vaccinations. She has no knowledge of menstrual health and hygiene, so there is no way of changing the attitude and rituals practised by the women here. Therefore, they continue to follow primitive methods. There are no health facilities nearby and the nearest district health centre is in Phulwani, which is 130 km away, and accessible only by bus.'

Accessing medical facilities is a real challenge for those living in remote villages. During an NJPC session, the Goonj team met with a group of fifty women and girls, which included staff, frontline workers, cancer survivors and teachers. Many of them shared their views on menstruation, and what came to the forefront was how the lack of proper medical care and attention exacerbated a situation. One woman, a cancer survivor, said:

'I started menstruating when I was twelve years old, but my menstrual cycle was not regular. I did not tell my mother about this. One day, I was bleeding heavily and had to be taken to

Emergency where I was diagnosed with uterine cancer. I had a surgery and my uterus was removed. Now I no longer menstruate.'

As highlighted here, there are multiple difficulties and challenges around menstruation, but Goonj has tried to address them by taking a multi-pronged approach through initiatives such as the NJPC.

What is innovative about Goonj's Not Just a Piece of Cloth initiative?

Over the last fifteen years, Goonj has used the surplus cloth it collected through contributions to create cloth pad packs. These cotton and semi-cotton cloths are segregated and converted into 'MY Pads'. This is a unique project which upcycles old, seasoned products, reduces waste and helps women. Sustainability and the environment are important aspects of the project.

Goonj's MY Pad is based on Reusable Menstrual Management Technology (RMMT) which is fundamentally linked to protecting health and the environment. Cloth-based sanitary pads can help overcome many of the hurdles when it comes to menstrual hygiene in rural India. These products are priced at a much lower cost than factory-made pads which makes them more affordable than commercial sanitary products. Since the material can be locally sourced, they can be made available even in remote areas. As more women begin to realize the benefits of cloth-based alternatives, there will be a gradual decline in the use of factory-made products. An advantage is that the majority of women in rural India use cloth to manage their periods. The same cloth, once it is upscaled into a more hygienic product, has the potential to change menstrual hygiene management in India, as menstruators will have options other than leaves, ash and commercial sanitary pads.

Cloth-based products have the environmental benefit of being reusable and biodegradable. In many parts of rural India, commercially manufactured sanitary pads are often discarded in drains and in the absence of efficient waste disposal facilities, these turn into a breeding ground for germs which can lead to the spread of diseases. No doubt, improperly discarded cloths can cause similar problems, but they are the best alternative because the amount of waste generated is reduced dramatically. Overall, Goonj found that through education and information dissemination, menstruators have begun to understand the need to be environment-friendly and use biodegradable products.

How else has Goonj helped improve menstrual health?

In rural India, open discussions about menstrual hygiene products and underwear are considered to be shameful. Many menstruators from these areas lack access to undergarments and are often unable to afford any form of menstrual hygiene products. Goonj has been supplying undergarments to menstruators in rural India for more than a decade. Even though menstruators in both rural and urban areas of India are exposed to many diseases, the causes are not widely discussed. In fact, the subject of accessibility to affordable undergarments is not yet part of the mainstream discourse on menstrual hygiene management. So far, more than 1.8 million square meters of surplus cotton cloth have been converted into MY Pads by Goonj since 2005, while more than 7 million MY Pads have reached menstruating adolescent girls, women, transgender men and non-binary people across the country.

Goonj works with rural village communities in a project called Chuppi Todo Baithaks (CTB) or Break the Silence

(BTS). A local resource person is identified who supports us in mobilizing the community to conduct meetings. The discussions at these meetings are conducted in phases, and the agenda includes garnering support for long-term interventions with the community to influence a positive change in knowledge, attitudes and practices around menstruation. The gatherings are considered to be safe spaces for listening, open dialogue and action by the community. In urban areas, Goonj's focus is on motivating the city dwellers to contribute their surplus cloth to the organization. They can do this in person, by donating at exhibitions, stalls, and also by spreading the word on social media. Since 2015, through its CTB meetings, Goonj has reached more than 2,26,000 participants and distributed more than 3 lakh undergarments.

How has Goonj tackled the issue of lack of privacy for women in rural India?

In a study conducted by Goonj in 2018, which included 599 girls and women from the villages in Odisha, Rajasthan and Karnataka, the majority of participants admitted to the absence of private bathing spaces where they live. In Odisha, for instance, it was found that 81 per cent of women and girls bathed in open ponds and near wells, where they were often humiliated and harassed by passers-by in addition to suffering the embarrassment of walking home in wet clothes. In rural India, it is a common practice for women to bathe fully clothed near ponds, wells and hand pumps. Their need for privacy goes unnoticed perhaps because it impacts the invisible gender of the society. Nearly 55 per cent of rural households do not have any kind of enclosed bathing space within their living premises.

The construction of private bathing spaces has become a core objective of Goonj's NJPC campaign. In 2018–19, Goonj built

113 private bathing spaces in the hope of having a positive impact on women's health. Through support groups and meetings, it encourages women in the villages to demand and make private spaces in their homes and actively adopt safe, hygienic sanitary practices and products with the aid of local resources. Other Goonj activities during 2020–2021 included: construction, repair and cleaning of 1,700 water points; establishment of 1,500 nutrition gardens through provision of vegetable and fruit seeds; creation and repair of 700 private bathing spaces and the execution of more than 2,000 sanitation-related activities.

Are there voices missing from the current dialogue on menstruation, and whose voices are they?

Goonj's work, spanning over a decade and a half, led to the creation of 'Menstruation Dialogue; Missing Voices, Missed Out Issues' in 2019. This forum sought to direct attention to the challenges of menstrual hygiene. It strived to highlight the voices of invisible women and include them in the mainstream discussion on menstrual health to bring in a more textured and nuanced understanding and drive more strategic work on the ground and at the policy level. Goonj has identified three groups missing from the debate: people with disabilities, migrant workers and tribal communities.

Some stories from the field will shed light on the challenges these groups face. For example, the parents of a girl with a disability wanted her to remove her uterus because they could not cope with the management of her menstrual cycle. They also believed she could easily be abused and become pregnant because she was vulnerable.

Homeless women have no safe space to rest or access to private bathing spaces. They are forced to share public toilets with men or wash in public spaces out of desperation, just as tribal communities have little or poor access to soap or running water. It is also quite common for migrant women workers working as labourers on construction sites to defecate and bathe out in the open using dirty water without any privacy. The story is the same for millions of women living in remote tribal communities, harvest workers, flower pickers and others.

Goonj did some work in Odisha State, which is primarily forest area, in Kandhamal, one of the poorest districts of the state, and very difficult to access by road. The women from the region are particularly vulnerable. A harvest worker from the Kui tribe in Kandhamal told Goonj: 'When I have a period emergency and I'm in the field and have no cloth, I'm forced to use *sal patta* [leaves of the sal tree].'

Another Kui woman, also a harvest worker, said: 'We don't have enough undergarments, and here it rains all the time. Often, even the few cloths we have, aren't dry. We make do with whatever we have. I wash my menstrual cloths with wood ash. I soak them overnight in water and ash. In the morning, I dust off the ash and dry the cloth in the sun.'

What were some of the unexpected outcomes of NJPC?

One positive outcome has been that as the women have started prioritizing their health and bodies, they have also started demanding and reclaiming space for their privacy and security. They have become emboldened to ask questions about their health and future and learnt to make more informed choices about their menstrual needs. Our initiative has empowered them to come together to support each other and take collaborative action. We have witnessed how improved menstrual health has contributed to an overall sense of each woman's well-being.

Over the past few decades, through the NJPC initiative, Goonj has been able to increase awareness about menstruation to people from diverse backgrounds, and help them talk openly about a subject which has been ignored for far too long. Goonj has been able to support and encourage menstruators across India to make informed decisions about their health and lives. This sense of agency has increased their self-confidence and dignity, and it has empowered them to strive to become self-reliant. Goonj has created an enabling and positive environment for enhanced participation in different spheres of life and promoted gender equality and freedom. Goonj's efforts to improve menstrual hygiene have also included minimizing the use of non-biodegradable menstrual products, promoting better nutrition, improving water, sanitation and waste disposal facilities, generating opportunities for sustainable livelihoods for low-income groups, encouraging participation and success rates at school and work, and raising overall community aspirations.

My Menstrual Rights Bill: Awakening a Nation

SHASHI THAROOR

THE NATURAL MONTHLY PHENOMENON OF MENSTRUATION comes with its own set of implicit challenges in the lives of girls and women, which in India are aggravated because of a lack of proper facilities. Compounding this problem is that in India, menstruation is often dealt with in awful secrecy and exclusion: the country has suffered a long-standing tradition of placing restrictions on menstruating women and girls. Instead of addressing the myriad health problems associated with menstruation, they are usually ignored or seen as the individual's concern. Statistics from various studies and reports depict a sad state of affairs.

Conscious of the positive impact that parliamentary legislation can create, moved by the plight of menstruating women and girls, and outraged by the blatant denial of basic rights that should accrue to women naturally, I decided to introduce The Women's Sexual, Reproductive and Menstrual Rights Bill, 2018 in the Lok Sabha (the elected lower chamber of the Indian Parliament) on 28th December 2018.

The Bill seeks to establish legally protected menstrual rights for girls and women in an unprecedented way. It advocates eradication of menstrual untouchability in public establishments by requiring them to facilitate easy access to sanitary products in their toilets to all individuals going through this involuntary biological process. These products are to be provided free of cost as one of the essential elements of personal care, just as water is.

Through amendment of The Right of Children to Free and Compulsory Education Act, 2009, my Bill creates the additional requirement of providing sanitary pads in girls' washroom facilities in schools.

The Bill recommends removing the stigma attached with women's sanitary pads and establishing the availability of menstruation products as indispensable basic bodily necessities, just like other common toiletries in the washrooms of our society.

The Bill, apart from promoting access to sanitary napkins, also restores a married woman's autonomy over her sexual rights (by making spousal rape a criminal offence) and ensures that unrelated facts such as her clothing, education, race and sexual history are not used to presume her sexual consent. It also secures the abortion rights of women.

Though (for reasons known only to the present government) the Bill could not see the light of the day as legislation, I am glad that it has at least served to propel the discourse in a meaningful direction. Constructive debates over the implementation of this suggestion have been initiated. It has also contributed a fair bit towards creating awareness as well as soliciting community participation. My hope that the government would consider backing the Bill were, however, belied.

A couple of months later, on 19 July 2019, I re-emphasized this pivotal issue when the opportunity arose to raise a question to the concerned minister on the floor of the Lok Sabha. The question sought details about the government's efforts in recognizing access to menstrual hygiene products as an essential right of women and enquired about the distribution schemes of these products in schools and public institutions. I highlighted the swelling number of girls who drop out from the eighth standard onwards, to reiterate the role of girl's education in transforming society and to seek the government's response on their willingness to bring about a legal mandate for facilitating such access.

The government placed reliance on its Rashtriya Kishor Swasthya Karyakram, a health programme by the Ministry of Health and Family Welfare promoting reproductive health amongst adolescents in the age group of ten–nineteen years. Guided by the belief that all women are equally entitled to gain awareness and access to menstrual hygiene products, I, therefore, suggested to extend the purview of this scheme to all age groups (instead of the existing age group of ten–nineteen years) and to urban areas as well (instead of rural areas only).

Though it is heartening to see numerous initiatives being undertaken, particularly the release of popular films demystifying the taboos around the subject of menstruation, a change in mindset as well as a new legal framework for policy implementation at the grassroots level is needed. Breaking the continued silence around menstruation will, in turn, allow our women to shatter the glass ceilings holding them down. Destigmatizing the issue of menstruation and creating a congenial environment for women's freedom to grow would be the only way forward for women to fulfil their potential in our nation.

The idea of ensuring access to menstrual hygiene products extends beyond the notion of better sanitation: to include dignity, bodily integrity as well as overall life opportunities for women and girls. Its passage would mark nothing less than the awakening of India to the needs and rights of women.

To be introduced in Lok Sabha

<u>Bill No. 255 of 2018</u>

THE WOMEN'S SEXUAL, REPRODUCTIVE AND MENSTRUAL RIGHTS BILL, 2018

By

Dr. Shashi Tharoor, M.P.

A

BILL

further to amend certain enactments to emphasise on the agency of a woman in her sexual and reproductive rights and to guarantee menstrual equity for all women by the State.

BE it enacted by Parliament in the Sixty-ninth Year of the Republic of India as follows:—

CHAPTER I

PRELIMINARY

    1. (*1*) This Act may be called the Women's Sexual, Reproductive and Menstrual Rights Act, 2018.

    (*2*) It shall come into force on such date as the Central Government may, by notification in the Official Gazette, appoint.

Short title and commencement.

2

CHAPTER II

AMENDMENTS OF THE INDIAN PENAL CODE, 1860

Amendment of section 375.

2. In section 375 of the Indian Penal Code, 1860,—

45 of 1860.

(*a*) for the words "Fourthly.—With her consent, when the man knows that he is not her husband and that her consent is given because she believes that he is another man to whom she is or believes herself to be lawfully married", the words "Fourthly.— With her consent, when the man knows that he is not the person she believes she has given consent to engage in sexual intercourse or sexual acts and that her consent is given because she believes that he is another man with whom she wants to engage in sexual intercourse or sexual acts."; shall be substituted; 5

10

(*b*) Exception 2 shall be omitted; and

(*c*) after the proviso to *Explanation* 2, the following proviso shall be inserted, namely:—

"Provided that the women's ethnicity, religion, caste, education, profession, clothing preference, entertainment preference, social circle, personal opinion, past sexual conduct or any other related grounds shall not be a reason to presume her consent to the sexual activity." 15

CHAPTER III

AMENDMENTS TO THE MEDICAL TERMINATION OF PREGNANCY ACT, 1971

Amendment of short title.

3. For the short title of the Medical Termination of Pregnancy Act, 1971 (hereinafter referred to as the principal Act in this Chapter), the following short title shall be substituted, namely:— 20 34 of 1971.

"This Act may be called the Legal Termination of Pregnancy Act, 1977."

Amendment of long title.

4. For the long title of the principal Act, the following long title shall be substituted, namely:— 25

"An Act to provide for the legal termination of pregnancies by both medical and surgical methods by registered health care providers and medical practitioners and for matters connected therewith or incidental thereto."

Amendment of section 2.

5. In section 2 of the principal Act, after clause (d), the following clause shall be inserted, namely:— 30

"(*e*) "registered health care provider" means—

(*i*) a registered medical practitioner; or

(*ii*) a practitioner who possesses any recognized medical qualification of Ayurveda, Unani or Siddha as defined in clause (h) of section 2 of the Indian Medicine Central Council Act, 1970 and whose name has been entered in the Central Register or State Register of Indian medicine; or 35 48 of 1970.

(*iii*) a practitioner who possess any recognized medical qualification of Homoeopathy as defined in clause (g) of section 2 of the Homoeopathy Central Council Act, 1973 and whose name has been entered in the Central Register or State Register of Homeopathy; or 40 59 of 1973.

(*iv*) a nurse or auxiliary nurse midwife who possesses any recognized qualification in general nursing or auxiliary nurse midwifery as defined in section 10 of the Indian Nursing Council Act, 1947 and who has been enrolled as a nurse or auxiliary nurse midwife in the Indian Nurses Register or the State Register; 48 of 1947.

and who has such training and experience to terminate the pregnancy as may be prescribed by rules made under this Act. 45

3

(*f*) "prescribed" means prescribed by rules made under this Act; and

(*g*) "termination of pregnancy" means a procedure to terminate a pregnancy by using medical or surgical methods."

6. In section 3 of the principal Act,— Amendment
of section 3.

5   (*a*) in sub-section (*1*), for the words "registered medical practitioner", the words "registered health care provider";

(*b*) for sub-section (2), the following sub-section shall be substituted, namely:—

"(2) Subject to the provision of sub-section (4), a pregnancy may be terminated.

(*a*) medically by a registered health care provider, who is affiliated to a place as 10   described under section 4, where the length of her pregnancy does not exceed twelve weeks; or

(*b*) surgically by a medical practitioner where the length of her pregnancy does not exceed twelve weeks; or

(*c*) by a registrered medical practitioner, where the length of the pregnancy 15   does not exceed twenty weeks, if not less than one registered medical practitioner is of the opinion, formed in good faith, that,—

(*i*) the continuance of the pregnancy would involve a risk to the life of the pregnant woman or of grave injury to her physical or mental health; or

(*ii*) there is a substantial risk that if the child were born, it would suffer 20   from such physical, mental or genetic abnormalities, as may be prescribed.

Explanation 1.—Where any, pregnancy is alleged by the pregnant woman to have been caused by rape, the anguish caused by such pregnancy shall be presumed to constitute a grave injury to the mental health of the pregnant woman.

Explanation 2.—Where any pregnancy occurs as a result of failure of any device or 25   method used by any woman or her partner for the purpose of limiting the number of children, the anguish caused by such unwanted pregnancy may be presumed to constitute a grave injury to the mental health of the pregnant woman by a registered medical practitioner; or

(*d*) where the length of pregnancy does not exceed twenty-four weeks and the woman falls in the categories of a survivor of rape, person with disability or any other 30   related grounds as may be prescribed by a registered medical practitioner; or

(*e*) if not less than two registered medical practitioners are of the opinion, formed in good faith, that the termination of pregnancy is necessitated,—

(*i*) to save the life of the pregnant woman; or

(*ii*) by the diagnosis of a fatal foetal abnormality incompatible with healthy 35   living and life as may be prescribed; and

(*f*) where a child survivor of rape is pregnant, if not less than two registered medical practitioners are of the opinion that the termination of pregnancy will not involve a risk to her life.

7. In section 4 of the principal Act, for the word "No", the words "Save as otherwise Amendment
of section 4. 40   provided in section 3(2)(a), no" shall be substituted.

8. For section 5 of the principal Act, the following section shall be substituted by, Amendment
of section 5. namely:—

"5. (*1*) No person shall reveal the name and other particulars of a woman who Ban of
revealation of
identity of
women who
intend to
terminate
pregnancy or
terminate
pregnancy. may intend to terminate her pregnancy or terminates her pregnancy as per this Act.

4

(2) Whoever contravenes the provisions of sub-section (a), such person shall be punished with imprisonment for a term which may extend to one year, or with fine of minimum five thousand rupees subject to a maximum of ten lakh rupees, or with both.

Amendment of section 6.

9. In section 6 of the principal Act, in sub-section (2),—

(a) in clause (a) for the words "registered medical practitioner", the words "registered health care provider" shall be substituted; and 5

(b) after clause (a), the following clauses shall be inserted, namely:—

"(aa) the training and experience to terminate pregnancy of registered health care providers under sub-section (e) of section 2; and

(ab) the categories of physical, mental and genetic abnormalities under 10 sub-clause (i) of clause (b) of sub-section (2) of section 3; and

(ac) the additional categories of woman under clause (c) of sub-section (2) of section 3; and

(ad) the categories of fatal foetal abnormality incompatible with healthy living and life under sub-clause (ii) of clause (d) of sub-section (2) of 15 section 3;".

Amendment of section 7.

10. In section 7 of the principal Act, in sub-section (1),—

(a) in clause (a), for the words "registered medical practitioner ", the words "registered health care provider" shall be substituted.

(b) in clause (b) for the words "registered medical practitioner", the words 20 "registered health care provider" shall be substituted.

Amendment of section 8.

11. In section 8 of the principal Act for the words "registered medical practitioner", the words "registered health care provider" shall be substituted.

CHAPTER IV

AMENDMENT TO THE RIGHT OF CHILDREN TO FREE AND COMPULSORY EDUCATION ACT, 2009 25

Amendment of Schedule.

12. In the Schedule to the Right of Children to Free and Compulsory Education Act, 2009, in entry 2, in column (3) under the heading "Norms and Standards", after the words and figures "(iii) separate toilet for boys and girls;", the words and figures "(iiia) sanitary pads, preferably in the toilet for girls, which shall be provided at no cost to individuals who may use such facility," shall be inserted. 35 of 2009.

30

CHAPTER V

MENSTRUAL EQUITY FOR ALL WOMEN

Duty to provide sanitary pads.

13. Every public authority, as defined by sub-section (h) of section 2 of the Right to Information Act, 2005, shall make available sanitary pads, preferably in the toilet for women, which shall be provided at no cost to individuals in the premises of the public authority. 22 of 2005.

35

STATEMENT OF OBJECTS AND REASONS

Women, the biological equal half in the procreation of human beings, had been confined to just that for millenniums and even in that they had no autonomy. When they broke socio-cultural shackles and went on to govern countries, fight wars and excel in professions, these few exceptions were considered as enough representation. Society is content with the minimal representation of women in different spheres, even though they constitute half the population of the country. Women have been made vulnerable by the social construct of patriarchy, leading to their exclusion in every other social space. Unless we account for these inequalities and deconstruct patriarchal notions, we will fail in our constitutional mandate to ensure everyone's right to access justice.

In furthering this equality, the autonomy of the woman must be rightfully restored to her by granting her the agency over her sexual and reproductive rights. For this, marital rape must be criminalized to eliminate the loss of a woman's sexual independence post marriage. Further, unrelated facts about a woman's life such as caste, profession, clothing preference, personal opinion and past sexual conduct, among others should not be factors in presuming her sexual consent. By shifting from a 'No means No' to a 'Yes means Yes' regime, it transforms us from an era of women having to actively fight for them to be treated with respect and dignity to an era where they will be treated with respect and dignity.

Similarly, even with respect to reproductive rights, a woman must have the right to terminate pregnancy as a norm rather than an exception. A woman's right to terminate pregnancy should be only restricted to avoid female foeticide and when a foetus gains the right to life after it becomes viable. In all other circumstances, including when the foetus or the pregnant woman has any injury or threat to life, or when a woman is a rape survivor or has a disability, she should have the right to terminate her pregnancy. There must be no unnecessary distinction in the right to terminate pregnancy between married and unmarried women. To ensure women, especially rural women, can successfully exercise this right, the procedure must be relaxed accordingly. A major hurdle in the termination of pregnancy is the social stigma attached to it, which should be removed by absolutely protecting the privacy of a woman who intends to or terminates her pregnancy under the Medical Termination of Pregnancy Act, 1971.

Another major source of inequality is the absence of access to menstrual hygiene products that puts girls out of schools and women out of the work force, pushing them into the vicious cycle of dependency. The absence of an equivalent reproductive process in men has resulted in our failure to consider the lack of facility for women's menstrual hygiene. We have failed to admit that this biological process is a role women play for the subsistence of the human species as a whole. This disparity can be eradicated by obligating schools and public authorities to supply sanitary pads free of cost to any girl or women in their facilities.

Hence this Bill.

NEW DELHI;   SHASHI THAROOR
November 19, 2018.

FINANCIAL MEMORANDUM

Clause 12 of the Bill stipulates the provisions of sanitary pads free of cost by schools under the Right of Children to Free and Compulsory Education Act, 2009. Clause 13 provides for provision of sanitary pads free of cost preferably in the toilet for women in the premises of every public authority. The Bill, therefore, if enacted, would involve expenditure from the Consolidated Fund of India.

It is estimated that a recurring expenditure of about Rupees one hundred crore per annum, will be involved out of the Consolidated Fund of India.

No non-recurring expenditure is likely to be involved.

ANNEXURE

EXTRACT FROM THE INDIAN PENAL CODE, 1860

(45 OF 1860)

*   *   *   *

375. A man is said to commit "rape" if he—   Rape.

(*a*) penetrates his penis, to any extent, into the vagina, mouth, urethra or anus of a woman or makes her to do so with him or any other person; or

(*b*) inserts, to any extent, any object or a part of the body, not being the penis, into the vagina, the urethra or anus of a woman or makes her to do so with him or any other person; or

(*c*) manipulates any part of the body of a woman so as to cause penetration into the vagina, urethra, anus or any part of body of such woman or makes her to do so with him or any other person; or

(*d*) applies his mouth to the vagina, anus, urethra of a woman or makes her to do so with him or any other person, under the circumstances falling under any of the following seven descriptions:—

First.—Against her will.

Secondly.—Without her consent.

Thirdly.—With her consent, when her consent has been obtained by putting her or any person in whom she is interested, in fear of death or of hurt.

Fourthly.—With her consent when the man knows that he is not her husband and that her consent is given because she believes that he is another man to whom she is or believes herself to be lawfully married

*   *   *   *

Fifthly.—With her consent when, at the time of giving such consent, by reason of unsoundness of mind or intoxication or the administration by him personally or through another of any stupefying or unwholesome substance, she is unable to understand the nature and consequences of that to which she gives consent.

Sixthly.—With or without her consent, when she is under eighteen years of age.

Seventhly.—When she is unable to communicate consent.

Explanation 1.—For the purposes of this section, "vagina" shall also include labia majora.

Explanation 2.—Consent means an unequivocal voluntary agreement when the woman by words, gestures or any form of verbal or non-verbal communication, communicates willingness to participate in the specific sexual Act:

Provided that a woman sho does not physically resist to the act of penetration shall not by the reason only of that fact, be regarded as consenting to the sexual activity.

Exception 1.—A medical procedure or intervention shall not constitute rape.

Exception 2.—Sexual intercourse or sexual acts by a man with his own wife, the wife not being under fifteen years of age, is not rape.

*   *   *   *

7

EXTRACT FROM THE MEDICAL TERMINATION OF PREGNANCY ACT, 1971

(34 OF 1971)

An Act to provide for the termination of certain pregnancies by registered medical practitioners and for matters connected therewith or incidental thereto

Short title, extent and commencement.

1. (*1*) This Act may be called the Medical Termination of Pregnancy Act. 1971.

(*2*) It extends to the whole of India except the State of Jammu and Kashmir.

(*3*) It shall come into force on such date as the Central Government may, by notification in the Official Gazette, appoint.

Definitions.

2. In this Act, unless the context otherwise requires,—

(*a*) *   *   *   *

(*d*) "registered medical practitioner" means a medical practitioner who possesses any recognized medical qualification as defined in cl.(h) of Section 2 of the Indian Medical Council Act, 1956 (102 of 1956), whose name has been entered in a State Medical Register and who has such experience or training in gynecology and obstetrics as may be prescribed by rules made under this Act.

When Pregnancies may be terminated by registered medical practitioners.

3. (*1*) Notwithstanding anything contained in the Indian Penal Code (45 of 1860), a registered medical practitioner shall not be guilty of any offence under that Code or any other law for the time being in force, if any pregnancy is terminated by him in accordance with the provision of this Act.

(*2*) Subject to the provisions of sub-section (*4*), a pregnancy may be terminated by a registered medical practitioner,—

(*a*) where the length of the pregnancy does not exceed twelve weeks if such medical practitioner is, or

(*b*) where the length of the pregnancy exceeds twelve weeks but does not exceed twenty weeks, if not less than two registered medical practitioners are of opinion, formed in good faith, that,— (*i*) the continuance of the pregnancy would involve a risk to the life of the pregnant woman or of grave injury to physical or mental health; or

(*ii*) there is a substantial risk that if the child were born, it would suffer from such physical or mental abnormalities as to be seriously handicapped.

Explanation 1.—Where any, pregnancy is alleged by the pregnant woman to have been caused by rape, the anguish caused by such pregnancy shall be presumed to constitute a grave injury to the mental health of the pregnant woman.

Explanation 2.—Where any pregnancy occurs as a result of failure of any device or method used by any married woman or her husband for the purpose of limiting the number of children, the anguish caused by such unwanted pregnancy may be presumed to constitute a grave injury to the mental health of the pregnant woman.

(*3*) *   *   *   *

Place where pregnancy may be terminated.

4. No termination of pregnancy shall be made in accordance with this Act at any place other than,—

(*a*) a hospital established or maintained by Government, or

(*b*) a place for the time being approved for the purpose of this Act by Government.

8

9

5. (*1*) The provisions of Section 4 and so much of the provisions of sub-section (2) of Section 3 as relate to the length of the pregnancy and the opinion of not less than two registered medical practitioner, shall not apply to the termination of a pregnancy by the registered medical practitioner in case where he is of opinion, formed in good faith, that the termination of such pregnancy is immediately necessary to save the life of the pregnant woman. *(margin: Sections 3 and 4 when not to apply.)*

(2) Notwithstanding anything contained in the Indian Penal Code (45 of 1860), the termination of a pregnancy by a person who is not a registered medical practitioner shall be an offence punishable under that Code, and that Code shall, to this extent, stand modified.

6. (*1*) *   *   *   * *(margin: Power to make rules.)*

(2) In particular, and without prejudice to the generality of the foregoing power, such rules may provide for all or any of the following matters, namely:

(*a*) the experience or training, or both, which a registered medical practitioner shall have if he intends to terminate any pregnancy under this Act; and

(*b*) such other matters as are required to be or may be, provided by rules made under this Act.

(*3*) *   *   *   *

7. (*1*) The State Government may, be regulations,— *(margin: Power to make regulations.)*

(*a*) require any such opinion as is referred to in sub-section (2) of Section 3 to be certified by a registered medical practitioner or practitioners concerned in such form and at such time as be specified in such regulations, and the preservation or disposal of such certificates;

(*b*) require any registered medical practitioner, who terminates a pregnancy to give intimation of such termination and such other information relating to the termination as may be specified in such regulations;

(*c*) *   *   *   *

(*2*) *   *   *   *

(*3*) *   *   *   *

8. No suit for other legal proceedings shall lie against any registered medical practitioner for any damage caused or likely to be caused by anything which is in good faith done or intended to be done under this act. *(margin: Protection of action taken in good faith.)*

EXTRACTS FROM THE RIGHT OF CHILDREN TO FREE AND COMPULSORY EDUCATION ACT, 2009

(ACT NO. 35 OF 2009)

THE SCHEDULE

(*See* sections 19 and 25)

NORMS AND STANDARDS FOR A SCHOOL

Sl. No.	Item	Norms and Standards	
1.*	* * *	*	*
2.	Building	All-weather building consisting of—	
		(*i*) at least one class-room for every teacher and an office-cum-store-cum-Head teacher's room;	
		(*ii*) barrier-free access;	
		(*iii*) separate toilets for boys and girls;	
		(*iv*) *	*

LOK SABHA

———

A

BILL

further to amend certain enactments to emphasise on the agency of a woman in her
sexual and reproductive rights and to guarantee menstrual equity for
all women by the State.

———

The Women's Sexual, Reproductive and Menstrual Rights Bill, 2018

EXPLANATION NOTE

Purpose:

The purpose of the Bill is to vest in women an inherent right to their sexual and reproductive choices. The existing laws fail to recognize 'woman' as an individual capable of making her own choices, specifically her sexual choices as a wife and her reproductive choices when pregnant. Therefore, the Bill omits and inserts provisions that will grant her these rights.

It also grants menstrual equity to all women, in furtherance of which, it imposes the duty on the State to provide menstrual hygiene products for women in government schools and public authorities.

1. Marital Rape & Consent for Sexual Activities

Section 375 of the Indian Penal Code reads as:

"*375. Rape.—A man is said to commit "rape" if he—*

(a) penetrates his penis, to any extent, into the vagina, mouth, urethra or anus of a woman or makes her to do so with him or any other person; or

(b) inserts, to any extent, any object or a part of the body, not being the penis, into the vagina, the urethra or anus of a woman or makes her to do so with him or any other person; or

(c) manipulates any part of the body of a woman so as to cause

penetration into the vagina, urethra, anus or any part of body of such woman or makes her to do so with him or any other person; or

(d) applies his mouth to the vagina, anus, urethra of a woman or makes her to do so with him or any other person, under the circumstances falling under any of the following seven descriptions:—

First.—Against her will.

Secondly.—Without her consent.

Thirdly.—With her consent, when her consent has been obtained by putting her or any person in whom she is interested, in fear of death or of hurt.

Fourthly.—With her consent, when the man knows that he is not her husband and that her consent is given because she believes that he is another man to whom she is or believes herself to be lawfully married.

Fifthly.—With her consent when, at the time of giving such consent, by reason of unsoundness of mind or intoxication or the administration by him personally or through another of any stupefying or unwholesome substance, she is unable to understand the nature and consequences of that to which she gives consent.

Sixthly.—With or without her consent, when she is under eighteen years of age.

Seventhly.—When she is unable to communicate consent.

Explanation 1.—For the purposes of this section, "vagina" shall also include labia majora.

Explanation 2.—Consent means an unequivocal voluntary agreement when the woman by words, gestures or any form of verbal or non-verbal communication, communicates willingness to participate in the specific sexual act:

Provided that a woman who does not physically resist to the act of penetration shall not by the reason only of that fact, be regarded as

consenting to the sexual activity.
Exception 1.—A medical procedure or intervention shall not constitute rape.
*Exception 2.—***Sexual intercourse or sexual acts by a man with his own wife, the wife not being under fifteen years of age, is not rape.***"*

a. Criminalizing Marital Rape

Exception 2 to the Section decriminalizing rape assumes that a woman loses her sexual autonomy upon her marriage to a man. **The Bill whose central idea is the agency of women, omits this exception, criminalizing marital rape and restoring a woman's sexual right to herself.**

Additionally, the Bill also omits the clause "Fourthly..." that holds sexual consent obtained through misrepresentation as a husband is also rape because it is again derived from the assumption that if the man was truly the husband, then it would not amount to rape. **It is every form of misrepresentation that must be condemned and not just the misrepresentation as the husband.** Therefore, both these clauses that fail to respect the dignity of woman have been omitted.

b. Eliminating the standard of 'assumed consent'

The inclusion of Explanation 2 by an amendment in 2013 is a shift from 'No means No' to 'Yes means Yes'. While the former is a regressive thought that assumes consent on behalf of the woman unless she denies consent, the latter recognizes the autonomy of women and assumes no consent until she voluntarily articulates it. Despite this change in law, various High Court decisions in India have presumed consent based on unrelated factors such as a woman's past sexual conduct, nature of woman's relationship with the man, education of a woman. One such case is *Mahmood Farooqui v. State (Govt of NCT of Delhi)* where the Delhi High Court acquitted the accused from rape charges as the victim failed to prove that the accused had understood her lack of consent. This misinterpretation shifted the standard of affirmative consent in Explanation 2 to assumed consent based on unrelated facts such as the woman's educational qualification and her relationship with the man.[1] Therefore, to prevent the judiciary from using unrelated facts that are societal measuring tools to gauge a woman's desire to indulge in sexual activities in the future to assume consent, the proviso as is below has been included after the Explanation 2.

"Provided that the woman's ethnicity, religion, caste, education, profession, clothing preference, entertainment preference, social circle, personal opinion, past sexual conduct, nature of relationship with the accused or any other related grounds shall not be a reason to presume her consent to the sexual activity."

2. Laws relating to the termination of pregnancy

The Medical Termination of Pregnancy Act, 1971 has been hailed for being one of the most liberal laws of its times to have legalized abortion. However, the failure to resolve some of its anomalies and evolve with the changing times, has led to 1.56 crores (1.56 million) pregnancies being terminated where more than 75% were unsafe, in 2015 alone.[2] Aware of this problem, the NDA government in 2014 brought a draft Bill fixing almost all its loop holes, however, it was suddenly withdrawn for no evident reason. Some of the provisions from the draft Bill have been included in this Bill. The changes this Bill makes are:

a. Change in the name of the legislation to 'Legal Termination of Pregnancy Act'

The termination of pregnancy can be either medical or surgical. Medical termination is when medicines are prescribed for termination and surgical termination is when the termination is through an incision or operation. In case of a medical termination, there is a low probability of complication which may require medical supervision. The usage of the word 'medical' in the title of the Bill created ambiguity, which mainly impacted rural areas as the doctors there feared to interpret the law in case of an arrest under Section 312 of the Indian Penal Code. Section 312 punishes anyone who causes a voluntary miscarriage including the woman herself. Additionally, to further clarify the ambit of the Bill, it is clarified in the definition section that termination of pregnancy means termination by either medical or surgical method.

b. Adds 'Registered Health Care Providers' as professionals who are allowed to terminate pregnancy.

The Act only absolved Registered Medical Practitioners (RMPs) i.e. medical practitioners registered under the Indian Medical Council Act, 1956, from the criminality of Section 312 of the IPC. The Bill also absolves the new category of 'Registered Health Care Providers' (RHCPs) which includes, in addition to RMPs, practitioners registered under the Indian Medicine Central Council Act, 1970, and the Homeopathy Central Council Act, 1973, and nurse or auxiliary nurse midwife registered under the Indian Nursing Council Act, 1947, from Section 312 of the IPC. They are limited to terminate medical pregnancy until the 12th week of pregnancy. This has been added as professionals in the medical field, they can be trained to cater to a large percentage of unsafe termination of pregnancy which are usually medical terminations without any prescription due to unavailability of RMPs in rural areas.

c. **The right to termination of pregnancy until the 12th week of pregnancy**

The Bill grants all women the right to termination of pregnancy until the 12th week of pregnancy. While the Act did require the consent of the woman for any termination to be carried out, it only granted her a negative right against it. The Bill, recognizing woman's autonomy over her reproductive rights, grants her the right to termination of pregnancy where she may terminate pregnancy merely by her request until the 12th week of pregnancy. By granting her this right, the Bill has saved countless single woman (unwed/divorced/widowed) who took termination of pregnancy into their own hands. The right, however, is limited to 12 weeks to avoid the possibility of female foeticide as the gender of the foetus can be recognized after the 12th week of pregnancy.

d. **Conditional right to termination of pregnancy until the 20th week of pregnancy**

The conditional right to termination of pregnancy is a right to abort the foetus, if it involves a risk to the life of the pregnant woman or of grave injury to her physical or mental health, or there is a substantial risk of physical, mental or genetic abnormality of the foetus after being certified by at least one RMP. The Bill is similar to the Act in these provisions except for adding genetic foetal abnormalities as a ground for termination of pregnancy and reducing the number of RMPs who need to approve such a termination from two to one. Additionally, the Act in its explanations included rape and failure of contraceptives for a married woman as mental injury. The Bill extends this to failure of contraception for any woman.

e. Right to termination of pregnancy for only certain categories of women until the 24th week of pregnancy

The Act limited termination of pregnancy to the 20thweek of pregnancy unless the survival of the woman was at risk. This led to vulnerable women like victims of rape and disabled women who had no risk of injury, threat to their life or foetus with an abnormality be embroiled in a legal dispute for their right to abort.[3] In order to avoid an added trauma for these vulnerable women, the limit is extended to the 24th week. It is not indefinite, as around 22–24th week, a foetus becomes viable, i.e., it has the ability to live outside the womb of the mother, upholding the foetus/child's right to life over the choice of the mother.

f. Necessitated right to termination of pregnancy at any time during pregnancy.

While the Act allowed the termination of pregnancy indefinitely if it was necessitated to save the life of the mother, the Bill extends it to fatal foetal abnormality incompatible with its healthy life and living. It is to avoid further suffering of the child and the women.[4] As it is almost the last stage of the pregnancy, where most features of the child may be identified, the possibility of misuse is very high, therefore the specific abnormalities for which termination of pregnancy may be undertaken shall be prescribed.

g. **Right to termination of pregnancy of minor rape victims**

Reported cases of minor rape victims approaching the judiciary to terminate their pregnancy even after the 20th week of pregnancy has become a regular affair.[5] In the midst of court proceedings, minors lose out on the crucial time when they can terminate their pregnancy without a risk to their life. Taking cognizance of the situation, the Supreme Court has held that a minor rape victim should not be forced to knock the doors of the court for getting permission to terminate her pregnancy arising out of any sexual offence.[6] Moreover, due to the improbability of a minor being pregnant, guardians fail to recognize a minor is pregnant until late into the pregnancy. Therefore, a provision allowing RMPs to terminate pregnancy of a minor rape victim unless it involves a risk to her life has been added.

h. **Privacy of the woman who intends to terminate her pregnancy under the Act**

The Bill protects the privacy of the woman who may intend to terminate her pregnancy or terminates her pregnancy under the Act against the world at large and penalizes anyone who violates it.

3. Menstrual Equity for All

While the Right of Children to Free and Compulsory Education Act mandates separate toilet facilities for boys and girls, it does not even discuss menstrual hygiene products for girls. Similarly, the government spends crores on building toilets across the nation and everyone hails it, while they hesitate to make aware boys/

men about the biological process of menstruation experienced by almost the rest of the country. Unfortunately, the biological process of menstruation is not even as voluntary as others, where one may wait it out. This leads to large number of girls dropping out of school in the fear of embarrassment from menstrual stains, which returns them to the vicious cycle of dependence.[7] It is unfortunate that this issue is being debated at all. In this male dominated society, the absence of an equivalent biological process of menstrual periods in men has become an excuse to make it an issue of debate, rather than a societal norm. While no public authority is legally obligated to have toilet facility, it is shameful to not have one. However, we see no such keenness to make freely available menstrual hygiene products. Therefore, clauses to provide menstrual hygiene products free of cost in government schools and public authorities, irrespective of the availability of toilet facilities, have been included as below.

"In the Schedule of the Right of Children to Free and Compulsory Education Act, after sub-item (iii) of item 2, the following shall be inserted, namely: --
"(iiia) sanitary pads, preferably in the toilet for girls, which shall be provided at no cost to individuals using that facility.""
"Every public authority, as defined by sub-section (h) of section 2 of the Right to Information Act, 2005, shall contain sanitary pads, preferably in the toilet for women, which shall be provided at no cost to individuals visiting that authority."

Right to Bleed at the Workplace

RADHIKA RADHAKRISHNAN

PAID MENSTRUAL LEAVE (OR PERIOD LEAVE) GIVES A PERSON the option to avail paid leave from their employer if they are unable to go to work during their menstrual cycle. A 2012 study[1] found that 20 per cent of women experience menstruation that is painful enough to interfere with their daily activities (dysmenorrhoea). Period leave has been recognized in some countries including Indonesia, Japan, South Korea, Taiwan and Zambia. The debate over whether paid period leave should be institutionalized at all workplaces in India has been going on for a few years now. Bills have been tabled by members of Parliament, and activists have voiced support for period leave in keeping with other demands of women's movements.

At the same time, a large number of women (including those in positions of power) continue to vocally oppose period leave at workplaces. This seems counter-intuitive, and it is worth pondering why so many women might hold a stance that appears so contrary to their self-interest. I offer three possible ways to understanding this. First, young women are socialized into believing that they are impure and polluting when on their period, and the stigma extends to the workplace. Second, women are enculturated to tolerate pain in a world that is disturbingly comfortable with the fact that many women suffer debilitating pain while menstruating that we still do not have satisfactory medical solutions for. And lastly, toxic workplace capitalist cultures promote the prioritization of an individual's work productivity over their health. In this essay, I will analyze and respond to these points to highlight the necessity of paid period leave at the workplace in India.

Sexuality, Purity and Community

Women's bodies and procreative capacity are considered to be ritually polluting in many cultures. What is the genesis of such a belief in India? Sources point to different origins. The cultural meanings of menstruation as contaminating can be traced back to Brahmanical Hindu mythology from the Vedic times. In the Rig Veda, the slaying of Vritra (withholder of the waters, demon of droughts) by Indra is said to have manifested 'guilt caused by the murder of a learned Brahmana'[2], following which he 'ran to the women to protect him[self]' who took upon themselves a part of his guilt. That guilt of the Brahmin murder is believed to appear every month in women as the menstrual flow and is considered a mark of a woman's innate impurity as well as sexuality.[3] Since caste structures have historically been maintained through control over women's sexuality, and women are considered to be entry points into the caste system,[4] menstrual taboos are yet another means of control over women's sexuality in a caste-divided society. Even practices that seem contradictory to the narrative of menstrual pollution (such as the public celebration of a girl's first menstrual cycle) end up reinforcing the patriarchal and reductionist narrative that a woman's primary purpose is reproduction.

These are not mere outdated historic myths; they continue to seep into everyday rituals and practices prescribed for women in many Indian cultures. For instance, notions of purity and pollution are *central* to the practice of Hinduism in India. Some forms of human bodily excretions and processes are considered to be polluting, and by extension, so are the bodies that produce them. Childbirth and menstruation are two such processes, and hence, women are subject to various cultural restrictions during these periods such as being prohibited from entering the kitchen (as it is believed that a menstruating woman may contaminate the food) and the prayer room. Here, a menstruating woman is a powerful, corrupting 'thing'; a 'thing' to be feared and shunned.

Similarly, other cultures have their own practices in place for the regulation of women's bodies and sexuality during menstruation. Orthodox Jews observe the practice of *niddah* (separation), which includes the proscription of sexual intercourse during the wife's 'unclean' period.[5] With respect to Muslim women, there are at least two kinds of menstrual restrictions. First, menstruating women are forbidden from praying, fasting or visiting any place of worship during the month of Ramadan, as they are believed to be a threat to the sanctity of these practices. Secondly, they are not permitted to have sexual intercourse for at least seven days after their menstrual cycles begin, as they are 'unclean' until they have been through a ritual washing.[6]

Important to this discussion is the understanding that such menstrual taboos across cultures are aspects of a ritual of purity and contamination and play a role in cementing women's subjugated position in society, forming a basis for control over their sexuality. An impact of these deeply ingrained cultural practices is that women are socialized from a young age to believe that they are impure and dirty during their menstrual cycles. Like all physical processes that have to do with sex and childbirth, menstruation is considered a private activity and a public acknowledgement of the same is stigmatized. And these taboos extend to the public workplace. In the context of such stigma, demanding leave for menstruation is often not an option for all women. This is especially true for some industries where male employers tend to hire women primarily because they are cheap labour, easier to control, make fewer demands and less likely to unionize. Thus, women do not always have the bargaining power vis-à-vis male employers to request period leave every month. In a society plagued by menstrual stigma, period leave cannot be left up to individuals to seek when required. The provision of paid leave for menstruation must be *institutionalized* at the workplace for all women for non-negotiable accessibility.

Period Care as Healthcare

There are important health and hygiene concerns around menstruation that have been highlighted by feminists. For instance, in India, over 62 per cent of menstruating girls and women use reusable cloth instead of sanitary napkins.[7] While this is ecologically friendly, the inadequacy of washing facilities available to women in rural India increases the risk of infections. Moreover, around 88 per cent of women end up using newspapers, dried leaves and ashes to aid absorption. The health risks of these makeshift alternatives have been discussed extensively in the current literature on menstruation. The under-studied aspect of healthcare that I wish to focus upon in this essay is the normalization of women's period pain.

From a young age, women are enculturated to tolerate abnormal amounts of pain as though it were normal. A 'good girl' grits her teeth and gets through pain. Many of us are told right from the time of our first period cycle that it is going to hurt, and that we have to be strong enough to get through it. With such an initiation into menstruation, young girls' ability to recognize unnaturally severe period pain is thwarted. In fact, enduring pain in silence is so commonplace that no one takes a woman's complaints seriously. At what point is one supposed to stop tolerating it and consult a doctor, especially when everyone says we're supposed to put up with it?

This lack of interest is also sustained by the skewed distribution of medical research about women's pain. For example, researchers have conducted five times as many studies into erectile dysfunction as compared to premenstrual syndrome (PMS) even though it is reported that 90 per cent of women experience PMS symptoms as opposed to 19 per cent of men suffering erectile dysfunction.[8] Invasive drugs (such as the controversial injectable contraceptive, Depo-Provera[9]) that are marketed to women as part of global liberalization policies, have come under fire from women's groups for being sold extensively in the global south to be 'tested' on women in low-rights environments. The most frequently encountered side effect of Depo-Provera is the alteration in the menstrual cycle,[10] and yet there is a stark dearth of clinical trials and conclusive information about its efficacy and potential long-term risks. Women's pain is neglected and does not seem to warrant enough medical research to find safe and sustainable solutions for. Conversations around period leave provide an opportunity to highlight this gendered inequality in menstrual healthcare access and to encourage more medical research and development on menstruation.

The normalization of women's pain manifests at the workplace when a woman suffering from period pain is encouraged to take a painkiller and continue working. This is despite the fact that it is common knowledge that painkillers do not work for a large number of women who suffer from period complications. On the other hand, for non-gendered ailments, there is the provision of sick leave at the workplace. For example, when we get a severe headache, we are encouraged to avail sick leave. It is recognized that during sickness, individuals require rest, sleep and hydration, not just medication, because care is an important aspect of recovery to good health. And period care is part of good healthcare, therefore it must be provided for through paid period leave.

Moreover, asking women to endure debilitating pain while working is ableist as it excludes the experiences of millions of women who have period complications. Indeed, many cases remain undiagnosed due to the normalization of women's pain, the stigma around menstruation and the dismal state of public healthcare infrastructure. An apt comparison here would be the common practice of awarding children in schools for 100 per cent attendance. Every child will fall sick at one point or another; being able to attend school, or work, every single day only shows that you either fall sick less often because you have better immunity or have a higher endurance for physical pain or can afford quality and timely healthcare. But these are all markers of privilege. They are not achievements to be celebrated with medals or inadequate provisions for rest and care. This ableism excludes the experiences of those who have health conditions that prevent them from working every day. What period leave does in this scenario is recognize women's invisibilized pain, offer them the option to care for themselves while having to endure it, kickstart much-needed conversations and encourage better medical research around menstruation.

Toxic Capitalism

So far, this essay has analyzed how the opposition to period leave can be understood to be a manifestation of internalized and ritualized misogyny (wherein women are taught to devalue themselves and their bodies), and the normalization of women's pain. I will now argue that these factors are amplified at the workplace which is structured around the needs of men and excludes the lived experiences of women. It is within the context of a capitalist workplace that I place my arguments related to period leave.

Under toxic capitalism, women are denied period leave and asked to keep up with men to be equally productive at the workplace and reap the benefits of 'equal pay for equal work'. But the workplace is an inherently *unequal* space to begin with. An able-bodied man versus a woman enduring period pain for at least two days every month is an unequal and unfair comparison. Professional workspaces have historically been designed by men to accommodate male requirements and are thus ignorant of and even hostile to the needs of women. In such a scenario, the struggle for 'equality' at the workplace becomes one where women must strive to be included by adapting to the male way of life. Instead of downplaying our differences as women, we should be focusing on reimagining the workplace that puts us at a disadvantage. To that end, women should not have to keep up with men in the workplace, it's the workplace that needs to keep up with women's biological needs such as menstruation. We need to restructure the workplace by introducing period leave, not restructure women's natural lives for increasing workplace productivity.

Intersectional feminism recognizes that the playing field is not level for all communities as different people work under different structural constraints. It is well acknowledged that women have been historically marginalized, denied political representation and excluded from certain domains such as education. Thus, there are affirmative action schemes (such as quotas) to ensure that the playing field is levelled for women in these spheres. For example, The Maternity Benefit Act of 1961 protects the employment of women during the time of their maternity and entitles them to maternity benefits, including leave to look after their children. One can argue for period leave by taking the same approach to menstruation and demand equality in the workplace.

Many sceptics fear backlash and increased discrimination towards women by male employers if mandatory period leave is institutionalized. However, such backlash discrimination should be handled through penal or civil action against the employer (by prohibiting it specifically through legislation like Title VII in the United States[11]), not by withholding or withdrawing valid and necessary demands put forth by women. More recently, similar concerns were raised during public conversations around the Sexual Harassment of Women at Workplace (Prevention, Prohibition and Redressal) Act, 2013. Women feared that mandating a sexual harassment policy at work would disincentivize male employers from hiring women for the fear of harassment allegations. However, this crucial legislation was passed because it was recognized that irrespective of how male employers responded, safety at the workplace is an undeniable right of all women. Similarly, healthcare, and by default period care, is also a universal right.

At the same time, it must be acknowledged that the provision of period leave is likely, at least initially, to benefit the more privileged section of women who work in the formal labour sector. In the informal sector, which employs most of India's working women, there are other hurdles that need to be overcome before one can talk about institutionalizing period leave. In many areas, access to toilets and clean water for women is itself a significant challenge, complicated by the menstrual taboos that ostracize women in their everyday lives.

Though civil society organizations have been working to better these conditions, the period leave conversation will be applicable in the informal sector only after basic sanitation needs have been met. That being said, it is crucial that feminists demand paid period leave for those who can access it. While we do so, it is also important to keep in mind that the conversation of period leave also pertains to transmen who menstruate and their voices and needs are just as important as those of cis women.

These three arguments in defence of paid period leave are very much in line with the demands of women's movements in India. First, period leave must be necessarily institutionalized because, given the context of the deeply ingrained and widespread cultural beliefs about menstruation, it is difficult for women to individually negotiate with employers for period leave every month. Feminists have been fighting to eradicate menstrual taboos and myths around the perceived impurity of women, which forms the basis of control over women's sexuality. Besides educational and outreach efforts for women, feminists have also launched campaigns[12] to challenge cultural taboos around menstruation. Until recently, women devotees of menstruating age were not permitted to worship at the Sabarimala temple in Kerala. As a result of the efforts made by feminists, the Supreme Court of India lifted the ban on the entry of women in the Sabarimala temple in 2018, stating that discrimination against women on any grounds (including religious) is unconstitutional.

Second, period leave acknowledges and makes visible the pain that women experience during menstruation, and this will hopefully lead to more effective medical research and development around solutions for women's menstrual pain. Feminists in India have a history of arguing against the invasive drugs marketed to women as part of global liberalization policies.

And lastly, the provision of period leave goes a step further towards restructuring the workplace to include the needs of menstruating women. Feminists have worked extensively towards affirmative action policies for women in various domains where we are disadvantaged (such as education) and towards institutionalizing legal means for women to access these rights like maternity benefits and protection from sexual harassment for women at the workplace. Similarly, paid period leave affirms the right of women to healthcare. By institutionalizing paid period leave for women in India, we would be taking a step forward in realizing one of the current feminist goals of an unbiased and accessible workplace.

Blood on My Chair: The Need for Period-friendly Workplaces in Bangladesh

FARAH AHAMED | INTERVIEW

IN BANGLADESH, ALMOST 50 PER CENT OF THE POPULATION IS women but according to the World Bank, as of 2020, only 34.54 per cent of them were part of the labour force, as compared to 78.56 per cent of the male population.[1] The male-to-female ratio in different work environments shows that women constituted 56 per cent of the workforce in agriculture, 26 per cent in the service sector and 18 per cent in manufacturing and other industries.[2] Although the readymade garment (RMG) industry has seen an influx of female employees recently (almost 60 per cent of RMG workers are women), most have yet to move away from the agricultural sector.[3]

While the number of women joining the workforce has been increasing, they still have limited choices, control and decision-making power over their employment, finances and economic assets. Some of the reasons include the fact that more than one-third of women in the labour force are unpaid domestic workers and the high rate of underage marriages among girls. Marriage is the most common reason for girls dropping out of school, and despite the decline in child marriages in the last decade, six out of every ten girls in Bangladesh still get married before they turn eighteen.[4] Moreover, women are often not given rights to family property, despite their contributions, because of social prejudice.[5]

I interviewed five women in the RMG sector in Dhaka to try and understand the challenges of coping with menstruation at their places of work. They are amongst the 4.1 million working in this industry. The interviewees are from different religious, socio-economic and educational backgrounds and their roles range from supervisory to janitorial. Their names have been changed to protect their identities. My thanks to Zaeem Jamal and Jennifer Shahed in Dhaka for their help with facilitating the interviews.

◆

According to a study conducted by the United Nations Development Programme (UNDP) in 2020, almost 90 per cent of the global population was found to be biased against women.[6] This attitude is reflected in prejudices against women in the workplace, but also prevents them from entering the workforce in the first place.

Bangladesh is no exception; women are pressured into early marriages leaving them no choice but to abandon their educational and career aspirations and rely on their husbands economically. Added to this is the sociocultural assumption that women are better off staying at home taking care of their families, while anyone who deviates from this prescribed path is frowned upon. As a consequence, women are denied agency, opportunities for upward social mobility and financial freedom.

Discrimination against working women takes many forms: fewer promotions in comparison to their male counterparts, gender wage gap, disrespect from co-workers and exclusion from social events. In Bangladesh, generally speaking, human resource policies make no provision for the needs of women whether they be maternity leave, childcare facilities and, in some cases, even annual leave. In such a context, a period-friendly organization is a pipe dream.

According to a Dhaka-based NGO, Karmojibi Nari (Working Women) almost 95 per cent of female workers in Bangladesh get no breaks during the average ten-hour-long shift, except for lunch, which means that a woman who has her period is unable to change her clothes or take a shower, if necessary. The problem is exacerbated by the lack of clean running water and inadequate washrooms.[7]

Tasneem is a thirty-two-year-old woman with an MBA. She works as a supervisor in a private RMG organization. She learnt about menstruation from school friends, but it was her mother who taught her how to manage it 'hygienically'. Tasneem shared how she coped with her period. 'I use sanitary pads, and I've never faced any difficulties using them. My problem is that I've had irregular periods from an early age. I discussed this with my mother, and she took me to see a doctor. I change my pads regularly and keep separate underpants which I do not use on normal days. I've never tried using tampons or a menstrual cup. I know what they are, and I'm planning to try out the cup.' Tasneem is one of the fortunate few who can afford and has access to menstrual products. She told us that she always dreaded getting her period. 'The worst thing of all is the period cramps and my first day is awful. Sometimes the pain makes it impossible for me to function normally. If I need to go to the office or shopping, I have to carry painkillers with me. If it's a hectic day at work, I find myself taking the pills thrice a day. There's no other solution, I guess.'

Tasneem said that while growing up, she had never had any constraints imposed on her when she had her period. There were no restrictions on food or movement. She said she believed that she wasn't expected to get married when she entered menarche because her family was educated. But she acknowledged that it was a common practice in the villages.

Shaila, a twenty-nine-year-old Muslim woman, works as a fashion designer at a private company. She had this to say about her first experience of menstruation: 'I started menstruating when I was in class eight. It came as a shock because no one had ever explained anything to me about it. I thought I was dying. I started praying, thinking that my days were coming to an end. Luckily, on the third day of my cycle, my grandmother noticed I was acting strange and asked me what the matter was. I burst into tears and told her my days were numbered. Then she explained that what I was going through was normal for girls. I suffered from terrible cramps, so she told me not to run around or lift heavy objects. I was not allowed to eat sour foods like tamarind because she said they could thin my blood, but she made me eat more protein and fruits. Nowadays I use sanitary napkins, but fifteen years ago, when I first started my period, I used cloth, because pads were not available or were too expensive. I've had infections, of course, but if I have any problems, I tell my mom or sister, and my mom takes me to the doctor. I don't use tampons or a cup, and I'd never heard of menstrual cups until today. I understand that periods are linked to getting pregnant, but I would not be able to explain to you how, exactly.'

A recent pilot study conducted in Bangladesh found that more than two-thirds of women working in the RMG sector use dirty pieces of cloth during their period. Only 20.5 per cent of female workers bought pads, with 78.5 per cent percent

using rags and 1 per cent using cotton wool. It is common
for women to use a single piece of cloth for the whole day
because they cannot afford pads, and many were unaware of
the importance of practising proper menstrual hygiene.[8]

Like Tasneem, Shaila was not forced into an early marriage,
but she admitted it was not unusual. 'I know a lot of girls are
pressurized into marriage, even my friends and cousins.'

Twenty-two-year-old Zainul has completed her primary
education and works as a cleaner in an RMG factory. She learnt
about periods from her mother and when her first period came,
with painful cramps, her mother told her, 'It's very normal and
happens to all girls.' Zainul uses sanitary pads and had never heard
of tampons or menstrual cups. She said she had no food or social
or other restrictions imposed on her during menstruation, nor was
she expected to get married after starting her period. However,
she pointed out that she knew many girls who faced this situation.

Sualeha is thirty-one and from a Christian background. She
graduated from a secretarial college and now works as a secretary
at a RMG factory. Her mother educated her about menstruation.
'I started my period when I was in class five. When I told my
mother I was bleeding, she explained that it happened to all girls.
She warned me about the pain but told me to carry on normally
with my daily routine and try and get used to the cramps. When I
was in class eleven, I developed a cyst on my ovary and ended up
in the hospital. I've never tried using tampons or a menstrual cup,
but I know what they are.'

Sualeha expressed her concern for early marriages and how
they thwarted women's aspirations, highlighting corruption as an
additional problem. 'Currently in Bangladesh, fewer girls are being
married off at a young age because the legal age for marriage is

eighteen, but still there are gaps in the system. People are able to bribe officials to get fake certificates showing that the child is of age and then they marry her off.'

Parveen is a twenty-five-year-old supervisor at a garment factory. She learnt about menstruation from her friends, and after she got her period, her mother guided her on what to expect. 'My mother was friendly and so I could freely speak about periods with her and my family. My friend told me not to eat sour foods because they could cause me health problems. My family told me not to go outside while menstruating because I could be vulnerable to attacks by wicked spirits.' While menstruation was a not a taboo subject in her home, Parveen's understanding is coloured by myths.

In Bengali culture, menstruation is considered evil and shameful. For example, in a village in northern Bangladesh, the women of Char Bramagacha menstruate in secret because they believe malignant spirits will be attracted to their menstrual blood. They bury their used menstrual cloths in the ground or wash them before dawn while the rest of the village is still sleeping. This practice is not unique to this village; the taboos around menstruation are ubiquitous throughout the country.[9] In fact, cultural beliefs and social norms place an enormous additional burden on menstruating women, limiting their participation in the community and preventing their progress.[10]

When asked how she managed her period, Parveen said, 'Sometimes I use a pad or place a folded cloth in my underpants. Other times, I use a piece of tissue paper. It depends on where I am and what I can afford that month.' Parveen was not taught about menstrual hygiene management, but she tries her best to take care of it on her own. 'I'm not sure if it's hygienic or not but when I can afford it, I change my pad every six hours. But when

I can't, I use tissue paper. This is very inconvenient because every hour I have to keep going to the toilet, but I don't know what else to do.'

A survey by the World Bank[11] found that on average, Bangladeshi households find sanitary pads unaffordable, and only 23 per cent of women use menstrual products. Most others reuse old cloths which they do not wash or dry properly – this puts them at a high risk of contracting infections. The dearth of hygienic latrines in villages is yet another burden on women who often try their best to hide that they are menstruating.

More Inclusivity

The interviewees were asked for their opinion on the silence and stigma around menstruation. Tasneem believes that both men and women should speak frankly about periods. She said, 'The awareness should come from family. Without their support, especially the men, this topic will forever remain a taboo. And no issue can be solved if half of the country's population is not on the same page, right? In fact, during my menstrual cycle, I'm pampered by my husband and my mother. But that is also because of the privilege that comes with my socio-economic background. The picture in the rest of the country is not the same.'

Zainul was very clear that the government had a role to play by including men in menstrual hygiene talks. 'I thinks it's important for the government to support women; I wish they would do it. If men and the government had a better understanding of periods, I think men would be more helpful to us and this would benefit the country overall.'

Shaila thought that the government ought to be proactive and supply schoolgirls with free sanitary pads. 'I think it would be very helpful if they did this because many girls who want to use pads cannot afford them. Instead, they use rags which is not very hygienic.' She also pointed out the importance of educating boys about menstruation. 'Because when men find out about it, they find it odd, as odd as I did, when really it is a very natural thing.'

Similarly, Sualeha said, 'Men find periods very abnomal, even though it's a very ordinary biological process. Women need to talk more openly to men about menstruation, so they can understand us better.'

Workplace Experiences

In Bangladesh, period poverty is apparent across the country. Approximately two-thirds of the female population cannot afford sanitary pads which puts them at high risk of infections and increased absences from school and work.[12]

Schools, like factories and offices, are not period-friendly. Parveen talked about a period-shaming incident she had faced at school. 'During one of my HSC final exams I got my period. I had no idea that blood had seeped through my clothes onto my chair. My friend, sitting behind me, noticed there was blood dripping from my chair and the back of my skirt was red. In fright, she whispered my name aloud. The exam invigilator got annoyed and instructed me to get up and hand over my answer sheet, accusing me of cheating. Because I was so ashamed, I couldn't stand up. I pleaded with him to let me continue with the exam, but he refused. He came over and snatched my paper from me. I stayed on my chair and did not move until the exam was over and every single student and the exam tutor had left. It was the worst experience of my life. It was so stressful and affected me mentally.'

Similarly, organizations are not equipped to support the needs of menstruating women. A recent study showed that women working in Bangladesh's RMG sector did not have access to adequate sanitary facilities. This increased their risk of infections and led to many of them skipping work.[13] Tasneem had this to say: 'Unfortunately, all offices in Bangladesh, not just mine, do not have the mindset to understand women when it comes to menstruation-related matters. So, the answer is no, we do not get any kind of help either through the provision of sanitary towels, or period leave. But I wish we did. There are dustbins in the washrooms, but having a dustbin in an office washroom is common sense, right? But I know this is not the case in all offices.'

Similarly, Shaila was indignant at the lack of support for women. 'A majority of factories in our country do not have provisions for menstruating women – there are no sanitary napkins in women's washrooms and even the dustbins don't have lids. Often, even though there are separate washrooms for women and men, men sometimes use the ones assigned to us. This makes me very uneasy. We definitely do not get any kind of period leave.'

Zainul also revealed that she did not get any assistance with coping with her period at her place of employment. She said she did not want to elaborate further, except to say that it was very difficult when she had her period at work.

Commenting on the menstrual hygiene practices at her place of work, Sualeha said, 'In my organization we get nothing to help us with our periods. We're just expected to get on with it. Employers ought to be more sensitive about periods and what women have to go through every month. They should at least give us sanitary napkins and there should be dustbins in our toilets. Once I had to use the dustbin under my desk to throw away my pad, because I did not know what else to do. It felt dirty, but I had no choice.'

Sualeha's office is not unusual in this respect; in fact, the absence of any menstrual hygiene management provisions in the workplace is the norm. However, things are a little different for Parveen. The corporate social responsibility department at the RMG factory where she works invited an NGO to conduct menstrual hygiene workshops for female employees. 'I used to receive pads from them every month,' Parveen said, 'and I attended a few menstrual training sessions.' But while this may be reason for hope, information must be complemented with infrastructural support, or it will be meaningless. As Parveen explained: 'I usually have to carry my used pads with me in the evening and dispose of them in my own dustbin at home because there are none at work. And when I use cloth pads, I only change them at home in my own washroom. There are no proper facilities at work.'

Tasneem is convinced that the government ought to play a more active role in providing menstrual support to women. She said, 'I think the government of every country should get involved in this issue. Why not? I also think that pads should be free for all people who have periods. If not, at least pads should be easy to buy. What I mean is that pads are very expensive in Bangladesh. It costs ₹16 per pad on average, which is not affordable for two-thirds of the population. But the argument for making pads free or cheaper is gaining some traction; more people are realizing that sanitary napkins are not a luxury but a basic necessity.'

The Way Forward

In Bangladesh, taboos associated with menstruation, a culture of silence and biased workplaces result in a lack of sensitivity to the needs of menstruating women. The situation varies depending on whether one is working in the formal or informal sector. But it would be true to say that that overall, in Bangladesh, workplaces are neither period-friendly nor women-friendly.

Unfortunately, no state-level policy has been implemented to address the challenges of menstrual hygiene management in the workplace. Any support so far has come from civil society organizations. The government needs to take the lead and provide the private sector with comprehensive guidelines. Strict regulation and penalties are necessary to ensure compliance across companies. Indeed, according to an investigative report by the *Dhaka Tribune*, women are more often than not not given any maternity leave even though the law clearly mandates factories to do so.[14] Without regulatory enforcement, change will be slow.

Women must be educated about their rights so that they are not taken advantage of and subjected to inhumane working conditions. They should also be made aware of their right to pursue their own career interests.

Another initiative the government could take is to make sanitary pads more affordable and accessible. Encouraging entrepreneurial innovations through government incentives is one way of boosting the manufacturing sector. For instance, in 2021 the finance minister of Bangladesh proposed a VAT exemption on the production of local sanitary napkins to motivate entrepreneurs.[15]

Creating a period-friendly office or factory requires multilevel changes. It includes giving women respect by providing both male and female employees with knowledge and information about menstruation, ensuring they have adequate toilet facilities with clean running water, and disposal bins. Women must have access to menstrual products at work and period leave, should they require it. Companies should implement policies which protect women from discrimination and support their career progress. They should offer women maternity leave, medical insurance and other healthcare benefits.

Bangladesh has made advances in encouraging women to join the workforce, but women must be given the dignity they deserve, and which is their right. An integrated approach to making the private sector more period-friendly is critical for women to be able to realize their ambitions.[16] As Eleanor Roosevelt said, 'Where, after all, do universal human rights begin? In small places, close to home – so close and so small that they cannot be seen on any maps of the world. Yet they are the world of the individual person; the neighbourhood [s]he lives in; the school or college [s]he attends; the factory, farm or office where [s]he works. Such are the places where every man, woman and child seeks equal justice, equal opportunity, equal dignity without discrimination. Unless these rights have meaning there, they have little meaning anywhere.'[14]

Behind the Braided Coconut Leaves

K. MADAVANE

TRANSLATED FROM FRENCH BY SIBA BARKATAKI

GUNA'S HOME, BUILT ON A LONG PIECE OF LAND, WAS WEDGED between two massive houses several centuries old. The house in which Guna and his family lived was of modest dimensions. It had a red-tiled roof and opened onto the road. The main entrance consisted of a double door and two small columns. The house, with its washed-out green color, had the appearance of an ancient dwelling.

The backyard was half barren. The other half was a garden which had no plants or trees. In the left corner, close to a tiny well, was a red-brick wall about two metres high, overlooking a deep clay pit. This improvised site of solitude was an open-air toilet for the members of the household.

It was a deep cavity, dug into the earth and cleansed by the ruthless rays of the sun. Here, every man and woman took turns to answer the call of nature. One could take refuge here at any hour to relieve themselves or to ease their sorrow or pain in private. The clouds alone witnessed their most intimate thoughts and innermost desires. Inside the crevices of the cracked wall of a large two-storey house far away, parrots busied themselves making a frail nest for their chicks.

Guna emerged from the toilet, holding a copper pot in his hand. There was still some water in it. His feet were wet.

He heard his mother humming a Tamil song which his grandmother used to sing. She was busy hanging up small scraps of cloth on the side of the well's wall, so they could dry under the scorching sun. These were pieces of old rags torn into different sizes. Her movements were careful and precise, like those of an artist playing a piano. She smiled when she saw Guna, her fourteen-year-old son. 'Wash your feet thoroughly before entering the house,' she said. But her smile froze when she noticed displeasure and irritation on his face. She felt a sudden rush of nerves; she had forgotten that it was Sunday so school was closed.

'These old, smelly rags are filling the garden with their foul stench again. Are they so precious that you have to guard them this carefully? What sort of ritual compels you to hang up these wretched rags every now and then, like some work of art? Don't you realize how unpleasant their smell is?'

Stench? Might he be mistaking it for the foul smell coming from the toilet nearby? Could he not guess how important these bits of clothes were? How could she explain it to him? Did they really smell that bad, even though she had thoroughly washed and rinsed them many times? She had no choice; she could not do without them.

No old clothes of any kind were ever discarded in this household. There were two women in the house who got their period, and another was well on her way to puberty. These remnants of old cotton saris were priceless. Was there a way to explain this to a young boy like Guna? His mother had not anticipated such an awkward conversation between her son and herself. A vague sense of helplessness and bafflement came over her. She stammered a few excuses, but nothing she said made any sense.

How could she have forgotten it was Sunday? She could have, after all, avoided this unnecessary situation. She had always completed this task in the absence of men. Her face revealed, despite herself, an inexplicable sense of guilt. How could she let her son witness all this? And to think that Akka, her elder daughter, had also started menstruating. Poor thing! Akka had been bleeding heavily for the past few days. She needed to study for her upcoming exams. She had to be prepared with a good reserve of fabric scraps to avoid leaks, possible stains and keep it invisible.

Guna's mother wanted to explain all of this to him, but her son's expressionless face stopped her. She knew he no longer wanted to continue the discussion. Ill at ease, not fully grasping the situation, he ran inside the house to avoid the conversation, which he already felt was beyond him.

◆

Guna had two sisters. Only recently the children had suddenly lost their father, the sole breadwinner. Akka had just turned eighteen. Their mother, a housewife, was still quite young. She was cultured but had never received any formal education. They would have to wait another year for Akka to finish her baccalaureate and find a job to support the family. With each passing day, she became her mother's confidante, helping her get through difficult times after her husband's death. To Guna, his older sister was almost like a second mother. She assisted him with his lessons, helped him prepare for his exams. She would get him back on track every time his passion and excitement for games got the better of him. But he could never confide in her when it came to his other worries about growing up. Their conversations circled around studies, books and exams.

His younger sister Amba was the ideal companion for all his games and escapades. She never failed to accompany him when he followed the boys of the neighbourhood to climb the red hills and roam the forests of mango and tamarind trees. When punished by adults, they defended and consoled each other. And at night, lying on the big mat they shared with their mother and older sister, they laughed quietly at the stories they told each other. Their bond had slowly grown into a strong friendship.

Every Friday Guna's family liked visiting the Draupadi temple, dedicated to the heroine of the Mahabharata, wife of the five Pandavas. Guna felt great joy in accompanying his mother and his sisters on these visits. He loved the wide, open spaces of the temple and the steady stream of pilgrims who were never in a hurry.

But what fascinated Guna the most was the goddess Bhadrakali. He never understood why the fierce goddess was sometimes called Kali and at other times Bhadrakali. And he never received a satisfactory answer to his query. The statue of the goddess was tied to the floor with big iron chains. It was believed that on some pitch-dark nights, she tried to set herself free. A few residents of the street swore that they heard the goddess breathing angrily and clanking chains throughout the night. Everyone was afraid of this fearsome goddess, who would crush demons under her feet.

'Why are other goddesses not as frightening? Why did Bhadrakali crush a man with her bare feet?'

The answer to this question was: 'Because he was a monster.'

'Why are monsters always male?'

This question was met with silence.

'Why does Bhadrakali carry a bowl of blood? Why is her tongue protruding and red, as though she's been drinking from the bowl?'

The goddess's bowl of blood was always filled to the brim. Guna was haunted by the image many a night. He often saw himself wading through a pond of blood. Little by little, Guna's curiosity became tenacious. Over the years he began associating blood with women, but he wouldn't dare to share his thoughts with anyone.

During their school holidays, Guna and Amba spent many happy hours with a bunch of boys and girls from their neighbourhood playing marbles, or *kottipullu*, on the road. It was a rather difficult and complex game, played with sticks of different sizes. Amba had remarkable physical strength. Her keen intelligence and fierce determination ensured that, more often than not, she emerged victorious against her opponents. Amba was a member of her brother's gang of friends; he was the leader, she his lieutenant. She would help him win all his battles. During the weekends, these games kept them busy until evening. Their flights of fantasy and passion were interrupted abruptly only at mealtimes. Their mother was used to hearing the cries of brilliant victories or violent quarrels of her children. She lost count of how often the children came home with their clothes run down by sweat and dirt, their faces ruined by tears of loss and exhaustion.

During the week they dreamt of Sunday because this was when their games became more elaborate and structured. Groups were formed based on affinities and performances over the week. They worked hard during the evenings after school when they weren't allowed to play on the street. At night, free at last, they dreamt about their upcoming conquests. They would complete all their homework and assignments on Saturday nights in anticipation of the games that awaited them on Sunday.

Guna would never forget that particular hot and humid Sunday during the summer holidays when he and his gang were free to do as they pleased. It happened around two o'clock in the afternoon, when the parents were taking their naps or sitting on the thresholds of their houses. But Guna's mother never slept while her children were out playing on the street. A protective mother, she would sit on the steps at the entrance of the house watching them play. Sometimes a neighbour or two would join her and share the latest gossip. These were their only moments of respite after a long morning of household chores. They sat talking, all the while keeping a close eye on their children.

Guna's mother noticed that Amba seemed unsure of her movements. But immersed in her game, Amba hadn't realized that she had been dragging her feet. Her reflexes were slower than normal. And why was she limping? Amba kept wiping something off her right leg around her thigh. Her face was locked in a frown; pain and exhaustion, made worse by the unbearable sun.

'Amba! Amba!' her mother yelled. 'Come here! Come home immediately.'

The ladies of the neighbourhood had noticed their friend's concern and guessed what had just happened.

'Oh my God! Poor thing!' They all exclaimed.

They ran to Amba who stood paralyzed, looking at her mother with tears in her eyes. The boys were rooted to the spot, their game forgotten. What was going on? Why had their mothers run to Amba?

The women ordered their sons to stop playing.

The boys were perplexed. But why? Why did Guna's mother carry away Amba who'd suddenly collapsed into her mother's arms? It seemed as if she had fainted. There was a commotion on the street. The girls from the neighbourhood spoke in whispers.

Guna was as confused as his playmates. What had happened to Amba? His team had been about to win the game. He ran after the women and went to the house to find out what was happening. But the women had shut the door behind them. After a few minutes, Akka emerged and stopped him from entering the house.

'Amba is sick. She won't be playing with you.'

'What do you mean, Akka? What's wrong with her? How did she suddenly fall ill? A minute ago she was playing so well, and we were winning. Amba must return to finish the round.'

'It's impossible.'

Akka went back inside and closed the door.

Disappointed, Guna and the other boys waited outside the house.

'It's always like this,' a lone voice chimed in the melee. 'Don't I always tell you not to include girls in our games? It's complicated with them. What do we do now?'

The boys stared at the shut door with sad eyes. Everyone admired Amba and wanted her back in the game. Guna felt bewildered and could not look at his friends. He turned away to avoid their looks of disappointment and accusing eyes.

Suddenly a voice rang out, clear and distressed.

'Guna! Look there's blood on the steps of your house.'

The boys panicked; they did not want to be scolded for a crime they hadn't committed. They scampered off and disappeared from the street.

Guna peered at the drops of blood on the steps. He bent to take a closer look. Was it really blood? He touched the red blobs with his finger.

Amba was hurt. She was bleeding. How was that possible? How had it happened? Where did the blood come from? No one could get so seriously hurt in a game of marbles. He had not seen her

fall down either. Guna grew anxious. He sat on the steps and tried
to imagine what would happen next. One thing was for sure – his
mother was going to hold him responsible for Amba's injury. The
more he thought about it, the more upset he became with Amba.
She should have told him about it, warned him beforehand. But
she hadn't said a word. He felt choked by guilt. He was unable to
swallow his saliva. He went to the door, banged on it violently and
kicked it, shouting and crying. He wanted to understand what was
happening. He wanted to see Amba.

◆

Amba was sitting on an old mat at the end of the corridor, next to
the kitchen door. She had been isolated behind a screen of tender
coconut leaves, specially braided by hand for the occasion. Amba
could hardly be seen through the small gaps in the screen, but she
could peer through the holes. Amba had to be sheltered from the
sight of other people; such was the custom, Guna was told. For
all the women in the neighborhood, this was good news. *But why
are we stopping Amba from moving around the house?* Guna asked.
Akka explained to him that it was for the good of the family. She
also told him a ceremony would soon follow to announce that
Amba was no longer a girl but had become a young woman.

The leaves and tiny yellow flowers of the coconut tree adorned
the threshold of the house. Guna learnt for the first time that
these flowers were called coconut rice. Although he found the
arrangement beautiful, Guna thought it quite strange. Mothers and
young women from the neighbourhood visited in turns, moving a
section of the screen to talk to Amba. Sometimes they sat next to
her to share a chuckle. Guna could hear them congratulating her
on blossoming into a young woman. But for Guna, Amba was still

the same, his younger sister, the fierce Amazon of their games. Would she ever come back and play with him? Guna was curious. He asked Akka. 'You'll understand in due time,' was her reply. 'I'll explain everything after my exams. For now, leave me alone.'

Guna did not trust Akka; she would not keep her promise. With great trepidation, he approached his mother who was busy with the preparations for the upcoming ceremony along with his aunts who had come from out of town to help.

'Amba hasn't done anything wrong. Why are you punishing her? Why have you sent her to a corner? And for how long will you keep her there?'

'A week, maybe. We are waiting for the priest to tell us the day and the hour of the ceremony.'

'What ceremony, mother?'

'*Manjal nir vizha.*'

This was the first time he'd ever heard those words.

'Amba has become a young woman now, and we're celebrating this good news with this ceremony.'

'But then why have you put her in a jail of coconut leaves?'

'It is not a prison, Guna. We have confined her there because … because she isn't clean. We can't allow the impurity to spread throughout the house.'

'What impurity?'

'You won't understand. First, she has to have a purifying bath; only after that will she be allowed to move around the house.'

'Will she start playing with us soon?'

'No, never again.'

'Why?'

'Why? Because she's no longer a little girl who can play freely on the street. This is how things are. Let's not discuss it anymore. But don't worry, Amba isn't in any pain.'

'But she's bleeding. Shouldn't we call a doctor?'

'It doesn't mean she is suffering. The midwife has already seen her. Amba will stop bleeding in three days. For women, blood does not always mean pain. We all bleed.'

'You too, mother??'

'Yes, of course. And your Akka too.'

'Why didn't you ever tell me this before?'

Guna's mother was silent.

'Did Amba know this would happen to her?' Guna saw his mother nod. 'And why didn't she say anything to me?'

'Because you're too young.'

'What do you mean? Amba is younger than me.'

'Because ... because you are a boy.'

'What do you mean by that?''

Guna's mother tried to change the topic. 'You see, everything will be normal after her turmeric bath ceremony. Amba will be blessed by all the married women. After that they'll help her wear a sari.'

Amba in a sari? She'll look ridiculous. She's too short.

His mother was saddened to see her son's anxious face. She stopped stirring the yellow milk she was preparing for the ceremonial bath and went down on her knees. 'Guna,' she said gently, 'we were all like Amba at her age.'

'I don't understand a word of what you are saying. Why can't someone explain to me clearly why there were drops of blood on the steps of the house? Why are the blood stains still there?'

'Stop, Guna. Listen to me. The blood was cleaned a long time ago. Why are you so obsessed with them? And you're asking too many questions. Why don't you accept what I'm telling you?'

'That's right. Shoo me away when you don't have the answers.'

'Go now. Study for your exams.'

And with that she ended the conversation and told him to leave the kitchen.

'No, I will not study. One day I will find out what happens in this house.'

He stormed out of the kitchen, and as he crossed Amba's prison, he stopped and said to the figure behind the braided coconut leaves, 'Traitor!'

◆

And yet, it was Amba who helped Guna decipher some of the mysteries. One time, when they were alone, she told him whatever she knew about the mystery of the blood. He listened for a long time. But he did not understand everything she said.

'Guna, do you remember during our visits to the temple you were asking about the image of the goddess Bhadrakali and the bowl of blood in her left hand? Amma didn't answer your question. I think it's the goddess's menstrual blood in the bowl which she probably drinks. It's awful, isn't it?'

'What are you saying? It's disgusting. I don't believe you.'

'That's fine. You don't understand, because you're a boy.'

'Stop it. You're talking like Amma now.'

Guna was upset and kept quiet. But he continued listening, as Amba carried on.

'Kali takes on the name Bhadrakali when she is menstruating. Isn't it obvious?'

All these details rang in his head like the blows of a hammer. The image of Bhadrakali drinking her own blood pursued him in his dreams. But he didn't risk discussing it with anyone.

Amba used this rare moment to also explain the usefulness of the old scraps of fabric which their mother would hang to dry on the wall of the well. Guna felt stupid. He also felt guilty about the way he had behaved with his mother earlier. How could he have reproached her in that way? Was there a way he could say sorry?

'I hope Amma has forgotten my harsh words. But I wish she had explained this to me.'

'Life is like that, Guna. Full of secrets. We will figure them out as we go along. Maybe.'

'Is it true that you won't play with us anymore?'

'Yes, but you can play without me. You're a boy. I'll come and watch when you're playing. You can also tell me about your adventures.'

'It won't be the same. It's no fun without you. We won't play on this street anymore.'

Guna's words spoken in this emotional moment became prophetic. He never played with his friends from the neighbourhood on that street again. After the rainy season, hoping against hope, Guna and two or three of his friends tried to resume their favourite games, but their parents decided otherwise: they were no longer children. A few boys from the gang started working in their parents' shops. Their adult lives began the day they stopped playing outside Guna's house.

From his house, Guna looked out at the street which had lost its charm, its enigma, its actors and actresses. Those few drops of blood on the threshold had snatched everything from him. He could no longer hear children's passionate cries and the violence of their innocence. Instead, cars blasted their deafening horns. Strangers inhabited the street now. Who were these people? Where had they come from?

Akka cleared her baccalaureate exams with flying colours and the family was proud of her. She began working as a teacher in the school where she had studied. Then one day she got married and went away, leaving behind Guna and Amba. Her mother lost her closest confidante. Soon it was Amba's turn to leave her family home, the same way her mother and sister had. She too would adopt her husband's home as her own.

Guna sat with his mother on the threshold of their house. He tried to assess the intensity of the stains of blood which had appeared one day like reflections of the monsoon clouds on the surface of an infinite ocean.

Red Nectar of the Sacred Lotus:
A Buddhist Perspective on
Menstruation

TASHI ZANGMO

LOOKING BACK ON MY CHILDHOOD, AS A YOUNG GIRL GROWING
up in rural eastern Bhutan, I cannot recollect anyone ever
discussing or even mentioning menstruation. At one level, this
silence was a result of my own peculiar situation. At the age of
eleven, I started attending a boarding school which was almost
a day's walk from my village; it was the nearest one at the time.
Students from faraway villages came to study here and live in
the two-storey campus building, which was the school's only
dormitory. Since I was the sole female boarding student, I had to
share it with the boys. At least for the first year of school, I lived
with them, sleeping in the corner of the dorm, next to the mother
of a distant male cousin who was also a student at the school.

I survived like a wildflower among thorns. My mother and
older sisters used to bring my ration supplies once a month, and
my aunt would cook for me and her son. If I remember correctly,
there were seven other girls at the school. They were the daughters
of teachers and shopkeepers who lived around the area and
commuted to school from their homes. During school hours, it

was just us few girls as opposed to more than a hundred boys. But in the evenings and on the weekends, I was the only girl on campus.

In those days, everything related to the body was considered to be mysterious. People were secretive and did not expose any part of it. This was especially true for girls. We were embarrassed to lift our dresses and expose our ankles, even to keep our clothes from getting wet or muddy, on rainy days. There was no such thing as sex education. Nobody told us how our bodies would change during puberty or what happened when girls began to menstruate or what to do.

Yet, when the time came, nature seemed to whisper in our ears, and somehow we could understand, to some extent, what was happening to us. Amongst the eight of us, there was a girl a year younger than me. She was the first to experience that initial drop of red nectar from her sacred body. Some of us had realized what had happened and wanted to ask her about it, but we did not dare because she was extremely embarrassed. Aside from the fact that we were not well informed, we also had no means of taking care of ourselves. So whenever we got our periods, we chose to ignore it, even when red stains appeared on the benches in our classroom. Even so, despite our ignorance and embarrassment, there was a certain charm and excitement to it all. As is often the case, hidden things are more exciting than the mundane.

Although us living as a few wildflowers among a myriad of thorns exacerbated the silence, we were not alone in our reticence to discuss periods. Bhutanese people, in general, do not talk about menstruation because traditionally it is a closed subject. Despite the close bonds between children and parents, adults tend to keep certain subjects – like menstruation – out of bounds. They do not share everything with us as our friends do. In Bhutanese culture, parents are revered and hold a position of respect and moral authority and children feel shy or even distant from them. This is especially true when it comes to private matters like menstruation, which is deemed to be impure and shameful. It is only in recent decades that we have started talking about menstrual hygiene-related issues freely in public spaces, and this has led to more acceptance and open discourse.

◆

It is interesting to look into the origins of the negative attitude towards menstruation. Some of these beliefs are so deeply rooted in the Bhutanese psyche that it is almost impossible to unlearn them, even though they are not backed by science or logic. Since ancient times, the menstrual cycle has been viewed as impure and menstruating women were not welcomed in the inner sanctums of some designated temples. This was to maintain the hygiene and purity of the space. While some argue that this segregation is an extreme form of gender discrimination, I instead see it as an old custom, a prescribed and practised tradition. For instance, in some temples in northern Thailand, women have adopted self-imposed restrictions which prevent them from circumambulating religious monuments such as stupas (even though one cannot find such restrictions in the actual Buddhist texts).[1] One could argue that this has been more of a personal choice as opposed to an external imposition.

In some cases, traditions are followed even when the reasons for their existence have become redundant or irrelevant and, consequently, unverified beliefs and ideas continue to be associated with female physiology. The equation is reversed as restrictions end up being founded on gendered ideas instead of biological reasons, and over the years, the directive becomes solidified as a gendered prescription. One such example is women being forbidden from entering the inner chambers of sacred places irrespective of whether or not they are menstruating. Today, the question of whether or not a woman should be allowed to enter the inner sanctum of temples is based purely on a particular perception of menstruation. Is menstrual blood impure or is it just like the blood which flows through the human body irrespective of gender?

At the other end of the spectrum is Vajrayana Buddhism, one of three well-known Budhhist sects and the state religion of Bhutan. Vajrayana Buddhism considers menstruation to be holy and pure because it is the life source for many enlightened beings. In classical and traditional Tantric Tibetan Buddhist texts, the word for a woman's private part is *pema* or lotus, which is a beautiful and positive metaphorical term. By extension, menstrual blood can be compared to the nectar of the lotus. The lotus is a powerful symbol because it grows in dirt but is offered at many shrines.

The female figure has always been prominent in Buddhist traditions. It is generally believed by Vajrayana practitioners that Dakini Yeshe Tsogyal menustrated when she was eight years old. Yeshe Tsogyal, the consort of Guru Rinpoche, was a spiritual master and teacher in her own right, and a preeminent figure in the Nyingma school of Tibetan Buddhism. According to some Tantric Vajrayana Buddhist texts, an eight-year-old girl's menstruation or the menstruation of a virgin is very auspicious, and menstrual blood does not become impure until she starts having sex. Until then, it is considered sacred.

In Vajrayana Buddhism, women are considered essential because male–female unity is inherently sacrosanct. Women and men together make *thab* and *sherub* (wisdom and method) just like *yin* and *yang* in the Chinese tradition of complementing opposites. The female partner of a *yogi* (a Buddhist practitioner) is addressed as *chagya-ma* ('seal' or *mudra*), *sangyum* (sacred partner or consort), or *rigzinma* (wisdom holder). Wisdom and method work in tandem. For an enlightened mind, there is no gender and the understanding of the world transcends binary divisions of clean and dirty, high and low, haves and have-nots, men and women. When one reaches this level of acceptance of the world, everything becomes wholesome, and there is no impurity or negativity.

If we were to consider menstruation from a lay person's perspective, not a Buddhist's point of view, we would acknowledge that without menstruation, there would be no life. Today, we understand the biological function of menstruation better than before; we know menstrual bleeding is a normal phenomenon and part of nature's evolutionary process. Menstruation is a life-giving process which nature has gifted the feminine physiology. We are all products of the same process.

The Buddhist approach to a woman's monthly flow is based on common sense: 'Menstruation is a natural physical excretion that women have to go through on a monthly basis, nothing more or less.'[2] The Buddhist biological viewpoint reinforces the notion that feeling ashamed or embarrassed about menstruation is a residue from the past, and a primitive reticence. Today, many more women can be equipped with the necessary sanitary paraphernalia, and hygiene can be maintained as never before. The question is whether we are willing to let go of our primitive beliefs and approach the world more rationally and scientifically? Or will we continue to perpetuate beliefs of the past blindly and irrationally? Only when we are willing to accept menstruation as a natural phenomenon will the dilemma of women and the inner sanctum be resolved.

During Buddha's time, he saw the spiritual potential in both
men and women equally. He founded, after considerable hesitation,
the Order of Bhikkhunis (Buddhist nuns), as one of the earliest
organizations for women. The *sasana*, or church, consisted of the
bhikkus (monks), *bhikkunis* (nuns), laymen and laywomen so that
the women would not be left out of any sphere of religious activity.
The highest spiritual states were within the reach of both men and
women equally and the latter needed no masculine assistance or
priestly intermediary to achieve them.[3]

◆

It is interesting to consider how cultures interact, transmute and
evolve. Some believe that the negative perception of menstruation
in the Bhutanese Buddhist psyche has been incorporated from
Hinduism because Buddhism does not subscribe to these ideas
in any form. Even restrictions of access to the inner sanctum of
some temples are not a religious imposition per se, but rather an
unverified popular social norm. Though there are subtle gender
judgments and biases in Bhutanese society, unlike in other cultures,
there is no extreme and obvious gender-based discrimination and
exclusion. Many of these practices and beliefs originating from
the belief that women are unclean are 'root[ed] in Hinduism
where women are seen as religiously unclean because of their
menstruation'.[4] In the Hindu tradition, menstruating women are
excluded from domestic chores, particularly the food-related ones.
For example, they are not allowed near fermenting rice because it
was believed it would be spoiled by their presence.

My own childhood experiences and readings of Buddhist
texts and traditions have led me to conclude that many of the
negative beliefs towards menstruation migrated to Bhutan from

India, specifically from the Hindu tradition. Despite the absence of evidence in Buddhist texts and teachings supporting the stigmatization of menstruation, such beliefs have passed from one generation to the next in Bhutan, as though they were always part of our customs. A memory from my childhood comes to my mind as I reflect on this. We had many Indian teachers at school in my village and one of them was a 'Brahmin'. When his wife had her period, she was restricted from touching anything – especially utensils in the kitchen. She was not allowed to cook or do any household tasks. Sometimes, we would offer to help her out with her chores but when we served her food, we would put her plate on the floor because she was forbidden from taking it directly from our hands. She was not permitted to touch anyone for fear of contamination because she was bleeding and impure. If, by chance, she touched anything in the kitchen, her husband would yell at her. She literally became 'untouchable' during her menstruation. This was my first and very early encounter of ostracization of women during menstruation, and it left a very strong impression on me.

It is also interesting that in India the original reason for gendered restrictions in some temples was not the menstrual cycle of women, but rather the circumstances. Sadhguru explains how some believed that the temple's energy was not an ideal influence on women and harmful to their feminine energy. There are also some hill temples which have denied access to menstruating women because it was believed that the smell of the menstrual blood might attract wild, carnivorous animals such as tigers. Consequently, women were kept away as a protective measure. It was not a taboo that stopped women from visiting the temple during their menstrual cycles.[4]

Some cultural practices are residues of purposeful customs which may no longer be relevant but are practised today without thought, and therefore, steps initally taken to protect a person end up devolving into gender discrimination. With the passage of time and evolving contexts, traditions need to adapt to change.

◆

For the past twelve years, I have been working with female monastics in Bhutan, and today, the Bhutan Nuns Foundation (BNF), established in 2009 under the patronage of Her Majesty the Queen Mother, Tshering Yangdoen Wangchuck, carries out trainings and advocacy related to reproductive health with the support of UNICEF and UNFPA Bhutan.

A decade ago, while thinking about setting up the foundation, I visited many of the country's nunneries and talked to the nuns about how they took care of themselves when they were menstruating. I learned that many of the nunneries did not have proper toilets with running water and the nuns did not have access to pads. Once we established BNF, we were able to connect the nunneries with local and international donors to offer training on menstrual hygiene, as well as life skills, education and nutrition.

In the beginning, the nuns were not open to discussing their monthly cycles. During one advocacy trip to a nunnery, after the formal talks were completed, I sat with a few senior nuns and over a cup of tea, we talked about menstrual hygiene casually. I asked them how they coped, when they went to villages to perform prayers and ceremonies, and whether they knew how to keep track of their cycles.

One nun giggled and said, 'Usually we never keep track of our periods; every time it happens, I feel surprised. The worst is when it shows up during prayer ceremonies in the village households.

When that happens, we rush to the cornfields to look for scarecrows and pull the old clothes off them to use as pads.'

We knew that it was unsafe and unhygienic for the nuns to use such rags as pads, so after hearing these stories, we explored how to get more support for them, and began giving WASH trainings throughout the country. These soft-skill trainings were made possible with financial support from organizations such as UNICEF, UNFPA and SNV Bhutan (the Netherlands Development Organization).

During those early days at BNF, we realized that theoretical training and advocacy workshops were not enough – especially where there was a scarcity of basic resources, such as proper toilets and clean running water. We looked for additional funds to build proper living quarters for the nuns, with attached toilets and shower facilities with running water. Such projects are still being supported by charity organizations such as Firefly Mission in Singapore and individual donors from around the globe.

Now, after more than a decade, the nunneries have been transformed. It gives us a deep sense of fulfilment to see such significant improvements especially in those nunneries in the rural areas where they had neither the means nor the income to put such essential infrastructure in place.

Recently, with the help of the Honourable Health Minister of the Royal Government of Bhutan, the BNF joined a campaign focusing on the 'elimination of cervical cancer through universal access to preventive, curative, palliative and rehabilitative services'. As an organization working for women and young girls in nunneries, it is the BNF's responsibility to educate the nuns in health-related areas, so that they in turn can reach out to the larger society in their role as religious figures. Bhutan has a strong spiritual tradition, and when people – especially women – get sick, they first reach out to monastic institutions. Only after monks and nuns perform all kinds of rituals do lay people go to the hospital. After working with the religious body over the years, we realized that it is imperative that we train the nuns in the area of women's health, so that they are better able to advise vulnerable women and encourage them to seek medical attention while the nuns perform rituals and prayers on their behalf.

Ultimately, through this work, I have come to realize that education is the key to liberation. Without proper education, it is not easy to conceptualize, communicate and understand one's environment. Liberation does not only mean emancipating oneself from external oppression but also using education to unfetter one's ignorant mind to realize one's potential. The mission of the BNF is to help educate the nuns of Bhutan. Our aim is to train them to become counsellors, hospice workers, basic healthcare and palliative-care providers, leaders, managers, doctors and teachers deriving passion and compassion from their own monastic tradition. Improving their basic hygiene and menstrual health was the first step towards this process of empowerment.

I am confident that the twenty-first century is already a better world, where all women will be able to realize their full potential and become agents of change for the well-being of humanity. A world where every woman perceives herself as a sacred lotus with the privilege to experience the powerful drip of red nectar.

Aadya Shakti, or Primal Energy

LYLA FREECHILD

WHEN I WAS ASKED TO MAKE MENSTRUAL ART FOR THIS
BOOK, 'Aadya Shakti' had been on my mind for several months.
The political turbulence and ecological strife in my environment
had been upsetting me. I kept asking myself: what is the ultimate
answer to the violence and anger? The answer came to me in a
dream one night and I felt convinced that reclaiming the ancient
belief in the magical qualities of menstrual blood through art could
be one way of healing the ruptures that were plaguing our planet.
I decided I would illustrate the mystical aspect of menstrual blood
to portray how women are connected to Mother Earth through
their menstrual cycle. Menstrual blood has the power to create
peace and regenerate the earth, and I felt the strong need to bring
this vision of the feminine life force to life through my art.

The idea birthed in my dream was initially a motif of many
lotus flowers floating in a sea of blood. In India, the lotus is a
political symbol and the logo of a right-wing political party, but in
many cultures the flower is used to depict enlightenment, fertility
and rebirth. I resolved to erase the negativity and hatred through
my painting and reclaim the purity of the lotus.

My menstrual art was inspired by two things. One was the
striking image of a golden Lajja Gauri. Lajja Gauri is the lotus-

headed Hindu goddess associated with abundance, fertility and sexuality. She is also known as Aadya Shakti (primal energy) and Bhu-devi (Earth goddess). In my vision, I saw myself as her, which is why in my painting you will see Lajja Gauri wearing thick bangles, toe rings, anklets and armlets – the kind of jewellery I wear. In order to do justice to what I had imagined, I photographed myself extensively. I used those photos as a reference to draw the hair on the goddess's body because I wanted my art to be very personal and intimate. I had been harvesting my own menstrual blood for several years and had collected enough to use as paint. I was convinced that this medium would allow me to reclaim the purity of menstrual blood.

The second inspiration came from a book I was reading by Lara Owen, entitled *Her Blood Is Gold: Awakening to the Wisdom of Menstruation*, in which she writes about the creation myth of the Kogi Indians of Colombia. The title of the book and these words from the book about the Great Mother – 'from her comes life' – resonated with me. The Kogis believe that the earth was formed by the Great Mother during her menstrual cycle. Her blood seeped into the ground and became the precious gold that flows in the seams of the earth's rocky interior. According to the Kogis, menstruation is directly related to the survival of life on this planet and menstrual blood is the magical fluid from which human life was created. The blood from the womb that nourished the unborn child is believed to have *mana*, or magical healing power. The Kogis also say that whenever the earth stops receiving this magical, mystical fluid, violence increases, leading to great destruction, which will eventually consume the planet itself.

The Kogi culture is not the only one that holds such beliefs. Many other cultures also acknowledge that menstrual blood has mysterious healing qualities; some say it could cure leprosy, and others claim it is an aphrodisiac. Menstrual blood, according to the Tantric tradition, is sacred, and men could become spiritually powerful by ingesting it. However, over time, patriarchy and evolving value systems have made us forget and distorted these ancient ideas and rituals, turning a sacrament into a pollutant. I had other symbols in my mind as I conceptualized my art. Blood is closely linked not only to Mother Earth, but also to the moon and the snake. As women, we are of the earth in a powerful way. Together, we are the nurturers and givers of life. The earth is our home, and like her, we host homes within us. When a woman bleeds, her connection with the earth is activated in a cellular and magical way. We are connected to the earth at a subatomic level. The female body is a microcosm of the earth as much as it is a metaphor and a reflection. What we see around us is how our bodies are too. The soil of the earth is like the skin of our bodies, and the ocean is like the human heart which pumps life into the body, the trees are like our lungs, and the menstrual cycle mirrors the regeneration of the earth. The fact that women bleed without dying adds to their numinous power and emphasizes the earth's continual renewal.

Women have an intrinsic relationship of similarity with Mother Earth. When we bleed onto the earth, we reinforce this connection to Mother Earth who sustains all life. Earth, like the menstruating woman, has lost her status as the sacred mother because humans have become increasingly 'civilized' and distanced from nature. When a woman menstruates, it is a chance for her own rebirth and the renewal of her connection with Mother Earth.

The other icon I use in my art is the snake. Snakes and women share a pattern of cyclical shedding. The snake sheds its skin, while the woman discards the lining of the womb when she menstruates. The symbolism of the snake also demonstrates the different stages of life that a woman passes through – the shedding of childhood at puberty, of fertility at menopause, and life at death.

The moon also features in my painting as a representation of feminine power and marks the congruity of the lunar and menstrual cycles. There is a period of darkness before the moon returns to the height of its glory, akin to a temporary death. Death occurs before renewal, and menstruation marks the end of a chance at the creation of a potential life while also offering the promise of yet another opportunity for the same the following month.

When women share their menstrual blood in a sacred ritual with Mother Earth, either individually or in a ceremony, enormous positive power is unleashed which can help to rebalance and heal our planet. During this act of sharing, women act as a conduit between the generative forces of the moon and the receptive fecund energies of the earth. Women are the link between two celestial bodies – the earth and the moon – through their lunar cycle and earth-nurturing menstrual flow.

Each person has a role to play in healing our planet. The growing hatred around us is drawing up more borders inside our hearts and on our lands; love, compassion, equality and dignity are dwindling faster than the speed of light. We are sliding down the path of destruction into a dark period of the moon's cycle. Isn't it time for us now to turn to the Great Mother who created us? To join her as she renews herself for the rebirth of our planet, its beings and its systems through a magical communion between her and our mystical blood?

Increased Period Poverty during Covid-19 in Lahore, Pakistan

AYRA INDRIAS PATRAS

THE COVID-19 PANDEMIC AFFECTED THE MOST POOR AND vulnerable communities worst of all because they had to also navigate through challenges accentuated by intersecting points of gender, occupation, religion and class. It imposed multiple constraints on women living on the fringes of society and made managing their period more challenging. This essay attempts to highlight the problems of menstrual management during the time of Covid-19. It is based on eight informal interviews conducted with women from the minority Christian community in Pakistan working as domestic workers and peasants in three villages in Punjab situated in the surroundings of Narowal, Patoki and Kasur.

A large percentage of Pakistani Christians work as sweepers and are often subjected to discrimination. They are considered to be of a lower caste because of their historical legacy of being 'untouchables' as well as their 'menial' occupation. In the wake of the Covid-19 pandemic, the women of this community, especially those residing in villages and urban slums, found themselves in a situation of triple jeopardy when it came to menstrual management. Firstly, they belong to a caste which has been deemed untouchable;

secondly, the perception of periods as dirty and shameful makes them seem further impure; and lastly, social distancing rules and regulations vis-à-vis washing and restraints on physical contact added a third layer to their oppression.

Many low-income households found it difficult to survive especially because their principal breadwinners lost their jobs. While handwashing and sanitizing were emphasized through media campaigns, very little was said about the poor who faced challenges of water scarcity and found sanitizers unaffordable. They were at a loss as to how to cope with the pandemic and its fallout. Social distancing to mitigate the likelihood of catching the coronavirus did not hold any meaning for those who lived in cramped spaces, often with six or eight family members inhabiting a single room.

Before the spread of the virus, women from these poor communities could, to some extent, find personal time and private space within their homes to cope with their periods. They were able to rest, wash and dry their period rags and discuss periods freely with their sisters and friends. However, during lockdown, when everyone was forced to stay inside their homes, they lost this space. A forty-three-year-old Christian woman with four children – two girls and two boys – whom I interviewed in Lahore, said:

'As the male members of the family are mostly home, my daughters and I find it very difficult to change, wash our personal garments and deal with our period. We find it shameful to do this when there are men around. It is very difficult.'

In addition to this, there was a surge in domestic violence in Pakistan, as reported in the press,[1] putting women in a more precarious situation than ever. One woman, a forty-three-year-old with two children, told me about an instance of domestic violence related to period poverty: 'A man in our neighbourhood beat his wife when she asked him for money to buy pads. He refused, got angry and became violent.'

While food rations were being distributed by NGOs and corporates, menstrual products were not considered a priority, and women who had previously used pads now had to resort to using rags. The loss of livelihoods for many women also translated to a loss of access to menstrual hygiene products. A twenty-four-year-old woman who had been trying to build a career as a beautician shared her story with me.

'Earlier, before the pandemic, I had a good job at a beauty parlour and I could easily afford to buy good-quality pads from the market, but now I have lost my job due to Covid-19. My employer has shut down the parlour. I can no longer buy pads and am using my old discarded and worn-out clothes [instead]. I feel uncomfortable using them.'

Generally, women living in villages do not have access to sanitary napkins, and when they do, the quality of the napkins available is poor. However, because of Covid-19-related lockdowns and restrictions, the situation has become worse. In a village near Kasur, during a church seminar on menstrual health, women revealed their problems. I spoke to a family with four daughters.

'We are four sisters, and it is very expensive to buy pads because each pack costs Rs 150. One pack is enough for only one person, but it is unthinkable for us to spend that much on buying pads. During the lockdown, we have even less money, so my mother spends it on buying food. We are too poor to even buy underpants, so, during our menstrual cycle, we share our underwear and rags with each other. We wash the rags and reuse them, even though we do not like to do this.'

During the 2020 lockdown in Pakistan, the second-hand clothing markets were shut down. Previously, women would buy cheap clothes or fabric to use as pads from these markets, but during the pandemic this became more difficult. One woman, about thirty years old, who often used to shop at the market, had this to say:

'I used to buy cotton clothes from the second-hand market at a very low price which I would cut up and use as pads. Now I can't, because the markets are closed, and even if they were open, I can't afford to buy those clothes because I've lost my job. I don't have a choice, so I made a few pads from an old towel.'

Before the lockdown, those who could afford to, began hoarding toilet paper and sanitary pads which created a shortage in the market. This made it more difficult for women from lower-income groups to access sanitary products[2], forcing them to resort to using rags and cloth, making them more vulnerable to infections. Such concerns about menstrual hygiene are hardly ever highlighted in the media.

Due to the shame and stigma attached to the subject of menstrual health, women do not speak about the challenges they face even under normal circumstances. The silence and restrictions increased during the pandemic as privacy and access to medical help were curtailed, and the attention of healthcare providers was focused on responding to Covid-19 infections.[3] Additionally, the fear of contracting Covid made women hesitant about visiting medical centres and many opted not to seek help for their reproductive health. A thirty-five-year-old mother of two girls and a boy told me:

> 'My daughter has been complaining about cramps and pain after not having had her period for three months. However, I will not take her to the hospital because I'm afraid of being infected by the coronavirus. She will have to wait.'

Coping with the challenges of menstruation during the pandemic has been very difficult for many menstruators in Pakistan.[4] Dealing with one's menstrual cycle while managing the more general public difficulties brought about by the pandemic was a demanding task. The particular physical, cultural, social needs of women, including their access to menstrual products and appropriate menstrual hygiene are crucial parameters for a more complete analysis of the gendered implications of the Covid-19 pandemic.[5]

In Pakistan, menstruation is stigmatized and never openly discussed and the link between menstrual and mental health is all too often ignored. Women are more susceptible to mental health disorders[6] and, during the pandemic, the strain of coping with menstruation already aggravated by cultural taboos and poor education became worse due to lack of access to and unavailability of menstrual hygiene products and medical health, water shortages and poor hygiene facilities. Going forward, there is much that policymakers, healthcare professionals, NGOs and educational institutions can do to help alleviate the long-term psychological impact of the Covid-19 pandemic on women's menstrual and mental health.

The Worst Day of My Life: Menstruation and Dysphoria

INTERVIEW | FARAH AHAMED

JAVED[*] IS A THIRTY-TWO-YEAR-OLD MAN LIVING IN ISLAMABAD, Pakistan, who works in the civil service sector. He keeps his life as a transgender man a secret, and therefore care has been taken in this essay to protect his identity.

Javed is proud of being a *mutajanus*, which he says is the correct Urdu word for a trans person. In Urdu, the word for gender is *jinss* and mutajanus alludes to the two-gendered quality of a transperson. Incidentally, Janus is the name of the Roman god of doorways, usually depicted with two faces on opposite sides of his head, representing sunrise and sunset and reflecting his primordial role as a solar deity. In Latin, *janus* literally means gate or arched passageway. In Sanskrit, the word is associated with the word *yanah*, which means path. *Khwaja sira*, the more commonly used Urdu term, literally means the owner of a guest house and comes from the word *siraye* which were guest houses for travellers along the ancient Silk Route or the old Grand Trunk (G.T.) Road, Asia's oldest and longest road.

---

[*] Name changed

Untitled embroidery by Sarah Naqvi

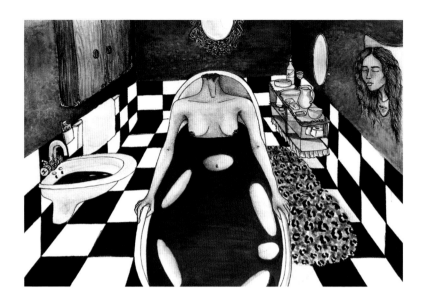

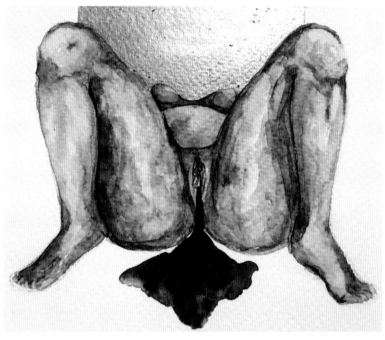

Untitled paintings by Sarah Naqvi

Nuns at Losel Yangchenling Nunnery in Mongar, Eastern Bhutan mark their cheeks as part of the Red Dots campaign to signify positive changes towards menstrual health

A sanitary pad incinerator installed at Losel Yangchenling Nunnery

Nuns celebrating International Menstrual Hygiene Day, 2020 at Losel Yangchenling Nunnery

'Period'
A Photo Series by Rupi Kaur

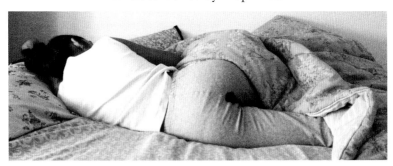

@rupikaur_

We removed your post because it doesn't follow our Community Guidelines.

Please read our Community Guidelines to learn what kinds of posts are allowed and how you can help keep Instagram safe.

OK

On 25 March 2015, Canadian poet and artist Rupi Kaur uploaded the first image from this photo series to Instagram. The images were part of a university assignment she was working on with her sister Prabh. Within twenty-four hours the photos were deleted by Instagram, not once but twice, and the explanation given was that the posts had breached the terms of their service. However, when the original post and Kaur's outrage at Instagram and Facebook was liked by 53,000 people and shared over 12,000 times, the company apologized. This photo essay highlights the indiscriminate censorship on social media platforms of artwork involving women's bodies. In Kaur's words, it is how they 'help keep the public safe from periods'.

'Menstruation is not a problem but a symbol of women's strength'
Mural on the wall of a community hall in Naya Bhadiyara,
Jharkhand, India

'Menstruation is not a burden, but nature's gift'
Mural near a well in Madransare, Jharkhand

The Scroll (1989-90)
Shahzia Sikander
WATERCOLOUR ON WASLI PAPER
34 x 162 cm

'The Scroll' is about 'the claiming of the freedom for the female body in the domestic setting'. Sikander says she wanted to illustrate the 'young adult female defying bodily restrictions by becoming an elastic, transparent, moving, morphing form, almost like a ghost' to show a woman's struggle to break away from 'the prevalent layers of patriarchy', because, ultimately, 'how one experienced space was all about restriction'.

Painted over a year and a half, 'The Scroll' reimagines the traditional vocabulary of the Mughal Indo-Persian miniature painting genre, and maps out everyday contemporary life in the artist's family home. Using the stacked, flattened-out style of the Safavid period, the painting shows the repeated image of a young woman moving through space and time; a day or a lifetime, past, present or future; menarche to menopause. In the artist's words, 'The protagonist is rendered in a diaphanous form where it is transparent and then opaque but never situated in the same time and space as the rest of the characters ...' Dressed in white, and painted from behind, the protagonist's spectral figure passes through each room filled with activities, reading, eating, and cleaning, until she's finally at an easel painting herself in an act of self-definition.

'The Scroll' illustrates flux and transition, inviting multiple interpretations. It highlights how a female experiences constraints of freedom of movement during puberty, makes a statement about the defiance and restlessness of youth and emphasizes her quest for identity.

Paintings by Anish Kapoor

'Blood Hole', 2018
Oil on canvas
274 x 213 cm

'Out of Me', 2018
Oil on canvas
274 x 213 cm

'New Blood', 2018
Oil on canvas
274 x 213 cm

Inside a Bashali in the Kalash Valley, Chitral, Pakistan

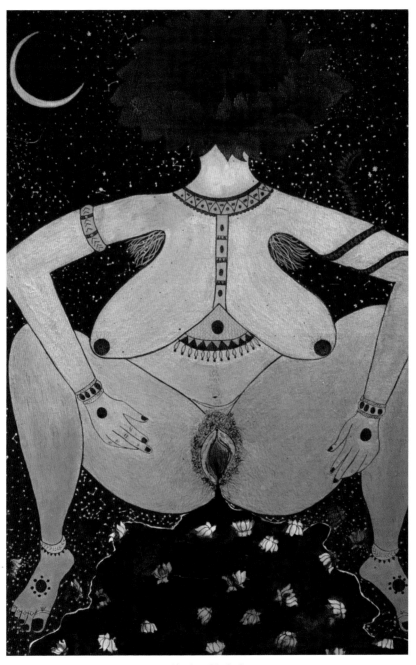

'Aadya Shakti'
by Lyla FreeChild

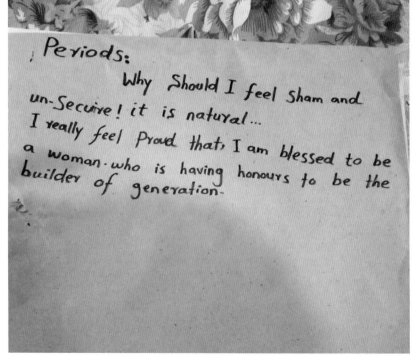

Creative expression by young girls at the first menstrual workshop in Balochistan conducted by Granaz Baloch

Stills from 'Raqs-e-Mahvaari', a menstrual dance
performed by Amna Mawaz Khan

Javed describes himself as 'basically a loner' and prefers not to share his life publicly. Most of his friends are either cis or gay, and he is not part of any transgender community. During my conversations with him, Javed shared that he did not really have to come out, because as far as he could remember, he knew there was something not right about himself. He had never felt internally aligned with his body, and despite what the world told him, he knew he was a boy.

For Javed, getting his period meant experiencing monthly episodes of extreme dysphoria, and every cycle was traumatic for him. Menstruation made his relationship with himself even more difficult. In this essay, I recount his journey to self-acceptance.

The following section is adapted from an exchange with Javed over the telephone.

◆

From the time I was very young, I never felt that I was a girl. I always knew that I was a boy, even though my body told me otherwise. I used to dream that one morning I would wake up and magically find myself transformed into a boy. Then I would truly be myself. So when I reached puberty and started menstruating, it felt like the worst possible thing had happened to me. All I could think was: I am a boy, and I am not supposed to go through this.

To counter the dysphoria, I started going to the gym and lifting weights, which would somehow lead me to feeling a modicum of congruence within my body, mind and soul. But every aspect of puberty was traumatic for me. I felt completely lost. And much to my mother's dismay, I began to rebel. She had no idea how to help me; my grades plummeted, and I barely made it through college.

Growing up, I was close to my mother. Before I started menstruating, she explained that it was a biological process and told me what to do when it happened. I was fifteen when I got my first period – and it was during the summer holidays. It was the worst day of my life. Deep down I knew I was a boy, so I actually believed I would never get my period. I remember thinking that this can't be happening. I'm not a girl. My mother didn't make a fuss about it and showed me how to use a pad. I never had any restrictions imposed on me, either related to food or attending social events and gatherings. I carried on with my life as I would on any other day, except that I felt an internal resistance to the whole biological process. There was a constant awareness that this was wrong. This was not me.

My mother was very open about her own period. I must have been nine or ten years old when I noticed that she would regularly feel unwell. Every month my younger brother and I would get worried and upset and ask her why she was always sick. She explained that women bleed every month, and it was normal for them to feel poorly during that time. She raised us to think of menstruation as a very natural process. She never hid her own cycle or hesitated to tell us about the pain she was going through. My brother and I would help her during those difficult days.

After I entered puberty, every month I dreaded getting my period and even through my twenties, I felt the same. But now, I feel a sense of compassion whenever I think about what women have to endure. Coping with menstruation is not easy.

When I turned twenty-eight, I started hormone replacement therapy (HRT). Within one month of my transition, my periods stopped. The day I realized that I would no longer have my periods was the happiest day of my life. My menstrual cycle had always been very regular, and when they ceased, I was relieved. I detested the blood, the smell, and dreaded the pain and the cramps; I hated everything about it. It was abhorrent to me. I was repulsed by every aspect of menstruation. I was not a woman, yet I suffered going through it every month. I could never accept it as something natural; it was abnormal for me. As a transman, managing my periods in public was also difficult because men's toilets often have no bins. But I never use public toilets, more for hygiene reasons than anything else. Undergoing HRT has changed my life.

I've been lucky because I've had a privileged upbringing. I went to good schools and studied at a university abroad. I did not face any discrimination as such, aside from snide comments, which I managed to deal with.

Masculinity is celebrated in South Asian culture. This has become even more evident to me after transitioning. I have gained far more rights and freedoms than I used to enjoy before. But discrimination against trans people is rife among the middle classes.

If we were to take a linguistic perspective and examine different languages – take for instance Urdu or Punjabi – you will find that our pronouns do not denote a gendered identity. There is no he/she, him/her in Urdu but instead the verb holds and indicates gender. This is unlike English and other European languages.

Gender fluidity, at least for the past five hundred years, has been intertwined with our culture. The law which the British imported to the subcontinent othered genderfluid people, especially the khwaja siras. As the upper and middle classes aspired to become more like the British, they adopted their attitudes and their prejudices. I would say this is more of a colonial hangover which plagues the middle and upper classes that have adopted a sort of Victorian prudishness and aesthetic. I guess everyone wants to be a 'kala angrez'. But this is not the case with the rest of the population, whom I have found to be more accepting and open-minded.

Advice for Pliny the Elder, Big Daddy of Mansplainers

TISHANI DOSHI

Great Man, now that you are dead, allow me to squeeze your hand. The sage
bushes in Umbria are heavy with bees, so I'm killing them with hypnosis. I
am a mere woman—inferior lettuce—but I understand swoon aka *mirabilia*.
I fill this cup with nectar and offer it to soothe your Vesuvian wounds. I share
your love of baths and classification and sure, if we had to point to a god in the
sky, why not call him Thunderbolt? I too believe sewers are *the* great architectural
invention. I do all my searching on roads. It has been two thousand years so we
can forgive some of your assertions. The sea mouse who helps whales find their
way by parting the brows above their eyes. The one-eyed humans and sciapods
with umbrella feet, the whole exotic bestiary. If I had no mouth but could live
off the smell of apples I'd move to Kashmir—scratch that, maybe Sussex.
Once a month, when the blood comes, I go out to lie in whatever field I
find to feel the scorch rise and the crops wither. Our powers are much
depleted. I can stand among men in full swing of my *menstruus* and
nothing will dim their ability to tell me about me. There are birds

at the window this morning I can't name and dogs in the valley
beyond, who are using their bell-shaped lungs to announce
their happiness again and again and again. Nothing has
changed. We worry about the wane and winnow. In
your time perhaps the ladies used bits of cut-up
smocks but these days we have menstrual cups.

Desire is still a kind of ruin—that silly bird
   fluttering against the window net,
   trying to get in, the body's steady
   lilt towards oblivion. They say you
   had a sister, like Shakespeare's—
   mostly overlooked. That it was she
   who first noticed the smoky clouds
   that sent you on your way. Dear
   Pliny, I guess you never heard the
   one about curiosity. The cat is real.
   The earth never tires of giving
      birth. If you get too close
      to a volcano, you should
         know it may erupt.

Menstruation in Fiction:
The Authorial Gaze

FARAH AHAMED

FICTION HAS ALWAYS BEEN THE PLACE WHERE 'FORBIDDEN' subjects are explored, and writers have dared to probe various aspects of sexuality, thereby offering readers a window into an understanding of the subject or an alternative perspective. Writers from all cultures have seen the breaking of silence as their main task. In her book *The Novel of the Future* (1947), Anais Nin wrote, 'The writer's task is to overthrow the taboos rather than accept them.'[1] In her short stories, she never shied away from illuminating moments of sexuality, no matter how transgressive they were. Similarly, around the same time, Ismat Chughtai, known as Urdu's wicked woman,[2] wrote about sexual experiences in verse with great candour.[3] She was charged with obscenity and put on trial for her short story 'Lihaaf' ('The Quilt') which had erotic and lesbian undertones. Later, in an interview, she said she hated the suffocation in the lives of her characters, and that being trapped in ideas of shame and honour was absurd. In the same way, Fahmida Riaz, known for breaking barriers, celebrated the unspoken aspects of womanhood in her works. Her poem *'Woh Ik Zan-e-Napak He' ('She Is an Impure Woman')* talks of 'blood, milk and menstrual discharge'.[4]

The writer is not without anxieties of her own, and writing about subjects likely to invite censure requires courage. Virginia Woolf described in her essay 'The Angel in the House' (1931) how she struggled to break free of society's expectations and was conscious of how they could hinder her, especially if she was writing about sex, morality and human relations. She wrote powerfully about wanting to be free to express her opinions without the sense of being controlled, even going so far as to illustrate as murder the extreme feeling of suffocation of the Angel's presence. *'Had I not killed her she would have killed me* ... She would have plucked the heart out of my writing.'[5] In a *Paris Review* interview, Ursula le Guin, an admirer of Woolf and a writer of courage and insight herself, said: 'Hey, guess what? You're a woman. You can write like a woman. I saw that women don't have to write about what men write about, or write what men think they want to read. I saw that women have whole areas of experience men don't have – and that they're worth writing and reading about.'

Female writers have written boldly about what disturbed them, as they tried to make sense of their bodies and relationships in spite of how society might judge them. Indeed, the same is true for male authors, such as Flaubert, D. H. Lawrence, Nabokov, Manto, Marquis de Sade and others charged with obscenity and whose works were banned because they went beyond the acceptable. As Evelyn Waugh said, 'an artist must be a reactionary', and a writer's purpose, according to Camus, must be to 'keep civilisation from destroying itself'.

So how did writers of fiction explore menstruation and what did they show? For both male and female authors, it has been a difficult subject to broach, and there has been a marked difference in their depictions. Female authors, when writing about menstruation, have shown a sensitivity to the cultural taboos surrounding it, an understanding of the accompanying bodily changes and the anxiety of lack of information. They have illustrated it as a time of healing and female solidarity, when women occupy a different space – metaphorically and literally. In contrast to this empathetic representation, male writers have presented their female protagonists as objects of male fantasy, obsession and voyeurism. I will begin by looking at the approach taken by female writers.

In the early 1960s, it was unusual and brave for a work of fiction to even mention menstruation, let alone explore it in any detail. In Doris Lessing's 1962 novel, *The Golden Notebook*, the protagonist, Anna, worries about her period and how it will affect the integrity of her writing. She says,

> A period is something I deal with, without thinking about it particularly, or rather I think of it with a part of my mind that deals with routine problems. It is the same part of my mind that deals with the problem of routine cleanliness.

Bapsi Sidhwa, in *The Crow Eaters* (1978), set in Pakistan, gives a clear depiction of the exile to which Putli, the wife of the main character, Freddy Junglewalla, is subjected during her period:

> Every Parsee household has its *other room*, specially reserved for women. Thither they are banished for the duration of the unholy state … Putli quite enjoyed her infrequent visits to the other room. It was the only chance she ever had to rest. And since this seclusion was religiously enforced, she was able to enjoy her idleness without guilt.

It is in fact only when Putli is kept isolated in the 'other room' that she finds some form of freedom. Nevertheless, she is reminded every month that 'even the sun, moon and stars are defiled by her impure gaze ... She knew she couldn't help herself to pickles or preserves for they would spoil at her touch. Flowers, too, were known to wilt when touched by women in her condition.' As much as Putli is 'able to enjoy' the segregation, she knows during these days she is considered to be the 'other': 'The family was permitted to speak to her through closed doors – in an emergency, they could speak directly, provided they bathed from head to foot and purified themselves afterwards.'

In Shashi Deshpande's *The Dark Holds No Terrors* (1980), set in India, the protagonist Saru has a similar but opposite experience; while Putli is sent to the other room, Saru is banished from rooms altogether:

It was just torture. Not just the three days when I couldn't enter the kitchen or the puja room. Not just the sleeping on a straw mat covered with a thin sheet. Not just the feeling of being a pariah, with my special cup and plate by my side in which I was served from a distance, for my touch was, it seemed, pollution. No, it was something quite different, much worse. A kind of shame that engulfed me.

Unlike Putli, Saru is alienated by every aspect of the experience which she associates with becoming like her mother, whom she hates. Deshpande uses melodramatic language to show her anger and resentment: 'You're a woman now, she said. If you're a woman, I don't want to be one, I thought resentfully, watching her body.'

Contrast this with Pettinah Gappah's (2009) short story 'The Maid from Lalapanzi' set in Zimbabawe, from her collection *An Elegy for Easterly*. Like Putli and Saru, Chenai is put in another space during her period, but a metaphorical rather than an actual one: 'When my period came, SisiBlandina was there to say, "Well you are in Geneva now, and you will be visiting regularly."' For Chenai, 'Geneva' connotes a foreign, distant and cold place where she has to go when she is menstruating.

Throughout the story, Gappah maintains a natural rhythm in the dialogue, suggesting Chenai's situation is the norm. Even when Chenai discusses a visit from Johnson & Johnson marketing representatives with the girls in her community, the tone is matter-of-fact:

> The women from Johnson & Johnson had come to the school and separated us from the boys so that they could tell us secrets about our own bodies . . . It was an unsanitary time they said. Our most effective weapon against this effluence was the arsenal of sanitary products that Johnson and Johnson made with young ladies like us in mind, they said, because Johnson cared.

Similarly, in Elena Ferrante's first Neapolitan novel *My Brilliant Friend* (2011), the protagonist, also named Elena, is kept in ignorance about the menstrual cycle by her mother. When Elena gets her first period, she is 'terrified by I don't know what, maybe a scolding from my mother for having hurt myself between my legs'. The lack of shared knowledge illuminates how shame is learnt and passed on. Later, when her friend Lila begins her period, Elena wonders whether Lila will become pretty, or ugly like herself. As it was for Saru, the onset of menstruation for Elena is fraught with anxieties about becoming like another, or even 'other'.

Miranda July's short story 'The Metal Bowl' (2017) could not be more different. Written in the first person, the narrator is candid: 'Our son, Sam, trotted in sleepily, and I warned him not to get in the bed: "It's all bloody."'... Sam pulled back the sheets and studied the mess, smiling giddily. "You got your period." This new generation of men has been taught (by me) to feel excited about the menstrual cycle ... I've been waiting a long time to have my period cheered on.' July's tone is cheeky: the narrator is aware she is pushing the boundaries of the modern-day limits of period-related conversation. She also, however, references 'tadpoles turning into frogs or the moon that follows them wherever they go', alluding to traditional menstrual myths: transformation, madness and sexuality.

Angela Carter, in her fairy tale retelling 'Wolf-Alice', from her short-story collection, *The Bloody Chamber* (1979), uses menstruation to explore what it means to become not only a woman, but also more human. Wolf-Alice is raised by wolves and uninhibited by her nakedness and dirt. After she secretes 'natural juices', Wolf-Alice recognizes a regular rhythm in her body unlike the 'filth, rags and feral disorder' from before: 'The flow continued for a few days, which seemed to her an endless time. She had, as yet, no direct notion of past, or of future, or of duration, only of a dimensionless, immediate moment.' And then: 'Soon the flow ceased. She forgot it. The moon vanished; but, little by little, it reappeared ... Sequence asserted itself with custom and then she understood the circumambulatory principle of the clock perfectly.'

Unlike Carter, whose imagery and vocabulary highlight the feminine, earthy qualities of menstruation, Jeannette Winterson's, *Written on the Body* (1992), uses figures of speech that are equally visceral, but more masculine. The unnamed narrator here is of ambiguous gender and says about their lover Louise: 'When she bleeds the smells I know change colour. There is iron in her soul on those days. She smells like a gun.' Iron is an obvious reference to blood, but 'in her soul' suggests a toughness, and 'smells like a gun' alludes to a masculine phallic representation, both explosive and violent.

This attention to smell is addressed differently in Lessing's *The Golden Notebook*, where Anna is repulsed. 'I begin to worry: Am I smelling? It is the only smell I know of that I dislike ... And resent. It is a smell that I feel as strange even to me, an imposition from outside. Not from me.' Anna's preoccupation with her hygiene and the wish that the days would pass quickly indicates how she is psychologically affected by her physical changes. She feels her period and its effects are not essential to her, but rather an intrusion.

In 'Bones' (1993), fantasy and horror writer Marcia Guthridge's male protagonist is attracted to the dark, messy, primitive side of human nature, including death. He notices everything that is conventionally considered dirty or spoilt; blood, urine, chipped and yellowing toe nails, slimy fish tanks, and even disfigured animals and maimed body parts. One morning as he is finishing his shower, his wife comes into the bathroom and stares at his naked body. He observes, 'What I continued thinking about after she left the bathroom, presumably satisfied, was how odd it sometimes seems to me that she has a wet sticky place on her like a sore. She wears a sanitary pad every day, even when she doesn't have her period, like a Band-Aid stuck onto her underwear.' What Guthridge is highlighting is male fascination and distaste with female effluvia, and how it is managed. In fact, it is these aspects which are accentuated in the representations of menstruation by some of the male authors I researched.

In her famous essay, 'If Men Could Menstruate: A Political Fantasy', Gloria Steinem considers what the world would be like if men, not women, menstruated. 'Clearly,' she says, 'menstruation would become an enviable, worthy masculine event.' In Steinem's imaginary world, male menstruation would be openly acknowledged, nurtured and celebrated, men would brag about it and, in the same vein, portray it as the essence of masculinity. But as it is in the real world, through repugnant depictions of menstruation, several male authors have implied that there is something 'wrong' with the female character's body and her mind.

My first example of this is the novel of Czech writer Milan Kundera, *The Unbearable Lightness of Being* (1984). He writes of his protagonist, Tereza: 'Whenever as a child, she came across her mother's sanitary napkins soiled with menstrual blood, she felt disgusted, and hated her mother for lacking the shame to hide them.'

These negative connotations are further compounded, when Kundera, as author-narrator, makes a comparison between Tereza's period and that of her dog, Karenina. 'Why is it that a dog's menstruation made her light-hearted and gay, while her own menstruation made her squeamish? The answer is simple to me: dogs were never expelled from Paradise.' The degradation here is palpable; for Tereza, women are sinful and repellent, and of a lower status than dogs.

We see an equally demeaning treatment of a menstruating character in Philip Roth's 2002 novel, *The Dying Animal.* In this story, Professor David Kepesh is told by his student Consuela about a boy who would 'want passionately to watch her menstruate'. She would call him over whenever she started her period, 'and she would stand there, and he would watch the blood run down her thighs and onto the floor'. Later we learn that he licked the blood from her legs. These graphic descriptions reveal that, as a character, Consuela is only an object of lust; the purpose of her menstrual bleeding is solely to fulfil the sensual needs of a male character.

A more lyrical illustration of this can be found in Nuruddin
Farah's *Secrets* (2016), set in a Somali village. In this story, the
protagonist, Kalaman, enjoys the precocious sexual attentions
of an older girl, Sholoongo, who is at various times his mentor,
companion and tormentor. He is encouraged by her to taste the
'feminine trust of blood', which he empties from the 'thimble
in a gulp' and asks 'for more'. Sprinkled with tribal wisdom and
parables, the novel highlights the fecund aspects of the menstrual
cycle with lush prose: 'menstrual blood scarlet ... dark as fertile
earth ...' Granted that the novel is in the genre of magical realism,
and that Sholoongo is a dynamic character, a 'shape-shifter', and a
practitioner of magic, Nuruddin Farah illustrates menstruation as
primarily serving to satisfy the male character's lustful greed.

The objectification of women is nowhere more chillingly
displayed than in Ammar Abdul Hamid's novel *Menstruation*
(2001), set in Syria. The main character Hassan's heightened
sense of smell enables him to identify a woman on her period,
even though 'it is the one he least desires', because 'no woman
is pretty when she's menstruating ...' Like the evil attributed to
Kundera's Tereza, Hassan believes that menstrual blood is 'the true
source of all evil in the world' and pregnancy is 'an infant vampire
nursed on menstrual blood'. His supernatural senses enable him
to detect the instant when 'a medium-sized spurt of deep, dark,
almost tarred blood' has filled a tampon and becomes aware of the
'invisible cloud of pheromones and odour molecules ... climbing
up from between her legs ...' and it 'fills his nostril, his mouth
and his lungs'. This is the stuff of both dreams and nightmares.
Hassan is drawn to what he fears. His obsession compels him to
sift 'through garbage in search of used tampons' which he then
classifies 'based on spectral differences of colour and odour across
different age groups', ranging from K to Tl, with subgroups of 1

to 9. This is a ruthless androcentric lens, with horrific and sinister implications; for Hamid's Hassan, menstruating women must be categorized and controlled.

By contrast, in *Carrie* (1974), Stephen King presents a more fully developed female character, even as he extrapolates the unpredictable and uncontrollable aspects of menstruation to the realm of the supernatural. In this horror novel, Carrie's late menarche is linked to her awareness of her telekinetic abilities, which she later uses to avenge her bullies. When she gets her first period, she is terrified because she has no understanding of it and her classmates use the opportunity to taunt her, using tampons and sanitary napkins as weapons, which they hurl at her. Although we get a stronger sense of Carrie as a rounded character, more so than Kundera's Tereza or Roth's Consuela, King nonetheless renders the female body as threatening and uses the period as a symbol of primitive violence.

MacLaverty and Joyce offer two gentler interpretations, but still very much filtered through the male gaze. Bernard MacLaverty's *Grace Notes* (1997), follows the life of a young composer Catherine McKenna, tracing her feminist and aesthetic development. She is a sympathetic, realistic and fully rounded character, until the moment when she thinks about her period. And then MacLaverty puts into question her presence of mind, as she reflects: 'Her period was due ... a woman was synchronised to the moon and there was nothing she could do about it.' This fanciful description reduces Catherine's character to someone subject to fatalistic reflection during her cycle.

And in *Ulysses* (1922), James Joyce's picture of Molly Bloom's observations on her period is heavily coloured by negativity. He describes Molly sitting on the chamber pot, realizing her period has begun, and contemplating the younger, attractive Milly who is wild and carefree, as she herself once was. 'There is always something wrong with us every 3 or 4 weeks.' Here again, a female character is found believing she is 'abnormal' during her period.

In the texts examined here, the male authors have shown little compassion or understanding towards their female characters, and have surrounded the subject of menstruation with eroticism, fantasy and superstition. There is an emphasis on sensual description which at times verges on obsession and depersonalizes and objectifies women. They are subjected to a restrictive male gaze which divests them of basic humanity and robs them of dignity and power.

Fiction which illustrates menstruation, be it by male or female writers, draws attention to the shame, myth and confusion surrounding it. And perhaps, inadvertently, it may also bring to light, in a way that is unusual for literature, the anxieties felt by the menstruating woman about her femininity and body, as well as a societal fear that a woman on her period is a threat.

In fiction as in the real world, there is a long way to go in removing the stigma from menstruation and normalizing it. However, hope lies in the fact that through the writers and artists, stories will be told, moments of truth illuminated, imaginations stretched and awareness spread.

When asked about the artist's task, especially in troubled times, Toni Morrison offered these succinct lines in reply: 'There is no time for despair, no place for self-pity, no need for silence, no room for fear. We speak, we write, we do language. That is how civilizations heal.'[6]

A version of this essay was published in Ploughshares *in 2019.*

A Caregiver's Perspective on Managing Menstrual Hygiene

AYRA INDRIAS PATRAS

I INTERVIEWED FAZILAT* AND HER FOURTEEN-YEAR-OLD daughter Reshma* one sunny winter afternoon in Lahore at a school for children with special needs. I explained to them that the purpose of the interview was to highlight the challenges faced by menstruators with disabilities for a book. Reshma is autistic and has a speech impediment. Each time I asked her a question, she was unable to respond. However, she kept nodding while her mother was speaking. Fazilat told me their story.

'At first, I didn't realize that my daughter was different, and it was only when she was almost three and a half years old that I noticed some strange changes in her behavior because she refused to speak, eat or stand. She was young and I did not know what to do, so I ignored this, hoping that with time she would learn and improve like children usually do.'

When Reshma was old enough, Fazilat enrolled her at a school. However, one of the teachers soon pointed out to Fazilat that her daughter was a special needs student and recommended that she consult a psychiatrist. The doctor confirmed what the teacher had suspected.

---

* Names changed

'The psychiatrist explained to me that Reshma had a neurodevelopmental disorder, and I knew then I had no choice but to teach myself to become more patient and learn how to care for her.'

When I asked Fazilat how she coped with Reshma's transition through puberty, she burst into tears. She said it had been very difficult for her as a mother and primary caregiver.

'I don't have a choice but to manage Reshma's menstruation and menstrual hygiene myself. She is not capable of understanding what is happening to her body. All I can do is remind her again and again, that she is a young girl so she should not sit beside, play with or hug young male relatives or any male members of the family. I told her these are sins.'

But Fazilat also explained that Reshma is a friendly and affectionate child who likes to smile at everyone she meets. So, Fazilat cannot help but be afraid that young men will bully Reshma and take advantage of her sexually.

'I've told Reshma she can't go anywhere without me. One time I went to the market and left Reshma at home with her sister. When I returned, I found Reshma had locked herself in her room and was crying because she had got her period and was frightened. Reshma does not understand why she bleeds every month, or how it is connected to getting pregnant. But she knows that she's not supposed to discuss it with anyone. She is aware that it is natural and not a disease, but it is shameful. She knows she must hide her soiled clothes and the pads from male members of the family. I've told her she must change her clothes when her underwear and trousers get soiled with blood, but she ignores this. It means that I have to check on her clothes, change her pad, shave her hair and give her a bath. I find this very challenging and upsetting, but what choice do I have?'

When Reshma experiences menstrual cramps or headaches and loses her appetite during her period, Fazilat takes her to a homeopath. She believes that homeopathic cures are safer than pharmaceutical medicines because they do not have any side effects. 'The homeopath usually prescribes drops and small pills that look and taste like sweets, which I give Reshma at bedtime. I don't know the names of these medicines, but I trust the homeopath.'

Despite the difficulties and familial pressure, Fazilat takes care of her daughter assiduously. 'I'm ready to do anything, no matter how difficult, to look after my daughter. Once my mother-in-law suggested that we remove Reshma's uterus because it would make her life and mine easier, but I refused to do it. I'd never think of removing her uterus or giving her any medicines [that would interfere with her cycle]. One of my relatives also has a daughter with disabilities. A friend gave her some medicines which she said would stop the girl menstruating. The medicines led to the girl developing a brain tumour and her health deteriorated.'

Fazilat's reluctance to a surgical procedure and allopathy also stems from her religious beliefs. 'I'm a religious person, and I fear God's wrath. It would be a sin if I went against the natural order and processes of the body which God has created. My husband and my mother are my only support. They remind me to be patient, trust in God, and pray for Reshma's recovery.'

When I asked Fazilat about her plans for Reshma's future, she became emotional. 'As you know in our society, unmarried girls are a burden and a bad omen for the family. Recently, my son got married, and Reshma asked me when it would be her sister's turn. She did not ask about herself and this pained me, because it meant she realized her future will be different from that of her siblings.'

Fazilat and Reshma's situation is not unique. I interviewed another woman, Soraiya, who has a sixteen-year-old daughter with a psychiatric disability. Soraiya explained how it disrupted her work because she had to keep asking her boss for days off, and this affected how much she earned. She said, 'Whenever my daughter gets her period, I have to request for leave to look after her. I don't have a choice because my daughter cannot manage her period herself.'

Shariffa, a fifty-seven-year-old domestic worker with a mentally challenged thirty-one-year-old son, said her life was consumed with looking after him. 'But I thank God every day that I did not have a daughter because if she had been born like my son, it would had been extremely difficult for me to manage her periods and protect her from the dirty eyes of men.'

It is a very common custom in Pakistan for cousins to marry, and there is research which suggests that children born from these marriages run a high risk of genetic disorders.[1] What this means is that in Pakistan, there are an increasing number of children born with disabilities in every family. The World Health Organization (WHO) estimates that around 31 million people in Pakistan live with some form of disability, but the figure is probably higher in reality.[2] People living with disability in Pakistan are largely isolated and have been relegated to the shadows because of the associated stigma. Some families even consider it to be a punishment for sins and are consequently ashamed and embarrassed to admit to having a child with a disability and try to hide this from the people around them. There are some who think differently and have attempted to overcome societal barriers, but they face many challenges.

Pakistan is not an easy place to live in if you have a disability. For instance, most buildings, educational institutions and places of worship do not have adequate facilities to accommodate those with mobility impairments. The government too, has not been proactive with legislation to promote the needs and rights of those with disabilities and the media has not stepped up to the role it could play in advocacy and promoting stories to help combat social discrimination. Even in the area of education, the situation is abysmal; the current undergraduate medical curriculum sadly does not include disability studies and even though there are more than fifty accredited clinical specialties, none of them have any dedicated module or training in the assessment and management of disabilities.[3]

As seen in the case of Reshma and Fazilat, the lack of support and understanding from healthcare professionals poses a huge problem. Parents of children with disabilities, especially the ones on the cerebral palsy spectrum and with neurodegenerative disorders, are often inadequately counselled by junior doctors and sometimes even told that their children will become 'normal' again after being prescribed a cocktail of multivitamins, neurotronic treatments and herbal medicines. The inadequate support from the state, coupled with the burden of social and cultural stigma, puts tremendous pressure on the caregivers of girls with disabilities. The caregiver's own uneasiness and embarrassment with regard to menstruation, as well as that of other family members, adds to the already difficult state of affairs.

Some recent initiatives undertaken by activists give reason for hope. One example is Tanzila Khan, a young disability activist based in Lahore, who developed a mobile app called Girly Things in 2018.[4] Her app aims to help people with disabilities purchase menstrual products with ease and efficiency by delivering products straight to their doorsteps. Users experiencing an unexpected 'period emergency' can also use the app's help button to request an

'Urgent Kit', which includes disposable underwear, three pads and a blood stain remover, to be delivered to them as soon as possible. Khan uses a wheelchair herself and so has experienced first-hand the challenges faced by people with disabilities. Such efforts are encouraging because they offer tech-savvy and scalable solutions.

Digitizing Menstruation: Algorithms for Cleansing Bodies

ALNOOR BHIMANI

A Period for Purification

FOR MANY WOMEN IN THE WORLD, MENSTRUATION IS THE MOST dreaded time of the month. Some societies regard menstruating women as being in need of rest and requiring isolation on the days they bleed. The idea that women are unclean during menstruation has been normalized across many cultures. Some men have held the belief that contact with menstrual blood or with a menstruating woman can 'sicken a man and cause persistent vomiting'[1] and that they would 'become ill if they are touched by or use any objects that have been touched by a menstruating woman'.[2] In northern European visual culture, menstruation has been considered 'dirty, disgusting, and embarrassing'[3] and thought to cause 'imbalance in taste'[4] in Japan. Nepalese menstruating women are isolated in mud huts or sheds called *chhaupadi*s because their blood is believed to be toxic. Banishing menstruating women from social spaces has been linked to religious beliefs. For instance, some Hindus regard menstruating women as ritually impure. Certain Buddhists prohibit them from entering temples.[5] Likewise, women are not allowed to enter Shinto shrines during menstruation, and instances exist where they have been banned from climbing sacred mountains due to their perceived impurity. Immersion in cleansing baths is part of Orthodox Jewish menstruation rituals[6] while some Christian church fathers defend the exclusion of women from ministry on the premise of uncleanness.[7] Jain religious texts state that menstruation kills microorganisms in the body, making women more prone to violence than males.[8] Across many cultures, shame continues to be associated with menstruation with most women believing that it is at least good manners, and sometimes necessary, to hide evidence of menstruation from public view if not also in private.[9] Some even see menstruation as the 'ultimate taboo'.[10]

However, digital technologies today are considered by many to provide a solution to the shame that continues to be associated with menstruation. This essay explores how digital period trackers are regarded as addressing issues of period cleanliness and the need for personal space whilst engendering greater self-understanding for menstruating women. It argues that although period trackers are presented as helping to address 'stigmatized topics such as menstrual health'[11], they also create digital spaces that are supposedly liberating, educational and private, but which silently extend norms of menstrual management tied to wider economic and social ambitions.

Monetizing Blood

The global market for all digital technology-based products and services focused on women's health could be worth $60 million by 2027.[12] Although South Asia comprises about a quarter of the world's female population, at present, 'femtech' investments in the region amount to only about 1 per cent. Of 1,323 femtech companies globally in 2021, only 41 were in South Asia.[13] Perhaps this is because less than 10 per cent of individuals in low-income countries can access the internet, and of the 3.5 billion people without internet access in the world, South Asian citizens are among the least well served. A further explanation may be that women in developing nations are 34 per cent less likely to have access to the internet, compared to men.[14] Nevertheless, women who can access digital technologies are increasingly using period tracker apps (PTAs), making them part of a fast-growing femtech product market.

PTAs enable the observation and analysis of menstrual cycles and a wide variety of related factors. Besides monitoring menstruation, they can be used to produce workout patterns, nutritional regimes and family planning tailored to one's body's cycles. The home screens of these apps usually display a numerical countdown and/or graphic illustrations of the number of days to the beginning of the next period or ovulation. Furthermore, most PTAs enable the tracking of menstrual cycle-related symptoms such as pain and mood swings, sleep patterns, contraceptives, sex life, effluvia, vaginal discharge, medication, food cravings and physical activity. Menstrual calendars included in PTAs provide statistical information on average cycle duration, changes in body weight, body temperature and other details, often through graphical, tabular and numerical depictions. Some PTAs also offer access to online forums and allow interaction with other users.[15]

PTAs require their user to give away personal data about their body. The user has to commit to the idea of enabling algorithmically generated data to be processed into calculative outputs personalized on an ongoing basis with the user's data inputs. A feedback loop between the app and the user is created, wherein continuous data exchange fine-tunes the self-tracked digital output. Purportedly, the greater the level of information given up, the greater the

accuracy of feedback from the app. As Karlsson explains: '… to
gain knowledge about one's own body entails giving away access
to data generated from that same body.'[16] The PTA user becomes,
in essence, a 'prosumer', one who produces as well as consumes
the data.[17]

Dozens of PTAs exist today with gynaecology and obstetrics
(G&O) experts extensively advocating their use. G&O Professor
Kudesia says of a PTA: 'I like its clean, modern interface, the
impeccable science behind it, their transparent citation of
supporting data.'[18] She also notes the importance of keeping track:
'If something suddenly changes with your cycle, or your period
is late, you may not realize it right away if you're not keeping
track.' Habitually updating the app ensures it is 'really' accurate.[19]
Professor Dweck, another G&O expert, suggests that 'the longer
you are tracking your cycle, the more data the app's algorithm
has to work with, and the more likely it is to be correct.'[20] Data
accuracy and reliable user information input are essential to
maximize the usefulness of PTAs.

We are accustomed to thinking that if we reveal something
about ourselves in a particular context, it will not be shared without
our consent. Privacy of information has been a 'key organizing
principle of social life'.[21] However, this is not entirely true in a
digital economy. The use of data by PTAs does not conform to
long-standing notions of privacy in many cultures. On the web, a
woman's body data becomes everybody's data. The intimate bio-
data gathered by the PTAs is extracted, analyzed and re-packaged
and aggregated into macrodata to make it relevant to the user.
This data has to have commercial, managerial and research value
in a form that is commodifiable and re-sellable.[22]

PTA users tend to be unaware that the personal information
they feed into these apps may also be sent to third parties. One app

has been reported to have been 'sharing some data with Facebook even before the user agrees to the app's privacy policy'.[23] The data shared by PTAs may include deeply personal information about women's health, moods, sexual practices, etc.[24] Typically, the intent is to deploy user data to send out targeted adverts or to develop consumer-related correlations that have commercial value to the app provider. Advertisers want to monitor consumers' moods and desires to make product offerings at times the PTA users are most likely to make purchases. For instance, women who are pregnant (or wish to be), will show shifts in their shopping behaviours. This can be useful market-segment information to target the most viable consumers.

Most femtech app users willingly commit to providing personal data in order to get personalized output. In the digital world, 'organizing principles' are shifting. Underlying this willingness to share intimate data in exchange for new insights about oneself is perhaps the notion that 'people are inherently interested in themselves ... because to be a person can be challenging.'[25] Giving up personal information is not challenged as much when it delivers new insights about oneself.

Quantifying Spills

There may be value in technology that allows the conversion of 'seemingly useless excess, the waste of the bodily system, into useful, exchangeable data'.[26] After all, none of this is new; quantification has played a role in assessing the health of women long before the rise of PTAs.[27] In ancient Greece, if a woman bled in variance with what was considered as normal in terms of number of days and amount of bleeding, she was considered infertile or diseased.[28] According to some advocates, the datafication of menstruation can hold much value. Researchers report that it can be an 'empowering practice'[29], arguing that not only can it distance one from having a sensory awareness of the smell, colour, texture or the visceral experience of 'feeling' a period and remove the person from the socio-behavioural dynamics of menstruating, but more importantly, calculations centred on menstrual blood are seen as providing a clean representation of information about a woman's body.[30] Quantification *disinfects* the dirt that inhabits the perceived reality of the object being quantified.[31] It creates for the PTA user mathematical distance from the embodied perceptual reference points inherently part of the menstruating physique.[32]

Data from apps can be cleansed so that when placed in the hands of women, it is seen as empowering them. PTAs give women access to the privileged world of 'dataism', offering a higher 'standard of knowledge about human behaviour'.[33] Some would say that it provides the 'power to de-stigmatise, radicalise, and feminise the non-inclusive patriarchal structures that have so far framed women's health and autonomy'.[34] Ultimately, quantified data on menstrual blood in the hands of a woman are argued to provide a means of enabling menstruation to be seemingly intelligently managed. Indeed, PTAs are viewed as permitting the control of the sensory experience of menstruation so the woman's personal experience can be improved upon.[35]

Purification for Greater Self-understanding

If everything a person produces is part of them, it also has its own way of being. Once what is produced is digitized, our perception of it changes, and when digital information is exchanged across platforms, the dualism perceived between heteronomy and autonomy is also altered. Digitization has shifted our understanding of the object-subject dichotomy. When things become connected – including people to each other – notions of how people relate to things changes. Digital trackers render the line between technology and the body less visible. As Capurro notes, 'Digitization changes the anthropological self-understanding of encapsulated world-less subjects facing objects in the so-called outside world.'[36] When we alter how we perceive an object, we also decentre how we make out our awareness of things via the interplay between the subject and the object. PTAs deeply affect this interplay because of their reliance on data input relating to the intimate and personal.

Quantifying menstrual information cleanses the reality of what is measured. In other words, data sanitizes what some have considered unclean.[37] Data as opposed to raw information makes the dualism of the subject and the object of the data more manageable.[38] The distancing from the 'unclean' that quantification proffers and the calculative engagement of the self with that produced by the self promote an internal understanding of how to systematically manage one's being. At the same time, digital self-trackers have also become bio-political instruments which assist in normalizing privileged notions of what should constitute effective health control.

PTA users engage with calculative forces that quietly prescribe bodily aspirations. They instil reflexive self-monitoring practices with a legitimacy that is derived from the interpellation of individuals in relation to other app users and wider population data. As such, PTAs are digital 'technologies of the self' that 'permit individuals to [reflect and act] on their own bodies and souls, thoughts, conduct and way of being, so as to transform themselves in order to attain a certain state of happiness, purity, wisdom, perfection, or immortality'.[39] PTA users abide by statistical standards against which comparisons can be made and through which they become compelled to assess themselves. They mobilize, in the process, 'reponsibilizing' norms[40] serving as 'regulatory ideals'[41]. The act of measurement cannot be neutral as all technologies of measurement legitimize certain forms of knowledge and experience and further enhance the 'datafication' of the person through their reactions.[42] Ultimately, PTAs make suggestions as to what constitutes normative behaviour based on tracked menstrual data to cultivate self-discipline in women.

Closed Spaces that Liberate

PTAs' calculative outputs reveal as much as they hide. They carry presumptions of truth embodying understandings of medical science, the legitimacy of big-data analysis and the propriety of algorithmic complex functions. They are presented as customizable, private platforms enabling women to act with freedom on data, which is seemingly transparent, robust and objective. In doing so, digital apps also offer the basis for re-stabilizing conventional gender arrangements and prescribed conceptions of femininity. PTAs embody a potential for reflexive expression and understanding of one's being. They offer women a wilful gateway to self-care and self-knowledge that embodies truths that elsewhere take more suppressive forms. PTAs silently advance idealized notions of calculative and transparent private spaces. They reconstitute their users as free and responsible individuals who may have previously ended up toeing the line established within more covert and coercive regimes of power relations.

PTAs are algorithmically constructed to endow a sense of emancipation and self-knowledge. They are offered as today's technologically intelligent solution, providing women private spaces that appear liberating but, in fact, uphold invisible structures of the feminine ideal. PTAs are potentially extending the reach of reconstituted economic and social norms, which imprisons the user like a digital chhaupadi in the guise of empowerment and emancipation.

This essay has benefited from inputs from Nadia Matringe, Ghazal Mir Zulfikar and Sheher Bano Mela, for which I am grateful.

Bleeding behind Bars: An Account of Menstruation under Incarceration

INTERVIEW | FARAH AHAMED

I INTERVIEWED ERUM, WHO SPENT SIX YEARS INCARCERATED in Pakistan, from 2003 to 2009. She had been charged with aiding and abetting a murder that her husband had committed under the influence of drugs because he believed the man he killed had been her lover. Erum insisted that she was not guilty, but the judge held that she had provoked her husband by having the affair and sentenced her to prison. When I met Erum, I explained to her that I was interested in understanding how she had coped with her period while in jail and what challenges she had to face with respect to her health and hygiene as an inmate. This is her story, which has been edited for clarity, without altering the intent of her testimony.

◆

After arresting me, the policemen took me to the *thana* [police station] and asked me to lie down on a bench and rest. I flatly refused because I knew they wanted me to fall asleep so that they could take advantage of me. I stayed awake for thirty-six hours because I was afraid.

In jail, I found myself sharing a cell with twelve other women. Some were there for no reason. They had been picked up by the police, who threatened to lock them up if they didn't sleep with them. So the women did what the police wanted, but they were still locked up. Others were drug suppliers or had committed crimes, like adultery or premarital sex, under the Hudood Ordinances.* My co-inmates were generous and supportive. I became best friends with a woman from Multan; we had become close, but I don't know where she is now.

The cell shared by thirteen of us was a room with a common washing area and a toilet. Sometimes the lines were so long that we would end up fighting and arguing about who needed to use the toilet more desperately. When I got my period, I tore my dupatta/scarf and made a pad. When I didn't have a scarf, I made a pad out of the old clothes given to me by one of the other inmates. Nothing was ever wasted. We had very little, but we shared whatever we had. Some of the inmates would receive visitors more frequently than others. I came from a poor family, and my parents and family members never came to see me, so I had no one to bring me the things I needed. I had to rely on the other inmates to help me. With so many women living together, naturally there were times when our cycles coincided. This was difficult but we would help each other with rags.

The wardens never assisted us in any way; in fact, sometimes they even stole our things like soap, shampoo and even pads, which were always in short supply. If we ever got pads, it was only a packet or two which never lasted long because it was distributed among all the inmates. Most of the time, we would share our

---

* The Hudood Law is part of Shari'a law and enforces punishments mentioned in the Quran and Sunnah for *zina* (extramarital sex), *qazf* (false accusation of zina), theft and consumption of alcohol.]

menstrual rags so there was never a shortage. You could always get a scrap of cloth from someone or the other.

Some women say you shouldn't wash yourself during your period, others say that we're impure when we bleed, and still others say that if we talked about our periods openly we would all go to hell. I don't believe any of those myths. I always keep my body clean, and I'm not ashamed to talk about it.

If any of us ever had cramps or headaches during our period, there was nothing we could do. Nothing. We'd bang on the prison doors and make a racket to call the warden, and hope that she'd get irritated with the noise and give us one Panadol or something just to keep us quiet. Usually, the wardens would scold us and accuse us of pretending or exaggerating our problems. Often we would be placated and told that a lady doctor would come and prescribe painkillers and treat our infections. But in reality, the doctor hardly ever came; she would only turn up once in a while.

One of the most frightening things about being in jail was that our food was laced with drugs. It made the food taste terrible, but our only choice was to eat it or starve. The authorities put medicine in our food to dampen our lust, anger and other natural impulses because they were worried that we would go mad and attack or kill each other. The medication kept us sedated. I learnt about this from the other inmates when they warned me that the prison authorities did this especially to suppress our sexual desires. Ask anyone if you don't believe me; everyone knows. You can find this medication in the bazaar.

Sometimes women from an NGO used to come and teach us how to sew or write and read. They never helped us with menstrual products. I don't expect anyone to do that, not even the government. Why should the government help? Menstruation is a woman's problem; it's her own body. Why should the government worry? It would be too much for the government to supply every woman with pads or medicines.

It was the friendships that I made with other women that helped me through that difficult time. Who am I? Just another poor woman. But the solidarity with other women helped me, without which, I would not have survived.

My husband is out of jail now, and we are back together. I know he's killed a man, so he can easily do it again. I live in fear, but I have accepted it. I try to keep out of his way. My four daughters live in a hostel – at least they're away from home and safe. They are getting educated, so their lives will be better than mine. I talk to my daughters openly about their bodies and their life choices. They've asked me about menstruation, and I've told them what I know. This is how God created a woman's body, so they should keep it clean and protect it to the best of their abilities and not be afraid. There's no point in being afraid of your own body.

I want to put the experience of being in jail behind me and think only of the future. I have four young daughters who I need to educate and marry off. I'm alive thanks to the kind bishop who got my sentence reduced, and now I have a good job. I'm trying to rebuild my life.

◆

According to the Ministry of Human Rights 2020 report, titled 'Plight of Women in Pakistan's Prisons', Pakistan's prison laws did not meet international standards, and the laws meant to protect women prisoners were being flagrantly ignored. Overcrowding was a major problem, with 66 per cent of the women in prison not convicted of any offence but awaiting verdicts of their trial in prison.[1] There were only twenty-four female healthcare workers available to provide full-time care to women and girls in prisons nationally. Majority of the prisoners suffered from diseases such as hepatitis, HIV and tuberculosis, and inadequate medical facilities and healthcare workers for prisoners have exacerbated the situation.[2] In such dire circumstances, menstrual health is completely ignored, forgotten and not treated as a priority.

Research carried out on Indian jails found the situation to be similar; women either bought sanitary napkins from the prison canteen or resorted to using old cloth and rags. At times, they relied on family members to provide sanitary pads during visits, but when it was a male member of the family visiting, they felt reluctant to broach the subject. Deep-rooted societal taboos across both India and Pakistan continue to restrict women's access to critical menstrual hygiene management.[3]

Steps must be taken to mitigate the difficulties women prisoners have to endure during their menstrual cycle. The Commonwealth Human Rights Initiative (CHRI), in collaboration with Boondh, has recommended a few important interventions for the same.[4] Their recommendations include providing basic necessities to the inmates like access to clean water and proper sanitation facilities, regular supplies of anti-bacterial soap, infrastructure which ensures privacy and dignity of menstruating prisoners, provisions for good-quality and a sufficient quantity of sanitary pads as well as facilities to aid their proper disposal and regular prison visits by female doctors for the better reproductive health of the prisoners. Another way to tackle the lack of resources could be the establishment of a menstrual product enterprise that teaches women inmates to make low-cost reusable pads. Finally, the need to raise awareness about menstrual hygiene among both the prison staff and the prisoners is crucial for the better menstrual health of the incarcerated.

What Has Dignity Got to Do with Menstrual Health?

MEERA TIWARI

THIS ESSAY PROVIDES AN OVERVIEW OF THE KEY CHALLENGES in menstrual health faced by women and adolescent girls in rural Bihar and Uttar Pradesh (UP), India, during 2018–19, within the framework of the literature on dignity. The purpose of the inquiry was to explore whether there was any link between social dimensions anchored in dignity and better menstrual health outcomes.

The literature on dignity, discussions with civil society organizations working on period poverty and menstrual health awareness both in the United Kingdom and India have been instrumental in shaping this inquiry with menstrual *health* and not menstrual hygiene at its centre, as has been previously done. By situating menstruation under the 'health' umbrella, attention is drawn to the normal functions of the female body, the well-being of women and their families, as well as the social dimensions that affect them. The reference to hygiene, on the other hand, has connotations of cleanliness and disease prevention. While hygiene may well be one of the dimensions of menstrual health, it certainly should not be the key focus when addressing poor menstrual health outcomes. Further, referring to it as menstrual hygiene may also suggest that menstruation is an unclean process thus reinforcing the 'taboo and stigma' discourse as noted by Bobel[1], and highlighted by the Bollywood biopic *Padman* and the Oscar-winning documentary *Period. End of Sentence*, among others.

Another outcome of this research has been the conceptualization of menstrual health as a societal concern, an issue that affects both men and women and not only women. This insight stems from grounding menstruation within women's health as an essential bodily function for childbearing because under the patrilineal norm and the preference for a male child in South Asia[2], childbearing acquires a higher function. On the other hand, the mother's well-being affects the health and nutrition of the children as well as the overall welfare of the family as per the comprehensive literature on mother and child well-being.[3] The family in this situation comprises children, teenage boys and girls, adult male and female members and the elderly. Hence, including women, adolescent girls and boys and men in this study has been central to capturing the perceptions surrounding menstrual health.

The Context

Improving menstrual health outcomes is crucial for tackling the global challenges of inequalities of opportunities experienced by girls and women in education, health and well-being.[4] The fundamental right of women to manage menstruation with safety and dignity is yet to be accepted globally.[5]

The UN's 2015 Sustainable Development Goals (SDGs) are a blueprint for ending poverty through a global partnership. The seventeen SDGs focus on improving health, education, reducing inequalities and spurring economic growth while addressing climate change and sustainability in all domains. According to the SDG Index India Report 2018[6], India's performance against SDGs 3 (good health and well-being), 5 (gender equality) and 6 (clean water and sanitation) were inadequate with a score of 52, 38 and 63 out of 100, respectively. Moreover, the states of Bihar and UP where this research was conducted, had the lowest scores in the country. The SDG 3, SDG 5 and SDG 5 scores were 40, 24 and 31 for Bihar and 25, 27 and 55 for UP.[7] Especially notable was the negligible progress India and its lowest performers Bihar and UP had made against SDG 5 for gender equality.[8] However, it must be mentioned that at the global level there is no target or indicator for menstrual health within the SDGs nor under Indian national or state-level plans for achieving SDG 6 relating to sanitation.

Research has established links between menstrual health practices and the rates of reproductive infections[9] but there is a lack of general public awareness about the same, though civil society activism and Bollywood have made some progress in this respect.[10] Recent data shows that 28 per cent of girls in rural India quit school soon after their first period, and a large proportion of them regularly miss school because of poor menstrual health.[11] Overall, 39 per cent of girls aged between 15 and 18 years in India drop out of school, far higher than the percentage for boys.[12]

Period shaming is common. For instance, at a women's college in the state of Gujarat, a complaint was lodged with the school authorities about female students breaking rules for menstruating women.[13] The social and cultural rules usually applicable to menstruating women were being extended to the school and classroom. Regularly observed restraints, including barring menstruating women from entering temples and kitchens, not touching other students during their periods, maintaining social distance while eating and washing their dishes separately were imposed by the school. Segregation was enforced in the classrooms where menstruating girls were expected to sit separately on the last bench. The female students were even forced to strip to prove whether they were menstruating or not. Such period-shaming incidents make this study even more relevant.

The Dignity Discourse

According to UNICEF's 2019 report[14], 1.8 billion people menstruate globally and millions of those are unable to exercise their right to good menstrual health and dignity due to discriminatory norms, cultural taboos, poverty and lack of access to basic amenities. Adolescent girls often face stigma and social exclusion during menstruation, resulting in school absenteeism and frequent dropouts. Women with lower literacy levels face additional chronic nutritional deficiencies and health problems. Cumulatively, these practices have far-reaching negative consequences on the lives of girls and women as they restrict their mobility, freedom, choices, affect attendance and participation in school and community life, compromise their safety and cause stress and anxiety.[15]

These in turn lead to unequal opportunities and chances of success in education and life.

To understand what UNICEF meant by 'menstrual health with dignity', the word dignity needs to be examined more closely. The literature on dignity can be traced back to the Aristotelian discourse on human flourishing. The Latin root of the word 'dignity' is *dignus* which means 'worthy of esteem and honour', and its meaning has been expanded to include the significance people have of themselves in their own eyes – self-respect and self-worth – as well as in the eyes of society.[16] Further insights into understanding the notion of dignity are offered by the capability approach discussed in the works of Sen[17] and Alkire[18], where human dignity is associated with being valued and having freedom from discrimination, shame and humiliation. Although closely linked to respect, the core focus of dignity is on *self*-respect, *self*-esteem and *self*-worth, implying one's perception of oneself. Respect, on the other hand, is measured in terms of value and honour received by an individual from the society and/or community based on another's perception and judgement. These notions of dignity and respect have helped shape this research.

Methodology and Findings

The densely populated states of Bihar and UP are the worst-performing states in terms of female well-being indicators such as maternal mortality (149 and 197 deaths per 100,000 live births compared to the country average of 113), female literacy[19] (51.5 and 57 per cent versus 65.5 per cent for the country)[20], female work participation (4 and 13 per cent as compared with the 23 per cent all-India average)[21] and declining child sex ratio (0–6 years), which has fallen from 927 females per 1,000 males in 1991 to 908 as per the 2021 census in UP and from 953 to 916 in Bihar.[22]

For this research, a sample of six villages was selected (three each from UP and Bihar) where there was an active presence of self-help groups (such as Jeevika and RGMVP). The self-help network comprises formal membership-based groups of poor and socially excluded rural women who function as a collective. The network platform enables the empowerment and financial inclusion of these women so that they are equipped to access better opportunities and public service provisions to improve their livelihood and well-being.[23]

The data set comprised 600 women and 300 men over the age of eighteen. The selected cohorts were representative of the rural socio-economic contexts in the two states in terms of low literacy, poor incomes and dependence on low-paying jobs in agriculture. In the female sample, 45 per cent had no schooling, while the remaining 55 per cent were split almost equally between having completed primary and secondary education. The male sample had 21 per cent with no schooling, 46 per cent with completed primary education and 33 per cent with secondary education. Almost 50 per cent of the women reported engaging in seasonal agricultural labour while 60 per cent of men identified themselves as being self-employed. A significant 81 percent of women aged between 18 and 25 were married.

A mixed-methods approach was deployed to capture the perceptions, practices and challenges of menstrual health. While conducting the research, it was found that there was strong reluctance from men to participate in the research, because they believed menstruation was a women's issue. To overcome this and encourage active male engagement, it was decided to share the key findings of an earlier pilot study via street theatre in the village squares. After conducting 900 interviews, two interactive performances at each research site were used as data-capture tools. During the performances, researchers collected observational data in terms of the number of villagers present – male versus female, their reactions and responses, how many left or stayed, etc. While the literature on theatre as a data-display strategy to engage new audiences in research is not novel,[24] using it to both nudge the respondents to react and record their interactions is the innovation in this research.

The performances while facilitating the study also educated the audience about the connection between menstruation and societal aspirations. Information on taboos and ill-conceived perceptions of menstruation, as well as the necessity of a regular menstrual cycle for a *waris* (heir/child /grandchild) to ensure the continuity of one's bloodline were discussed. The data collected from the audience at the performances revealed that 83 per cent of the men were aware that menstruation is linked with having children but did not think it was important for the men to be involved. However, connecting healthy menstruation directly with their aspirations for an heir made it evident to the men its critical role in the survival of the family lineage, thereby underlining the importance of and supporting dignified menstruation.

The responses gathered offer interesting insights into perceptions of menstrual health within the dignity discourse.

Taboo

Generally speaking, the word menstruation was not mentioned in the presence of young children, or men and elders. About 87 per cent of the women had no knowledge of menstruation until their first period, and the majority of the men learnt about menstruation only after getting married. The most common restrictions for menstruating women included not touching pickles or grains, avoiding cooking, not serving food, not going to school or work, and hiding the menstrual cloths from male members of the family. The religious prohibitions included constraints on praying at home, entering a place of worship, and participating in any religious ceremony or touching the offerings.

Shame/Worthlessness

About 62 per cent of the women admitted to feeling worthless, embarrassed or like a burden during menstruation. The remaining 38 percent emphasized the pain and mental stress they experienced during menstruation.

Menstrual Health Awareness

The women's understanding of menstruation was almost 100 per cent. This was captured in a focus group discussion where the women used the analogy of the relationship between fruits and flowers – the fruits being their children and the flowers being their menstruating bodies. Eighty-three per cent of the men were aware of the biological connection between menstruation and conception. Both men and women commonly held perceptions of menstrual blood being dirty, having a foul smell and being caused by heat in women's bodies. Further, unfounded claims and myths were also reported by the women. These included the idea that irregular or no menstruation led to blindness, gas, bodily swelling, filth accumulation in the stomach, infertility and other illnesses. The men believed menstruation was a way for women's bodies to expel poisonous, dirty blood and black filth.

Access

Three-quarters of the interviewed women used rags while the rest used menstrual pads to manage their menstruation. Rags made from old clothes were easily available but reusing them required washing which was a challenge because clean water sources were usually in open courtyards or public spaces. While pads were easier to use, they were expensive, even though the local brands were much cheaper, priced at ₹2 or ₹3 per pad. Over a third of the women used a room inside the house to change, while 50 per cent out of the remaining two-thirds used the toilet and the other 50 per cent changed outside due to the absence of clean running water and toilets. The disposal of either the pad or the rag was difficult, and women either buried the used product or discarded it in the open on a rubbish heap.

Dignity and Respect

An important difference in the way men and women understood dignity and respect emerged from their responses. While the men's focus was on pride derived from work and what society thought of them, for the women self-esteem and self-respect were based on their ability to care for the family, happiness in the family, offering hospitality to guests and being valued by their husbands.

Conclusion

An analysis of the data collated during this study reveals that the lack of appropriate menstrual health practices in rural Bihar and UP result in the women feeling dirty, worthless, ashamed and like a burden on their families. These sentiments were reinforced by their exclusion from social practices and religious traditions. The link between menstruation and childbearing is masked by myths that menstruation is a mechanism to expel dirt, poison, black blood, body heat and filth which accumulates in a woman's body, and irregular menstruation is linked to blindness and internal diseases.

While over two-thirds of the women reported feelings of shame and worthlessness during menstruation, their understanding of dignity did not directly mention menstrual challenges, even though they identified self-esteem and self-respect as part of their understanding of what constituted dignity. This suggests that the women perceived menstrual health to be a women's concern only. They associated dignity with the ability to care for their families but did not relate it to the idea that a woman who considers herself to be a burden, was unwell and felt worthless was unlikely to be able to take care of the family properly. Moreover, the idea of the 'self' was found to be absent from the women's conception of dignity. This suggests that the women did not prioritize their health and the misconceptions about menstruation added to them disregarding menstruation as a healthy bodily function. The study concluded that the idea of the 'self', including the menstruating self, is critical for women's understanding of dignity.

There have been efforts globally to improve the 'dignity' of menstruating women, and one solution has been to facilitate access to affordable sanitary pads. For example, since 2018, the UNFPA has been distributing 'dignity kits' to refugees in Angola. The dignity kit includes sanitary napkins, soap, laundry detergent and other essential hygiene supplies. This undoubtedly helps girls and women achieve better menstrual hygiene and respect for their bodies. However, the dignity kit does not help tackle the stigma and lack of information surrounding menstruation. Much more needs to be done to restore the essential dignity of menstruating women.

It is only with the eradication of misinformation and thereby the inclusion of the 'self' in women's conception of dignity that improved menstrual health will become possible.

Anguish of the Unveiled

VICTORIA PATRICK;

TR. AMNA MAWAZ KHAN

Underneath this canopy
Have I many years spent
Under the shadow of oppression
Helpless and alone

The One who is my master
The guardian of my fate
To his yes, I nod yes
To his no, I say nay

Who am I? I do not know
Where am I from? I do not know
Why do I here lie?
How much time have I let fly? I do not know

Day and night, I lay exposed
Four hundred hungry eyes on me
I am human, not cast of stone
How can I guard my dignity?
During my monthly bleed

I survive in hiding
But there is no resting place
No space, no solace

Terror of diseases at every turn
And a perpetual dampness
I find only pain, and no cure
Oh God! Oh God!

No cloth nor rag
Neither privacy nor shelter
None come near me
Don't let them come near me

May Allah show me mercy
May my life be easy
May my simple needs be met
May there be redemption from this stench

بے پردگی کا کرب

اک سائبان کے تلے
کٹی ہے میری زندگی
ظلمتوں کے سائے میں
بے کسی و بے بسی

جو شخص ہے آقا میرا
میرے مقدر کا امین
اس کی ہاں میں ہاں میری
اس کی نہیں میری نہیں

میں کون ہوں؟ پتہ نہیں
کہاں سے ہوں؟ پتہ نہیں
کیوں پڑی ہوئ ہوں میں
کب سے ہوں؟ پتہ نہیں

بے پردگی دن رات ہے
نظریں ہیں بھوکی چار سو
انسان ہوں پتھر نہیں
کیسے بچاوں آبرو

ماہواری کے ایام میں
بچتی پھروں میں جا بجا
گوشہ کوئ آرام کا
نہ در کوئ نہ آسرا

بیماریوں کا خوف ہے
رطوبتوں کا سلسلہ
علاج نہ معالجہ
میرے خدا! میرے خدا!

کپڑا ملے نہ چیتھڑا
نہ پردہ نہ بیت ا لخلا
نہ پاس ہے آتا کوئ
نہ پاس آنے دے ذرا

مجھ پر بھی ہو نظرِ کرم
ہو زندگی آسان میری
اشیا ضروری ہوں بہم
بدبو سے چھوٹے جان میری

Cloth, Ash and Blood: Conversations with Homeless Women about Menstruation

INTERVIEW | FARAH AHAMED

IN 2019, WHILE TRAVELLING AROUND MULTAN IN PAKISTAN, I spoke to several homeless women living near the numerous shrines dotting the city. I asked them how they came to be living there, and what challenges they experienced during their menstrual cycle. Initially, they were very reluctant to open up about their lives, let alone their bodies, but after I explained to them that I was compiling a book on menstruation experiences, they were a little more forthcoming.

My first meeting was with a woman whom I found sleeping roughly at the roundabout near the Shah Rukn-e-Alam Tomb. Sakina* was about sixty years old and had been living near the shrine for almost a decade.

'About eight years ago, my family abandoned me. They said I was useless as I could no longer help them with household chores because of my age and ill health. They said they did not have the money to feed me, so they pushed me out of the

---

*Name changed

house. I had nowhere to go, so I came to this shrine because I knew, if nothing else, at least I would get free food from the *langar*. This place is my home now, and I sleep on the streets or behind the shrine, in the backyard.

'I pass my days here on the roadside or on the footsteps of the shrine begging. At first it was difficult, but now I'm used to it. I have no choice. At mealtimes, I go to the langar at different shrines where I get free food. This is how I expect to pass the rest of my days.

'When I was younger and used to get my period, I would make a pad using my old clothes which I'd cut into strips. My sisters and I would shape ash from the charcoal stove into thin blocks. Once these were dry, we would fold one into a strip of cloth to make a pad of sorts. The ash block absorbs the blood and prevents leaking. After using the pad, we'd bury it. I learnt this from my mother and aunts who said that's what their mothers had taught them. I know these days women use pads from the shops, but we didn't have enough money. We often did not even have enough old clothes, so our rags were precious, and we had to make the most of what we had.

'At home, many restrictions were imposed on me during my period. I was not allowed to eat mutton, eggs, rice or anything sweet like halwas or mithai. Even drinking cold water was forbidden. Nowadays, I eat whatever I get at the langar, I know I won't starve. In any case, I no longer get my period and so I don't care about those constraints. In a way I am freer here than I was at home.

'There are some younger women who are also homeless and live with me in the shrine's backyard. I teach them what I know, and what they should do when they get their period. When we get infections, if we have money, we go to the doctor and get medicines. If we don't have money, the only option is to live with the pain. We rely on public latrines at the shrine for bathing and cleaning. Behind the langar at the shrine, there is a private area for women; no men are allowed there. We wash our few personal clothing items there and hang them to dry. It is easier in the summer when there is sun, but in the colder months our things stay wet, and we have no option but to put them on when they are damp.

'Even though I've been living out here on the streets for many years, I can say I have never been embarrassed or shamed by a man. Obviously, at my age I've learnt how to protect myself and maintain my dignity. I don't let a man speak to me disrespectfully. Every woman should know what to do; this is the way it is, after all.'

◆

After hearing Sakina's story, I met a group of young women living in a rough shelter behind the shrine of Pir Shams Sabzwari. Parveen, Farida and Husna* said they were between sixteen and eighteen years old, but they could have been much younger – it was hard to tell. I found them begging by the entrance of the shrine. Initially they refused to tell me their names, and while we were talking, they kept turning and looking at the men who were manning the kiosks on the side of the shrine watching us. It was obvious that the men seemed to have some sort of control over the girls, and the girls were afraid of them.

The three young women spoke quickly, interrupting each other; below is a gist of their responses:

---

* All three names changed

'We have always lived here; we were born here and will die here. We rely on the goodwill of the Pir. He provides us with food, shelter and protection. We have never experienced any difficulty relating to any area of our life. As you can see, we are fine and happy. Of course, we have some problems when it comes to money and, when it is cold, we need extra warm clothes like sweaters and shawls, but otherwise, everything is fine. People around here are kind and look after us.

'We live behind the shrine and use public latrines. We are used to it. During our period we use rags or cut our old clothes into strips and wash and dry them. We know what we have to do; our mothers and grandmothers did the same things. We don't make a big deal about it. All women get their period – it's a natural thing – and we cope with it. It's how Allah made our bodies, so we accept it. Sometimes we collect ash from the shrine, make it into small, thin blocks and then we cover it with cloth. The ash absorbs the blood, and we use this during our period. No one bothers us; this is our private affair. We rely on the Pir's goodwill, and people around here would not like us talking to you about our lives and such personal matters.

'No, we do not believe we are unclean or dirty during our period. We are not allowed to eat langar or enter the shrine during our periods, but this is normal. The shrine is a clean and pure place, so it's right we should not go there when we are bleeding. There are no restrictions on us of any kind. We've never had any infections. Why would we? The shrine is a place of worship, so Allah protects us. Sometimes, if we have a headache, we get medicines. Otherwise, Allah has looked after us and we are grateful to him and the Pir.'

◆

A few days later, I came across Amina*. A young gypsy woman, she was sitting on the steps of the open-roof, carved-brick shrine of Hazrat Sheikh Sadan Shaheed. Locally known as 'Farishton ka Darbar' or 'Angels' Court' – because it is believed to be constructed by angels – the seven-hundred-year-old mausoleum is situated near a village called Jalaran, on Muzaffargarh Jhang Road, about three hours from Multan. Amina was sitting outside the shrine, playing her harmonium, singing a Sufi qawwali. A couple dropped a few coins into the small cup at her feet, but Amina stayed engrossed in her music. When I approached her, she refused to give me her name or speak to me. She said her husband would get upset and say she had brought dishonour to the family by discussing her life with a stranger. I explained I was collecting stories for a book, and she agreed to speak to me behind the shrine, where her husband would not see us.

Amina's main worry was that she had not become pregnant even though she had been married for two years. She clarified straightaway that she was sitting outside the saint's tomb to sk for prayers, not money. The shrine of Sheikh Sadan Shaheed is considered to be an auspicious place for offering prayers, especially for women who cannot conceive. The trees around the shrine have ribbons tied to the branches and their trunks are wrapped with scarves with Quranic inscriptions. Around the entrance of the shrine, thousands of small, coloured ribbons flutter in the wind – a testament to the many female devotees who come from afar with hope. Amina had similar hopes pinned on Sheikh Sadan Shaheed's blessings.

'We live behind the Pir's shrine, just beyond the graveyard. It is difficult because sometimes we have money and at other times

---

*Name changed

we do not. When we have none, we stay hungry. When we do, we buy food and eat. We rely on whatever money people give us when they come to the shrine. But I am not concerned about food; I have a bigger worry.

'I grew up never thinking much about my period. My mother had explained to me what to do, and I accepted it. We use old clothes, which we cut to make cloth pads. The men don't interfere with the women's business, so my husband never asks me about my period. My periods were irregular, but I didn't care. Whether I bled or didn't, I didn't take notice. It was only after I got married that I was told that periods were related to getting pregnant. Before that, nobody had told me, and I didn't know the two things were connected. I've been married two years now, and I haven't had a baby. All my sisters and friends are mothers. They make fun of me. They call me *be-aulaadi* – the barren one – and the men look down on me.

'My biggest fear is that my husband will leave me for another woman who can have children. There is nothing I can do about that. Every month, when I see the blood of my period, I become very depressed. I know the bleeding will stop when I get pregnant, but when will that be? I don't know. That's why I come here every day to pray, in the hope that the Pir will have mercy on me and answer my pleas. I am desperate to have a child. Many women's prayers are answered after coming here, so why shouldn't mine be?

'There is nothing else for me to do all day, except come here. If I had a child, I'd be busy looking after it. I'd be with other women. My time does not pass sitting and singing here day in and day out. I'm not concerned about periods, or infection or anything else. Every woman gets those problems. I only want a baby. There is no life if you do not have a child. I know my life is cursed. Only Allah can help me. I do not think that my inability to conceive has anything to do with an infection, or disease or is related to my husband. If I am sick and there is no money, there is nothing I can do but suffer. When there is money, I will get some medicines. Allah is the one that gives children, and he can do anything. He is the one who decides what will happen; I have no control over my body or my fate.'

◆

Pakistan has a population of about 220 million, out of which 20 million are homeless with children, with women being the most affected and vulnerable.[1] Without stable shelter and security, proper nutrition, education or healthcare, the women live precarious lives. They spend the day guarding their temporary shelters, trying to find temporary work or selling things on the street. In the absence of other suitable options, they often have to use male public washrooms. Their transient lifestyle means that they have no regular and easy access to proper sanitation, clean running water and menstrual hygiene. They have no privacy, no dignity and no safe space to rest.

Despite the challenges they faced, I observed that all the women I interviewed were remarkably resilient. They saw menstruation as a natural phenomenon and had devised ways to deal with it. While periods were associated with youth and fertility, which were desired by family members, there were many restrictions around menstruation.

Sakina suggested that once a woman was unable to bear children, or help with chores, she was useless. However, in contrast, Amina was ostracized by her family and friends, even though she was young and still getting her period. While Sakina's story illustrated the challenges of ageing for women from a certain socio-economic and cultural background, in Amina's case, getting her period every month was a reminder that she was cursed because she had not been able to conceive. My conversation with the group of three young women pointed to a reluctance towards speaking about the subject openly because they were conscious of being watched by men. It is probable that they were worried about being shamed, ridiculed or scolded later. The hesitation to engage in discussions about menstrual health because of societal norms needs to be overcome to make menstrual health a priority.

Memory and Imagination: Reclaiming Menstruation

SIBA BARKATAKI

LET ME BEGIN BY TELLING YOU ABOUT THE AMBUBASI MELA, a sacred festival celebrated at the Kamakhya Temple in Guwahati, a city in northeast India. As part of the celebration, devotees of the temple goddess Maa Kamakhya also venerate a phenomenon that women usually do not talk about. For someone like me growing up in a family of *devi bhakts* (devotees of a goddess or a feminine power), menstruation had both physical and spiritual significance. My family, like other worshippers of Maa Kamakhya, believe that during Ambubasi, the goddess experiences her annual cycle of menstruation. During the four days of the festival, the gates of the temple are kept shut. No one is allowed to enter the temple for fear of disturbing the goddess. It is also a time of meditation and contemplation for her devotees – a time for aligning one's energies with the supreme feminine force. During Ambubasi, yogis, sanyasis and sadhus who usually meditate in isolation and in secluded spaces like mountain caves, camp outside the temple during the course of the festival, believing it to be in its most powerful state. On the last day of the festival, the head priest bathes the shrine of the goddess and performs rituals before opening the gates to devotees once again. This story, recounted every year during the Mela, with all its imaginative power, has remained etched in my memory since my childhood.

As a girl, I used to love listening to the stories of sadhus with psychic powers going into trances and performing mystical rituals during the Ambubasi Mela to increase their spiritual energy. When I entered puberty and became more conscious of my gawky teenage body, I began to feel a special affinity with the bleeding goddess. I became curious to know more about the significance of the feminine force. It was no longer an abstract story for me; I felt a visceral connection with the goddess and her potent vitality. The Kamakhya Temple is the site of the vagina, or *yoni*, of the goddess Sati, and in the inner sanctum there is a stone which resembles a yoni, and from it flows a natural underground spring. The yoni is worshipped because it is considered to be the most powerful Shakti *peeth* – a sacred shrine for the followers of Shaktism – as it is believed to host the goddess's potent body part. Over the years, I have come to believe that my menstrual cycle reinforces my connection with the goddess. In spite of the blood and the pain, I feel powerful and exhilarated.

◆

At school, menstruation had important social implications. I was almost fifteen years old and had not yet started getting my period, while the entire class of forty girls, including my closest friends, had already had their first brush with menstruation. It was terrible because I felt I was being left behind. My friends shared stories of their experiences, how they discovered the blood, what their mothers told them, and how they used sanitary napkins. I witnessed an intimate kinship forming within the group, but I could not be a part of it. Among the girls there was empathy, compassion as well as excitement about the future, while I had nothing to say.

But the awaited day finally came. I woke up one Saturday morning and found I was bleeding. My younger sister, two years my junior, was asleep in the bed next to mine. We were close; we played, fought and shared every aspect of our lives with each other. But in that moment, something changed for me. I realized that this was something I could not tell her. This was different, because I felt different. While there was relief and excitement, I was also anxious about what would happen next. I knew the conversation with my mother was going to be awkward. Despite the communal celebration of Ambubasi, menstruation was not discussed freely in my family. My mother had never talked to me about periods or how to deal with them. Whatever I knew, I had learnt from my friends. Even now, I can recall the exact conversation. We were standing in the garden, taking in the cool morning air when I broached the subject with trepidation, trying to keep my tone matter-of-fact.

Me: Maa, I got my period.
Maa: What did you say?
Me: I got my period.
Maa: When?
Me: I saw the blood this morning. Don't worry, I know what it is.
Maa: How do you know?
Me: All my friends in school have it.
Maa: You'll have to use a pad. Do you want me to show you how to wear it?
Me: No, no, it's fine, I know how it's done.
Maa: If you saw your period this morning, then today will be counted as the first day.

After this my mother took over. I had to stay in my room for a week and wasn't allowed to go to school. Shortly after, female members of my family came to visit, bringing me gifts of fruits, curd, cream, jaggery, sticky *bora* rice and other food items that I relished. I remember how my aunts congratulated my parents because their daughter had 'grown up'. I recollect feeling embarrassed at seeing how disconcerted my father was. But my aunts, now that I had transitioned into adulthood overnight, decided it was time to share stories of their first period. One of them revealed how, on seeing blood for the first time, she went into a frenzy because she thought she'd burst her liver.

There were a few peculiarities about my seven-day quarantine. The curtains were kept drawn to stop sunlight from entering the room. I wasn't allowed to eat the usual family diet; foods such as daal, rice, vegetables or fish curry were not served to me. Instead, my meals were restricted to porridge mixed with milk or curd, jaggery, fruits and water. The week seemed never-ending, and I remember, even now, how towards the end of the quarantine, I would dream of eating rice. On the seventh day, my mother presented me with an elaborate array of pastes made from different pulses and herbs. Some were for washing my hair and body, and others for massaging my body.

After the bathing ritual, I was informed a special *puja* was going to be performed in my honour. In my household, rituals were a part of our daily lives, and it was not unusual for us to have such a ceremony. But this puja was extraordinary because it was being conducted for me. I was the only one participating in it; it was my rite of passage. At the time I was reminded of my older brother's sacred thread ceremony and the puja when he turned fifteen. Now it was my turn to feel special.

From my room, I spied a beautiful arrangement of flowers. Diyas were lit, and I could smell the fragrance of burning incense. Fruits, coconuts and betel leaves were arranged on the floor in readiness for the puja. Our family priest Pobitro Sarmah sat at one end of the small ceremonial set up, and I at the other. He began chanting *shlokas* in his slightly hoarse, low-pitched, soft voice. At intervals throughout the ceremony, he asked me to repeat a few shlokas and sprinkle rice, flowers and water over the floral arrangement. An hour later, when the ceremony ended, I was asked to wrap a moist *gamusa*, a traditional Assamese towel, for a few minutes around my upper body, like a shawl.

When I returned to school after seven days, my friends welcomed and congratulated me. I did not have to tell them what had happened. They all knew.

◆

Life is a narrative. We are a version of the story we choose to tell ourselves and others about ourselves, and our biography changes with time. Writing about my memories of menstruation makes me wonder if those recollections are still a part of who I am today.

When I relocated from my parental hometown to follow my dreams in the big city, I also moved away from the traditions and customs of my culture. The importance that my first period had for me, as well as the associated Ambubasi rituals of menstruation, receded into the background. Over time, those memories faded.

However, menstruation was still an integral part of my life, banal even, because it was so predictable and repetitive. It was something I had learnt to cope with, without thinking. On the first day, I'd pop a painkiller to numb the cramps and pain, and then I'd get on with the usual routine. Menstruation further lost its importance when my daughter was born, eight years ago. After that I stopped marking the date on the calendar and worrying on which day my cycle would begin, because I was no longer anxious about conceiving. The thought of my period briefly crossed my mind while preparing my grocery list. I dealt with it practically, ordering sanitary napkins along with other household items. There was nothing spectacular or special about it. But now, as I reflect, I realize that when I get my period every month, I feel like that young vulnerable girl in Shillong again.

Memory is, in many ways, also about a sense of loss, and it is this feeling of privation that makes us yearn for that lost time. In writing about my memories of menstruation, I have reclaimed and found a part of myself again. When I reminisce about my first period and the festival of Ambubasi, I am transported to my childhood and to those early events which shaped my creative and spiritual subconscious.

Now that I've found that memory, it makes me wonder how different I might have been if I had reconnected with the memory of Ambubasi sooner? Maybe, when you unexpectedly gain a sense of wholeness, you begin to appreciate what you lacked.

I asked myself, what are the consequences of retrieving that story from my subconscious and making it a part of my personal narrative again? Has it changed the way I perceive myself and other women?

Ambubasi is a fertility festival. It is a celebration of how the feminine existence goes beyond the body, and is intimately connected to the earth's soil, its abundance and well-being. This suggests that by virtue of their essential nature, women have a deeper connection and resonance with planet Earth. It sometimes crosses my mind, how women could play a more dominant role in influencing environmental changes for the betterment of the planet. The Chipko movement and the non-violent protests led by the rural womenfolk in the Himalayan region of Uttarakhand is one example. This was a forest conservation movement started in the early seventies, and women were its backbone because they were the ones most affected by deforestation.[1] It was unusual because it saw mass participation from women and spread fast around the region mobilizing female support around a shared concern.

Menstruation is how my body reminds me every month to reconnect with cosmic feminine energy, rejuvenating by dint of this force of nature. Can menstruation therefore not be a time when we focus on rekindling the feminine imagination? In a compelling essay on the subject of finding a female tradition, Elaine Showalter noted that women have generally been regarded as 'sociological chameleons', taking on the class, lifestyle and culture of their male relatives.[2] In reality, the conditioning is so thorough, that more often than not, women adopt the male perspective and worldview. It is therefore not surprising to see grandmothers and elderly aunts reinforcing the patriarchal order and control in the family, especially when it comes to the dressing habits and code of behaviour they prescribe to the younger women in their family. This suggests that the feminine vision is hidden, and evident only, as Viviane Forrester pointed out, 'in what you don't see', what is absent and not visible.[3] Can't menstruation be a time when women focus inwards, searching for the inner woman and articulating the feminine perspective?

Over time, rituals evolve. We know today that in the past, rites and restrictions connected to menstruation were a consequence of circumstances and notions of impurity associated with menstruating women, and their consequent isolation was due to a lack of proper menstrual support. Isolation of menstruating women is irrelevant today because we have better access to menstrual products and hygiene.

Reclaiming menstruation through a memory, for me, means re-establishing the feminine continuum. Today, as I remember my first period, I am taken back to those seven days that I spent in my room, the food I ate, and my aunts. Their jokes and discussions on menstruation and pregnancy were my first lessons in sex education. I had never felt so close to the women of my family before, and I remember feeling privileged knowing that I had become a part of a community; a sisterhood that would accompany me on my journey to womanhood.

Shared rites and rituals reveal the memory of an ancient society. When I think of my daughter, I ask myself: How will I carry my family traditions forward? After all, reinstating the memory of menstruation in my life narrative will remain incomplete if I do not restore the legacy of the feminine continuum in my own family. The puja and other rituals will take on new meaning for my daughter if I explain their history and significance, particularly in the context of our family traditions.

I sit here at my desk, in Delhi, miles away from Shillong, and visualize an interaction with my daughter. I reminisce about getting my first period, allowing her to envision her own. Remembering the past allows us to imagine a future.

Sowing the Seeds of a Menstrual Revolution: The First Menstrual Workshop in Balochistan

GRANAZ BALOCH

THE FIRST TIME I GOT MY PERIOD I HAD NO IDEA WHAT IT WAS. But this much I knew – that from then on, my family would start thinking about my marriage to an elder cousin because I was no longer a young girl. In Baloch culture, generally speaking, from the moment a girl starts menstruating, the clock starts ticking: the family aims to have her married within two years. I knew I was soon to be married off. Teenage weddings are the norm in my culture. Getting your period, even though talking about it is veiled in shame, is a family matter. Everyone finds out that you have started menstruating because the head of the family is informed that you have become marriageable, and a husband must be found as soon as possible.

In Balochistan, the subject of menstruation is taboo and shrouded in myths of shame, dirt and impurity. Ignorance and lack of information are passed on from one generation to the next. Even health problems – such as excessive bleeding, PCOS (polycystic ovarian syndrome), amenorrhoea – are not discussed, and no help is sought for afflicted family members. During their period, girls are usually forced to stay home because of a lack of access to menstrual products and proper toilet facilities. According to a 2018 UNPO study, the dropout rate for girls is as high as 90 per cent and female literacy is as low as 26 per cent. More than 40 per cent of girls in Balochistan never attend school.[1] Their lives are restricted to domestic housework and bringing up children.

The position of women in Balochistan society is complex. On the one hand, women are highly respected and protected at all costs, especially during times of war. On the other, the Baloch system of ruling is extremely patriarchal and unequal in relation to the rights of women, whether it be in regard to their studies, ownership of land or decisions about marriage, educational progress and career choices. As a result, a vast majority of Baloch girls are still confined to their homes and forbidden from pursuing higher education or professional activities. The only option available to a girl from a poor family is to get married, often to a man at least two decades her senior. In such a society, women tend to not discuss their personal challenges with each other. Every woman has her own set of difficulties which she is expected to deal with, and this includes menstruation. Mothers, aunts, teachers, sisters or friends, no one wants to talk about this subject. I learnt about menstruation from the internet when I was in my teens, relying on Google to tell me what was happening to my body.

I grew up in Balochistan, which is the largest province of Pakistan, spread over 347,190 square kilometres and covering 44 per cent of the country's total area. To the north, it shares a border with Afghanistan, to the west with Iran and on the east and south side, the Pakistani provinces of Sindh and Khyber Pakhtunkhwa. Balochistan's population is just over 12 million and is made up of several multi-ethnic groups, the majority of whom are Baloch, Brahvi and Pashtun. Consequently, it is multilingual with the most popular languages being Balochi, Brahvi and Pashto. Despite its size and strategic geopolitical position, Balochistan is the poorest province of Pakistan where unemployment, poor health and malnutrition, gender inequality and illiteracy are the norm. The region has never been stable politically or economically for many reasons, including the lack of representation at the capital, in Islamabad. Most of the Balochi population depends on the smuggler trade of oil from Iran and, for the tribes in the west and north, seasonal agriculture provides subsistence. Balochistan is by and large a secular province, but few areas still enforce a tribal system of governance, especially on the Quetta side. Religion rarely features in everyday activities and, while the population is Muslim, it does not overtly practise Islam. However, Baloch cultural values – Baloch Mayar or the Baloch code of honour – is of paramount importance and always at the forefront, even more than tribal allegiances, political ideology or national or geographical identity. Ultimately, no price is too high to protect this 'honour' – killing oneself or another to do so is considered normal. Growing up here, I understood at a very early age that everything I was taught was based on Baloch Mayar, and I would always be judged by how I upheld it.

I lived and studied in Balochistan until I completed my undergraduate studies. I did not come face to face with the worst consequences of not understanding menstruation until I started my first job at a village public school. There I discovered the challenges girls faced during their periods. They had to miss an entire week of classes because there were no toilets at school and also because of the long distances they had to cover on foot between their school and homes. Many of these girls were very poor and could not afford sanitary napkins, so they preferred to stay at home. I began talking to them about menstrual health and hygiene, well aware of how little they understood about it based on my own upbringing. I supplemented my knowledge by reading health blogs on the internet.

It is extremely difficult and very challenging to talk about menstruation because of the conservative and patriarchal Balochi society. However, I am determined to help these young women because I can see how their chances to progress and succeed in life are being hampered because of ignorance.

When I was approached to write an essay for this book, I was conducting a menstrual health workshop for young women. This was the first of its kind and I faced resistance towards the idea. Many women said it was unacceptable for me to talk about periods in a public space and holding a workshop to discuss the subject was unthinkable. I explained it was about women's overall health and well-being, but many refused to accept that poor menstrual hygiene is linked to diseases and infections. I decided that rather than giving in to the pressure, I should take a bold stand and be a role model. Maybe after seeing me, other young women would be inspired to follow my example.

The aim of my workshop, which was held on 6 December 2019, was two-fold: to educate a group of students on the subject and also gather data on their menstrual experiences and challenges. For this, I also invited a qualified gynaecologist to be a part of the workshop. The target group was seventy female undergraduate students, between the ages of eighteen and twenty-three, attending XYZ college (anonymity is preserved to protect the students as they fear repercussions from their community leaders). The workshop offered a safe space for the participants to learn, discuss and share. They were encouraged to think about menstruation creatively and express themselves through writing or art. This came as a surprise to them as they had never been asked about it either at home or at school. The girls had a chance to ask questions about the myths they had grown up with, and I used the opportunity to explain what happened to their bodies biologically which had nothing to do with the 'stories' they had heard.

One theme that emerged was that the girls perceived menstruation as a burden or curse. It was always a time of pain and suffering. It caused them to miss school or university, stay apart from everyone else and compromised their chances of success. Some girls said there had been times when they had to miss their final exams because of heavy or painful periods and inadequate menstrual products.

Another subject that fuelled discussion was the fact that most of the girls did not eat a balanced diet, nor did they follow any healthy menstrual practices. When they faced problems during their periods, their families did not support them with the necessary products or medicine. This was due to the many misconceptions and unrealistic ideas about menstruation, one of them being that periods are supposed to be painful and there was nothing anyone could do about it. That's the way it was and always would be. You just had to accept it.

Many of the students said they had irregular periods and suffered from extreme pain which made it impossible for them to move. They did not mention going to see a doctor or trying to seek medical advice but explained how they resorted to traditional herbal remedies instead. They said it was too embarrassing for them to ask for help. During the month of Ramadan, when they were menstruating, they stayed away from the male members of the family and pretended they were fasting. They could not tell their family members the truth. I shared whatever information I had about nutrition, exercise, health and hygiene and showed them how they could protect themselves during their period using clean menstrual products.

Despite the initial hesitation and resistance, I took the opportunity to ask the participants about their thoughts on women who were less fortunate than them and how they coped during menstruation. This is what they shared. Disabled women and girls are invisible, have no access to anything and are completely ignored or silenced. Because of their situation, they are always dependent on a caregiver in the family. One girl told me the story of a blind woman in her neighbourhood who would hide at home during her period because she was ashamed and too afraid to come out and buy food even when she was starving. She had been dependent on her mother for support, but after her mother's death, she had no one to help her and was at the mercy of her neighbours.

Most of the participants said that in their communities women or girls with disabilities were kept locked in the house when they were on their period because their family members would feel embarrassed and uneasy. One participant mentioned a girl with polio who was being looked after by her mother. She said that during the girl's period, her mother would lock her in her room and leave her there. If she suffered any pain, she was given an injection.

Another story was about a blind woman who also suffered from a mental disorder. She had neither a caregiver nor proper clothing or shelter. She often roamed the streets wearing dirty, blood-stained clothes. One of the participant's cousins had a bone disease and was usually looked after by her mother. However, during her period she too was kept locked in her room and not allowed visitors.

I asked the participants if they were aware of the experiences of transgender people and what challenges the LGBTQ+ community faced during menstruation, and how they were different. The LGBTQ+ community in Pakistan does not enjoy equal rights as their heterosexual normative counterparts, and same-sex relationships are criminalized[2] by the Pakistan Penal Code.[3] They face discrimination and stigma, stemming from religious and cultural beliefs, which makes it challenging for them to disclose their sexual preferences and have open, steady relationships. However, some have been able to secretly socialize, organize, date and even live together.[4] In 2018, seventy-nine transgender people were attacked in the Khyber Pakhtunkhwa province, which neighbours Balochistan. In reality, the figure is likely to be higher as anti-trans violence is poorly reported.[5] Therefore, it was not surprising when the participants replied they had no idea about any of this because of the conservative nature of Baloch society.

The participants were invited to paint, draw or write about their experiences of menstruation. It was very exciting to hear their responses. One young girl aged eighteen said, 'This is the first time in my life I am expressing my feelings about menstruation on a page with writing and paints. It had never occurred to me that I could do that. I hate talking about my period because of the pain I always suffer, but now having shared my feelings, I feel relieved.'

Out of the exercise also emerged a painting of a girl drowning in a red river with a small boat in the distance. The artist explained she resented having her period every month because she had no resources for protection, had never received any education or guidance and had no money to buy menstrual pads. The river symbolized menstrual blood and the overwhelming depression she felt every month because of her inability to cope, while the boat was a metaphor for a sanitary pad. Still another said, 'I had never realized how such a deep, suppressed fear could be illustrated through art or poetry. Now I appreciate how transformative and freeing the experience has been – I was able to express how emotionally and physically disturbed I become during my menstrual cycle.'

A recurrent theme was the taboos associated with periods and one girl drew the foods that were prohibited during periods according to traditional superstitions. These included cucumbers, cold water, tart, bitter and spicy foods, onions, Mountain Dew, red meat, eggs, potatoes, pickles, lemons and limes, and tamarind.

The workshop inspired one young woman to record all the medicines used to alleviate stomach cramps, backaches or heavy bleeding. The list included Panadol, painkiller injections like Voren and traditional Balochi herbal medicines extracted from medicinal plants like neem.

I asked the participants to calculate the number of days of school they had skipped because of their period. Many girls could not attend up to a week of school every month equivalent to more than ten lessons per day. One of the students in the group reported to have lost out on eight months of school because of heavy bleeding and another said that she had never received any medical help despite suffering from severe cramps. The reasons cited for lost attendance included the lack of proper toilet facilities at school, the unavailability of adequate menstrual products and no means of transport to faraway schools.

It was not surprising to find that all the women believed that menstruation was a shameful 'female' problem which should be kept hidden and not discussed – certainly not with men – and that all menstrual products should be kept out of sight.

At the end of the workshop, the women were given undergarments and sanitary pads. They went away feeling empowered and more confident about their bodies. At least 80 per cent said they felt they would be able to conduct similar sessions in their neighbourhoods and villages to help other girls. I was very encouraged by this, and it led me to hope that we could start a revolution, step by step. However, while these small attempts to educate women continue, at the heart of the matter lies the problem of an entrenched patriarchal system. Unless it loosens its firm grip on women and allows them equal status as men, their professional mobility and progress, including the exercise of their rights over their own body and health, will not be possible, and women and girls will continue to suffer ill health and remain restricted to traditional domestic roles.

I am aware that by conducting the first-ever menstrual workshop in Balochistan and writing this essay, I was breaking Baloch Mayar. However, I am not afraid of challenging my culture and its outdated norms because I believe that girls and women deserve hope and a chance at a better future.

Hormo-baha: Flower of the Body

SRILEKHA CHAKRABORTY

LET ME START WITH A STORY OF DISCOMFORT. ONE THAT engulfed me every month when I was working as a researcher. I came to realize that I was not only an ethnographer and a woman, but above all else, I was an outsider in the small tribal village community where I was conducting my research. This discomfort has a strong pungent smell. And even though it emanated from me, it took me time to accept it as a part of, and integral to, my everyday life and identity. This story is also about one of the remotest states of India, Jharkhand, where I have been working for the last eight years with the Adivasi community and other backward castes (OBCs). Adivasi is an umbrella term used for the tribes of the Indian subcontinent which are considered indigenous. My work is mainly with a tribe known as the Santals. Their survival is centred on struggles of *jal, jungle* and *jameen,* a legacy of colonialism that has left them impoverished and without dignity.

Menstruation is a natural bodily function. But in many marginalized communities of India, including those in Jharkhand, puberty is a time of extreme shame. Because a girl is misinformed, and has no understanding about her body, she struggles with taboos and social stigma. These stay with her throughout her life.

My research and activism over the past few years have been around educating the Santal community about how that can improve their health, and teaching them about their menstrual rights, especially in relation to gender.

◆

In 2017, I was in Jharkhand, working in the Santhal Pargana region on a health project. Every morning, for the next three years, I travelled around twenty kilometres to reach remote villages as part of the project. Over time, I started developing strange symptoms. I would feel nauseated every time I thought about my fieldwork. I felt repelled by the thought of the discussions I would have to have with the villagers. I had to force myself to conduct interviews, and sometimes, I found myself vomiting at the prospect of carrying out day-to-day field activities. After two weeks of torture, I sat down and reflected on what was upsetting me so much. One of the rules of ethnographic research is that the researcher should identify every change they experience during fieldwork. On greater self-examination, in keeping with this guideline, I realized it was the conversations with the women that were making me ill. Our discussions were mostly about menstrual stigmas; patterns of sexuality and horror stories of abortion and menstruation every day had taken a toll on me.

As someone born and brought up in a relatively liberal Hindu Brahmin family in Bengal, the stories were forcing me to confront my own privileges and accept the fact that at the end of the day, as a researcher I was a *diku*. Diku is a derogatory Santali word for outsider, foreigner or even intruder – someone hostile, not from the tribe. I had to accept that I was an outsider, no matter how much I struggled with it. Even though I felt strongly bonded with the women of the community, I realized that I was not one of them, we were not all the same and did not form one homogenous category of women. I was not there to absorb their pain and make it my own, but to recognize and acknowledge the differences between them and me. With this realization, my symptoms began to fade to some extent.

I share this story here, as part of this essay, because whenever I am asked to write about my work on menstruation and tribal communities, I become conscious of my position. Am I a researcher? An outsider? Am I writing this essay about them, for them? Or am I writing about my understanding as an outsider? Or as a researcher? Or both? My approach has been that of an outsider narrating her experiences of working with young girls from the Santal tribe. In this essay I want to explain how my own understanding of menstruation and my body was challenged through interactions with the Santali women and girls.

Living with a Leech

In Santali, menstruation is called *hormo-baha,* although because of the influence of Sanskritization, it is often referred to as *mahina* and *mahvaari* by young girls. 'Hormo' means 'body' and 'baha' means 'flower', so the words mean flower of the body. *Baha-parab* is the Santali festival of spring when the entire community congregates to celebrate the birth of new flowers.

I grew up in Bengal, where the phrase *shorir kharap* was the colloquial way of referring to periods. 'Shorir' means 'body' or 'health' and 'kharap' means 'bad', so 'shorir kharap' literally means 'when you're not in good health'. Until I met the Santali people, the notion that my menstruating body was bad or ill governed my views. Learning that periods could also be referred to as a flower of the body changed the way I viewed myself when I was menstruating. This newly discovered name encouraged a positive attitude in my own perceptions of menstruation.

During the summer of 2015, I started collecting stories from young girls about their first menstruation experience. At the time, I was working with Network for Enterprise Enhancement and Development Support (NEEDS) for a project called Stories of Life. This was an innovative programme aimed at sensitizing young people about sexual and reproductive health through short informative videos that were tailored to their needs and relevant for improving their knowledge, skills and practices. A typical session was conducted under a huge banyan tree in a corner of a field where a group of ten adolescent girls would share their experiences. At one of the sessions, a young girl named Fulmoni had this story to tell.

'One day when I went to take a bath in the river, I saw something red and sticky in my skirt. I checked and saw to my horror that I was bleeding from my vagina. I thought to myself that a leech from the river has entered my body through my vagina and that it was going to suck all my blood, I was surely going to die. But I was too frightened to tell anyone about this at home, so I kept quiet. For the next five days, I did not sleep because I was sure that if I did, I would never wake up. I just stood straight against a wall and stayed still because I thought moving my body would encourage the leech.'

When Fulmoni finished narrating her story, the girls laughed, including Fulmoni herself, but I sensed her horror and anxiety and could not make light of it. And as I heard more stories, I realized Fulmoni was not alone. Many of the young Santali girls had had similar experiences with menstruation; there were times when they too had believed that they were going to die because a leech, an insect or some terrible disease had entered and taken over their bodies.

Their fear stemmed from a lack of education and ignorance about puberty and the changes their bodies were going through. While I appreciated the beautiful Santali name for menstruation, I could see that the girls had little or no knowledge about the process itself. Fulmoni's leech story reinforced my motivation to try and do whatever I could to provide the young girls with appropriate information about menstruation.

Labour, Myth and Menstruation

I grew up in a middle-class family in Kolkata and am an only child. I had a lonely and somewhat difficult adolescence. When I began menstruating, I had to figure it out for myself, because there was complete silence around the subject at home. During my menstrual cycle, I was not allowed to enter the kitchen or touch any utensils containing drinking water. I was not even allowed to touch my mother's wardrobe, which came as a shock, because we used to share our clothes, especially when we went to the temple. My normal bed clothes would vanish, and instead, a thin blanket and old pillow would take their place. I could only return to my usual comforts at the end of the cycle. The period pillow and blanket were then washed and sanitized. The first one and a half days of my period were always terrible. I felt ostracized and rejected by my family, and that experience would colour the rest of the month. I lived in dread of my next period, knowing it would bring the same constraints. All I could think about was how this could be done to me, every month, in my own home.

During my fieldwork in Jharkhand, I spoke to the Santali girls to uncover any taboos and stigmas related to menstruation practised by the community. I was surprised to find there were very few. The young girls were not restricted from working in the fields, fetching water, or performing household chores like cooking and cleaning. They said, 'Who will do the work if we don't? We are allowed to do everything.' During the harvest season, a young girl can earn between ₹200 to ₹250 for a day's labour in the field. This revelation shed light on an aspect of privilege that I had never considered before. For the girls, a day off during menstruation would result in no pay, and consequently no money for a family's meal. I began to grasp that the sacred and profane are not only determined by patriarchy but are also deeply rooted in privilege. The notion of leisure during menstruation is a privilege for one class of women who have the luxury to rest their bodies during their period, while for another, such a period of rest is unthinkable.

The Santali girls spoke only of one restriction during menstruation which was that they were not allowed to enter the garden and touch or pick flowers or vegetables because it was believed that if they did, the plants and vegetables would decay and wither. One girl I spoke to was curious about the claims and told me how she decided to verify the truth for herself. She said, 'One day while menstruating, I entered the garden. I did this without informing anyone in the house and plucked some vegetables. I wanted to see if they would rot. I waited for several weeks, but nothing happened.' The other girls in the group giggled at the story, suggesting that they were aware that the restrictions were baseless. Like all young girls, they were curious and rebellious.

The Santals follow the Sarna faith which advocates respect for the sal tree, mountains and nature. In the Santali culture, ancestors or *bongas* are held in great importance and menstruating girls are not allowed to participate in religious festivals – *parabs* – or touch anything used in religious rituals for fear of offending the bongas. A girl told me how she pretended she was not on her period because she wanted to attend a religious ceremony.

'I'd been waiting all year to worship Goddess Saraswati, the goddess of knowledge. When the time of the festival came, I got my period. I did not know what to do. I thought: why should I miss the chance to worship because of it? I decided to keep quiet and went to the temple to pray. When I returned home, I told my mother what I had done, and she became angry with me for defying a tradition. But I defended myself and told her that if I had not prayed, Goddess Saraswati would not have helped me at school, and I would have failed my exams. I was sure the goddess would have been more disappointed in me about this than anything else. My mother kept quiet.'

In my own home in Bengal, unless I told her, my mother would never know whether I was menstruating. However, I found the Santali girls were very open with their peers and knew who among their friends, sisters or cousins were on their cycle. When I asked why their mothers were the last to know, one girl said, 'We're too shy; we're told never to discuss it with anyone, so we don't even tell our mothers.'

Indeed, there were some instances where mothers discovered that their daughters had started menstruating during community discussions, and when confronted, the girls would reply, 'Yes, for two years now.'

This revelation about mother-daughter relationships with respect to the subject of menstruation in the Santali community was a mystery to me, and I was interested in finding out where the girls obtained whatever they knew about menstruation, if not from their mothers. I gathered that they learnt about periods from their sisters-in-law, friends and sisters. Village schools generally did not have classes on menstruation and healthcare workers from the government tended to prioritize care for pregnant women and lactating mothers over adolescent girls.

Not a Priority

The majority of Indian health policies for women focus on maternal health, pregnancy and childbirth while a few like Janani Surakhsha Yojana have had a considerable impact on maternal health. However, so far policies catering to adolescent health have been scarce. One example is the Weekly Iron and Folic Supplementation (WIFS) programme, but this has not been consistently promoted. Some adolescent health projects have been piloted in phases; for instance, the 2014 Rashtriya Kishor Swasthya Karyakaram (RKSK) programme which was rolled out in a few districts in each state. Unfortunately, the Menstrual Hygiene Management Scheme, which was supposed to provide sanitary pads in schools through the Accredited Social Health Activist (ASHA) project, has been a failure and, consequently, far-flung communities like Santali girls and women continue to struggle for access to basic menstrual hygiene services and products.

In 2017, I began exploring what men thought of menstruation. I questioned male health officials I met while working in Jharkhand to initiate a dialogue on periods, but the response was always the same: 'Could you please speak to a female officer? I can't help you with this.'

When I insisted that as decision makers it was important they took part in the conversation and opened up the discussion they still refused. This made me realize that menstruation was being perceived as a women's-only issue, and not really a public health concern.

On several occasions I was told by male state officials and policymakers that menstruation did not have political economy, and that's why politicians did not take any interest in it. As one official remarked, 'As long as no one is dying and as long as it's not yielding votes, it's not the priority; it can wait.'

A Campaign for Impact

By 2018, I was more determined than ever to ensure that the Santali girls in Jharkhand were able to make better and more informed choices. I wanted to bring about permanent change, and started an online petition at Change.org, urging the Ministry of Drinking Water and Sanitation of Jharkhand to guarantee that young girls would be provided with menstrual knowledge and health services. I argued that in areas where there was hunger and poverty, even though it was equally important, the dialogue around gender, sexuality and menstrual hygiene had taken a back seat. My aim through the petition and campaign was to bring to the forefront the many issues affecting poor tribal women at the grassroots. I wanted to highlight the challenges they faced and ensure that the 'menstrual rights of indigenous women' were prioritized.

In Jharkhand, the state already had a strong network of Anganwadi workers, who educated the women in villages about health and nutrition. However, most of them were not trained to talk about menstruation and had no printed material like brochures and posters imparting health education. This made it difficult for them to disseminate accurate information. From my own work with the Santali girls, I knew that they required appropriate materials, training and sessions on menstrual health and hygiene. My campaign made a pitch for the same.

◆

I want to end my essay with an anecdote of something revolutionary done by a group of young artists, NEEDS, and the local community of Jharkhand. In 2014, the central government, under the flagship of Swachh Bharat Abhiyan, promised to bring 'Comprehensive Sanitation and Hygiene' to people in rural India. However, the programme was mainly focused on the construction of toilets and cleanliness, without any mention of menstruation either as a hygiene agenda or an issue which needed to be destigmatized. The government had put up various posters and slogans on walls around the village, but none touched upon menstruation. For a semi-literate population, slogans on a wall and other visual modes of social messaging are an important medium of communication and a way to reinforce important messages. I decided that one way of getting menstruation noticed by the local authority was to create a wall mural.

In May 2019, on International Menstrual Hygiene Day, after a four-day workshop with thirty-five youth and social workers from the community, we began working on two murals. We rallied adolescents, both young men and women from the community, to participate in the project. The location of the murals was of paramount importance, and we decided, after visiting many villages, that the murals should be on the walls of the community centres and on the main road, so that every passer-by could see them and engage with the messages.

Challenges were aplenty. The scorching heat at that time of year meant that we would have to start painting at five o'clock in the morning. Because it was so early, villagers came up to us and asked what we were doing, while brushing their teeth. During the day, others sat down and watched us paint, curious to see what we were up to. Over the course of the month, many adolescents joined us, asking for more information and we handed out pamphlets about menstrual health. Even motorcyclists and truck drivers stopped along the roadside for a better view of the murals and asked for pamphlets. It was very exciting.

One of the murals is in Naya Bhadiyara village on the side wall of a community hall, near a busy highway. It is hard to miss. Today, the mural on the wall appears surreal, as if it were from a dream; it shows a young girl in a yellow dress surfing on a red ocean of huge waves. The red waves symbolize menstrual blood and the surfboard is a sanitary pad which the girl manoeuvres with ease. The mural appeals to young girls to feel safe, confident and informed during their periods and sail forward confidently in the direction of their dreams. The slogan on the mural translates to, 'Menstruation is not a problem but a symbol of women's strength.' Oh! How lovely a sight it is!

The second mural is near a well in a village called Madransare. The well is a strategic place for a mural because everyone comes there to fetch water, and no one can avoid seeing or talking about it. The girls in the village were known to be a crazy bunch of hooligans because they kept climbing trees, and it was they who came up with a mural of a Gulmohar tree. The tree has red flowers symbolizing period blood, and under the tree are young girls plucking fruits, playing on swings and reading a book. The slogan translates to: 'Menstruation is not a burden, but nature's gift.' What a way to destigmatize menstruation. This is the power of young people!

Homa Istrizia Azan Asan:
Our Women Are Free

FARAH AHAMED

IN NORTHWEST PAKISTAN LIVES A SMALL COMMUNITY OF
3,000 people, the Kalasha, who have been there since the eleventh
century. They follow a culture where women are 'azat' or free, and
have 'chit' or choice. They live in three tiny valleys, Bumburet, Birir
and Rumbur in Chitral District, of Khyber Paktunkhwa Province,
and speak Kalasha or Kalasha-mun.

If you were to walk along the side alleys and streets in all the
small villages, you would see wooden signs with arrows pointing
to 'Bashali: maternity home'. When I enquired what Bashali was,
I was told it was the village menstrual building where Kalasha
women went during their menstruation and to give birth. I asked
if I could visit a Bashali, but was told the place was completely
forbidden to outsiders, anyone not menstruating and not almost
due to have a baby. No one, not even the women's own female
family members were allowed to disturb the women inside the
Bashali. Men were never allowed to enter, nor touch the walls or
the doors of Bashali. This was a private space created and curated
by Kalasha women for themselves.

It was my good fortune to meet two young women who
were able to help me understand the Kalasha culture better.

Rabia Kausar, working in the Directorate of Labour and Bureau of Statistics, Khyber Pakhtunkhwa, as an Observer, assisting with the Child Labour Survey, and Safina Safdar, a Third Party Field Monitor with the Health Department, offered to take me to visit a Bashali after I clarified that I was writing a book on menstruation experiences. They also accepted to act as my interpreters if I wanted to interview the women there, and provide me with supplemental information from their Kalasha friends. Rabia and Safina asked for permission for us to enter the Bashali, speak to the women and take photographs. The Kalasha women, who very rarely allow visitors, kindly accepted to allow us inside the compound.

The Bashali or Bashaleni which I visited in Bumboret was a bungalow with a wide porch, situated on a large compound with leafy trees. Two large rooms, with six beds in each, opened on to the verandah. There was a small kitchen with utensils, cooking implements and firewood. Around the back was a space with a tap with clean running water for washing clothes. The compound was clean and organized, and I was told the women had a shower room at the back with hot water and toilets. The house was well swept and clean and the atmosphere was one of calm. It is probable that decades ago the Bashali was quite different, but it has obviously evolved; the house is now a solid building, self-contained and modern.

The garden had different varieties of trees, including pines, chlghoza, deodar and oak. Noisy mynas twittered in the branches and a cat was curled up in a garden chair. In the shade of an old oak, a woman sat behind a sewing machine stitching a black skirt, while talking to her friend who was relaxing on a charpoy. In the front of the house, another woman was busy at her sewing machine. Someone else was washing clothes. By the door, seated on the steps, were a young girl and a woman intent on embroidering a Kalasha headdress. Rabia explained that the women were busy preparing their outfits and headdresses for the upcoming Chilam Joshi spring festival in May. In one bedroom, two girls were lying on their beds chatting, and by the door was an empty baby's cot.

Safina asked Mazdana, the woman who was busy with her embroidery, to explain the Bashali segregation ritual to us, how she felt about it and what happened here. Mazdana looked about forty years old, but could have been younger – it was difficult to tell.

'I come here every month for five days during my period,' she said. 'This is my chance to rest from the pressure of family and household chores. During this time, I don't do any heavy work, any cooking or lifting or anything that puts strain on my body. I rest, sleep, talk to my friends and do embroidery or knitting. In the evenings, we sit together and share stories, sing or dance. We do whatever we want to, whenever we feel like it. We feel free here, we enjoy the time with our friends.

'We bring our own blankets from home, and every day someone from each of our households brings us food. They'll leave it outside the door. We are not allowed to see them or touch them. Even the utensils used for our food for this time are kept separate.

'During these five or seven days, or however long our periods last, we do not take a bath or shower. We do not change our clothes. Only after the bleeding has stopped will we shower, wash our hair and change our clothes. Then we will return home.

'If there is an emergency we can leave Bashali, but only after we have showered and changed our clothes. It is not that we are dirty, or anything like that – we just have to stay separate from everyone so that our bodies get some rest. In Kalasha culture we always say, 'homa istrizia azat asan', which means, our women are free.'

While the Bashali's compulsory rest of five days sounds welcome, if there was a festival or important occasion, the women inside the Bashali would have to miss out, because they were not allowed to socialize as they were menstruating. This was inconvenient. Also, during the cold winter months, some of the women did not like coming to the Bashali, but most of the times, it was a relief for them to be able to escape their intense domestic routines.

While the Bashali people did not consider menstruation shameful, there was an aspect of impurity associated with it, even if it was a matter-of-fact belief and not an overtly negative judgement. Safina and Rabia told me that they would not be able to visit any household that day because they had been inside the Bashali. The Kalasha people did not allow anyone who had been in contact with the menstruating women in the Bashali to enter their homes.

Rabia enquired from the young fourteen-year-old girl, Ratumi, who was stitching a traditional belt, where she had learnt about menstruation. She said: 'My mother told me, of course. While I was growing up, I knew when my mother got her period every month by observing when she would come to Bashali. Everyone knows this. This is our culture. It's normal. I knew I would have to do the same when my time came. Even my brothers know about Bashali. There is nothing to hide. When I got my period for the first time, my mother showed me how to use cloths. We don't use anything from the shops like pads or anything like that. We look after Bashali and we keep it the way we like it. I like coming to Bashali because there is *wa slaw* [space].'

The Bashali is a central point for nurturing female culture and a community of sisterhood. It enhances a Kalasha woman's sense of agency, both personally and collectively. Safina explained that there were rituals to support younger women as they pass through puberty, including purification ceremonies and offerings. When a girl starts her period and enters the Bashali for the first time, a ceremony is conducted in front of the wooden statue of the goddess Dezalik. According to Kalasha culture, Dezalik is the goddess of fertility, childbirth, the hearth, and a life-giving force. She protects girls and women, and is particularly responsible for them in the Bashali. When the first-timer is ready to leave the Bashali after her period is over, her clothes and beads are washed by the other women, before she sets out to walk through the village. This completes her initiation into the sisterhood. In the Bashali, the women talk candidly about sex, their cycles and reproductive health. They support one another with knowledge, advice and humour. Through monthly visits to the Bashali, a young girl becomes connected to all the women in her village. She will get a chance to socialize with different women and make friends because not the same women come every time. She will learn knitting, sewing and other traditional skills of craft-making.

There are certain rituals which are practised in the Bashali. Before touching any food, the bed, floor or their feet, the women must wash their hands. Shoes worn inside the Bashali must never be worn on the streets, and food must not be placed on the floor or the bed. In the Bashali, women do not have to wear the traditional headdress, their beads and the belt. They do not have to worry about their braids. But before they leave, everything must be thoroughly scrubbed; their bodies, the beads around their necks and their headdresses.

While I was walking through the village after my visit to the Bashali, I met a woman walking with a bundle of clothes under her arm; her hair was wet and her headdress was worn sideways. My male tour guide asked her if she was returning from a Bashali, and she said, 'Yes, I just finished bathing.' Her tone was matter-of-fact, and she showed no embarrassment at being asked. Everyone in the village must have known where she was coming from – it was quite obvious. Visits to the Bashali are an ordinary part of Kalasha life.

The Kalasha people are polytheists and nature plays a significant role in their spiritual life. Going to the Bashali is akin to a religious act, a conscious effort on the part of each woman to play her role in maintaining the order of the wider community. Women's religious expressions are vibrant in the rites they practise in front of the wooden statue of the goddess Dezalik. The women ask Dezalik to bless new entrants, for help when a woman is in pain or has bad cramps during her cycle, or is experiencing a difficult labour. Dezalik is a goddess just for women, and they believe she is their special connection to the divine. Menstruating women are not allowed to touch Dezalik's statue, which is about eighteen inches tall. The triangular figure has an indented oval circle at the top and a diamond-shaped hole in the middle. The oval represents the goddess's face and the hole her vagina.

'Dezalik is a messenger, even though she is a goddess,' Ratumi explained. 'So we call her name, easily and with conviction, and believe that God hears our prayers and answers them.' One of the rites involves throwing three cracked walnuts at Dezalik's head, while praying for relief. 'The walnut is a symbol of fertility and sexuality,' Rabia said. 'In this way, Bashali rituals support girls and women as they move through menarche, maternity, childbirth, possible miscarriages and menopause.'

The Bashali is the only place where women speak freely about childbirth. Here, the women learn from one another about what happens during this time and how they can lend support. Rabia clarified what happens at childbirth. 'When a pregnant woman's labour pains start, she is taken to the Bashali by her close female friends or relatives and an older women is called to come and do the delivery. There is no professional nurse or doctor, and very few painkillers are used. In cases of extreme labour and prolonged pain, rituals are performed to ask Dezalik for help.' Safina said the standard prayer was something like this, "Oh, my Dezalik of the Bashali, make her deliver quickly, bring the new flower into her arms, don't make things difficult; your eating and drinking." And while reciting the prayer, walnuts are cracked and thrown at the figurine of the goddess. If the birth is especially difficult, the pregnant woman's beads are placed around Dezalik's neck. These are returned to the mother after the child is born. After six days there is a special birth celebration inside the Bashali. A mother will stay in the Bashali for two or three weeks, cared for by the other women, until she feels strong enough to go home.

The Bashali offers women the space to think of themselves as a community. The women are bound together through their bodies, the rituals to Dezalik, their creativity and their experiences. It contributes to the *jamilishir* or the sisterhood of women and reinforces their identity and claim to freedom. As the Bashali is off limits to men, they are not privy to any of the 'secret' discussions that take place here. Kalasha women take the notion of privacy and secrecy in the Bashali seriously. So even while menstruation is openly acknowledged, what happens inside the Bashali is never disclosed.

The women at the Bashali use the time to get to know one another better. All Kalasha marriages are love marriages, which means there is plenty of bantering and teasing. Kalasha women often refer to the Bashali as 'Bashali dur' which means family or house. The women live together in the Bashali as family members, sharing their problems, resources and supporting one another to look after their children. Of course, it can also happen that sometimes the women do not get along. But generally, in the Bashali, the women are affectionate, sitting close together, laughing, pinching each other's cheeks, holding hands and being completely unselfconscious.

I asked Safina if women ever pretended they had their period so they could escape to the Bashali. As it turns out, it is sometimes the case – women will now and then use their period as an excuse to get away from family or other social pressures. Some even extend their stay after their period is over, to delay returning home. Others go there to hide from angry or violent husbands. The Bashali is a place where women can exercise certain freedoms. It is a space where they can reflect on their lives without being harassed by domestic obligations. The fact that women who are not menstruating sometimes go there shows that the women seek out the protection of Bashali. It also obscures them from the view of anyone trying to assess their reproductive status. At the Bashali, the women are able to experience an expanded sense of themselves.

What if women were given the opportunity to explain menstruation on their own terms, and decide what they wanted to do during their cycles? Would the Bashali be one choice they would ask for? The Bashali highlights what could happen when women have control of their bodies and space and the menstruation conversation. Their response is one of emancipation, where they, a sisterhood of women, recognize and nurture their mutual needs and choices. The Kalasha men are supportive of this, because while the women are away, they have to adjust to their absence in the home as a normal monthly routine. Women, when allowed to be the experts on their lives, choose to honour their cycles. In the title essay of her book *Men Explain Things to Me*, Rebecca Solnit recalls Virginia Woolf's passage in *To the Lighthouse*, which even though from a different culture, resonates with the Bashali experience.

'For now she need not think about anybody. She could be herself, by herself. And that was what now she often felt the need of – to think; well, not even to think. To be silent; to be alone. All the being and the doing, expansive, glittering, vocal, evaporated; and one shrunk, with a sense of solemnity, to being oneself, a wedge-shaped core of darkness, something invisible to others. Although she continued to knit, and sat upright, it was thus that she felt herself; and this self, having shed its attachments, was free for the strangest adventures. When life sank down for a moment, the range of experience seemed limitless.... Beneath it is all dark, it is all spreading, it is unfathomably deep; but now and again we rise to the surface and that is what you see us by. Her horizon seemed to her limitless.'

Hothousing: Embracing Menopause at Thirty-seven

LISA RAY

I LOST MY PERIOD WITH THE FORCE OF A TEST DUMMY crashing into a wall. And this was how a doctor described it, when I was sitting across from him in his office. 'Normal menopause is a donkey and wagon; chemo-induced menopause is a Ferrari hitting a wall at 100 miles an hour.' I appreciated his vivid metaphor even as I spun in my seat, and in my head, I tried to peer down the corridors of my body.

In June 2009, when I was diagnosed with multiple myeloma, a deadly bone cancer, the sole intention and best outcome for me had been to survive. Months of heavy steroids and chemotherapy, bone-modifying drugs and countless hours spent on my back searching for patterns in popcorn ceilings had coaxed me into bland acceptance. But I was not prepared for this news. In the demolition zone that my body had become, the imminent loss of my period had not been discussed with the white coats. What did the doctor mean? Would the typical symptoms of menopause – hot flashes, night sweats, mood swings, vaginal dryness – descend on me like a thunderstorm?

The doctor went on to explain. 'Here's what's going to happen next. In preparation for your stem-cell transplant … yada … yada …

but before the final steps, you have to think about your fertility. You have two options; the first is to freeze your eggs. The second option, well, actually, is that you don't bank them and add a full stop to the propagation of your genetic DNA.' My menstruation career was over. Period.

Suddenly, every outline turned crisp, every detail came to life in sharp relief. I recall the musty smell rising from the stacks of manila folders stored on the shelf behind the doctor's desk. The fallacy of misplaced concreteness, as I had once read. This detail would be embedded in my experience of menopause, attached with a strong sensation and odour. The scent marking the end of my period.

I had never felt the socially mandated resonance with my fertility or feminine aspirations of marriage and family. When I was diagnosed with cancer I was in a new relationship, but in my mind and choice of habits, I was still single. What about sex? Sex for me had always been complicated. Every beginning was marked with starry voices in the dark and moans that lengthened like shadows, until arousal inevitably turned into lament. Then came the 'I do not exist for you,' and a line would be drawn through the name. But what about me? What did this sudden development mean for my body? My vagina? Oh god, and what about kids?

According to the internet, 'Menopause marks the end of a woman's menstrual cycle. It is diagnosed when twelve months have passed without a menstrual period.' Menopause can happen in a woman's forties or fifties, except in cases like mine: at thirty-seven, induced early by chemotherapy and a life-saving stem-cell transplant.

Meno-pause. I would dissect the dreaded word in my mind. Why is it called a pause, when it is not defined as a comma event? Why not call it a period, because it puts a period in front of periods? Considering the fact that menstruation is a biological process, it is worth asking why menopause is not placed within a larger context of life's natural cycles, like a dry season following the rain. When menopause happens, we are abandoned at the riverbed's parched edge, as it were. But surely, this is not the end. It cannot be. Another cycle must begin.

In my experience, womanhood is about cycles within cycles. From the archetypal maiden to the mother to the crone, I have always felt both inside and outside of time in each role, shifting and transforming, from creator to sustainer and destroyer, in what I can only describe as watery ways. I have never been particularly conscious of the four phases of the menstrual cycle – the menstrual phase, the follicular phase, ovulation and luteal phase – but the lore of lunar cycles exerting an influence on me feels real. Inside us, ancient stories circulate, and dreams gush through our veins ruled by tidal forces. A woman does not dream alone, but she moves the village to dream with her.

Until my ovaries stopped releasing eggs, I had never felt the biological ache to be a mother. I asked myself, why was that? In those moments of confusion and hurt, all I wanted was someone to tell me how to live. But to whom could I turn to for comfort? My doctors could only offer me prescriptions for the post-menopausal symptoms or the latest technological solutions to my sudden desire for motherhood. Much of contemporary medical advice has been shaped by the outdated male-dominated medical community bending their professional opinions to market pharma-backed hormone replacement therapy. It soon dawned on me that I needed female friends.

My mother had passed away a few months before I was diagnosed with cancer, so I had to seek out wild matriarchs and surrogate mothers. I had always cultivated relationships with older

women whose faces spoke as frankly as their words. Like my
Neeta Auntie for instance, who is more of a friend and confidante.
Her blowsy beauty alludes to a life of pleasure-seeking without a
care for the world's lacerating looks. 'I've had my kids. Now, I live for myself,' she told me. 'And my
period – I don't even remember when it stopped. I just use extra
lubrication now for my skin and down there, you know.'

Here then rests an opportunity to relinquish the inherited
power struggle that dogged most female relationships in my
younger years: Are you my rival? Or my ally? Who are we to
each other? How do we bask in each other's presence without
overshadowing the other? I had longed for sisterhood, but it
wasn't until my bleeding stopped that forming female ties became
effortless. And essential. It was a splash of cold water to the face.
Perhaps salvation lies not in blood ties, but in composites, in
tribes of women who instinctively bind themselves to each other.
Like kindred water spirits, we nurture one another by sharing
experiences and evolving together to accept the remnants of what
we once were.

Entering the 'meno-period' means I am no longer young, no
longer the object of desire, or the succulent ingénue. There will
be gutting around my hips and bum. After menopause, the full
stop of my period, I am no longer jam. Metaphorically speaking,
conventional ideas of menopausal women bring to mind dried
riverbeds and cracks on the pavement stained by the colours of
Holi, a shade of rust. Everything desiccated, the remains of the
party. The effluvia, the aroma of a possibility, passed.

Did I mention I had never longed to be a mother until the
possibility was taken away? Time. Time is always calling, shaping
our desires before we know it. Blood no longer drips and runs
down my inner thigh, spots my white jeans. But gradually, as

I healed from cancer and felt my pulse stronger than before, I started seeing the fact of my early menopause in a different light. I am not frozen or frigid. Rather, my blood is all mine. Since it was the diagnosis of multiple myeloma, a blood cancer, that triggered the premature menopause, it was a doubly powerful realization. I found myself entering the cycle of consolidation, the blood inside me seething between shore and shallows, alloying the elements that give me life and imagination. Replenishing myself. For myself.

In the beginning, striding out to meet the world as a menopausal woman filled me with apprehension. I began taking oestrogen and other replacement hormones. Even so, I noticed there was a subtle shift in how I was being perceived. It was a primal instinct and reaction. No longer a pomegranate, I was a fruitless tree. Or even better, a hothouse, growing myself in new and reckless ways, throwing off a long, primeval past.

I should clarify that my period never held me back, but this phase contains a surplus of grace. I met my husband and married him, post menopause. I wrote my first book. I moved across four Asian cities. My children were carried in another woman's womb and born when I turned forty-six. It might even appear that this phase marks a release from constrictions and self-imprisonment, a wildly fertile cycle. I have to admit there are times I look down at my thighs and midriff and wonder: how have I lost control of my body? Menopausal weight gain is real. I will never have the same silhouette I had at twenty. And that's all right. I see my mother's hands and sturdy arms expressing themselves in me, and it gives me comfort that this potent vein of connection is alive in my tissues and hips.

The postmenopausal period is as intrinsic a part of creation as the bleeding womb. No matter how it comes to a woman, whether as instant impact or perimenopausal flashes, and no matter how many times you have heard it, the end of fertility is not the decline of a woman. Menopause middle spread be damned! This phase should not be defined as deficiency by the one terrible thing that marks both menstruation and menopause – shame. Instead, it must be acknowledged for what it is – a passage to stature and empowerment.

Biographical Notes

Farah Ahamed is a human rights lawyer and writer. Her essays and short fiction have been published in anthologies and journals including *The White Review*, *Ploughshares*, *The Massachusetts' Review* and *The Mechanics' Institute Review*. Her short story 'Hot Mango Chutney Sauce' was shortlisted for the 2022 Commonwealth Short Story Prize. You can read more of her writing at farahahamed.com. Farah and her sisters have been involved in raising awareness about menstruation and increasing access to menstrual products in Kenya for more than a decade. Find out about their work at www.pantieswithpurpose.com.

Granaz Baloch is a PhD student researching water resource management, gender and violence with a particular focus on the gendered aspects of household water management in the rural areas of Balochistan, Pakistan. Her aim is to elevate the voices of Baloch women who have been excluded from policy and planning around water scarcity. Her forthcoming book, *A Glass of Water and Women: Stories from Balochistan*, will give visibility to the hidden and untold aspects of women's and girls' lives around disability, violence and denial of access to school and proper health facilities.

Siba Barkataki is Assistant Professor in the Department of French and Francophone Studies, English and Foreign Languages University (EFLU), Hyderabad. Her areas of specialization are the Swiss Francophone writings of C. F. Ramuz, memory of indenture in Indian Ocean literature and teaching French as a foreign language. She is also a professional translator.

Alnoor Bhimani is Professor of Management Accounting and the Director of the South Asia Centre at the London School of Economics and Political Science. His research interests include the digitalization of business, governance and economic factors driving societal changes. He sits on the advisory boards of universities in Asia, America, Africa and Europe. He is also Honorary Dean of the Suleman Dawood School of Business at the Lahore University of Management Sciences, the first 'period-friendly' university in Pakistan. The business school is the first to offer a 50 per cent scholarship to every woman admitted to a graduate programme.

Srilekha Chakraborty is a PhD scholar and sociologist working on gender and reproductive health rights with tribal communities in India. She uses art to promote sustainable behavioural change through her Change.org campaign 'Periods Pe Charcha' (Let's Talk Periods). In 2019, her work was recognized by the Ministry of Women and Child Development, India. In 2020, she represented the Global Shaper Community at the World Economic Forum, Davos and was awarded the IRC–WASH International Ton Schouten Award for her advocacy and storytelling skills to bring improvement in sanitation and hygiene.

Shashi Deshpande is an Indian writer based in Bangalore and has written ten novels, one crime novel, a number of short stories, a book of essays and a literary memoir *Listen to Me*. She has also translated works from Kannada and Marathi into English. Her latest book is a collection of essays titled *Subversions*. She has always attempted to make women's lives visible and their voices heard through her writings.

Tishani Doshi writes poetry, essays and fiction. One of her most recent books, *Girls Are Coming Out of the Woods*, was shortlisted for the Ted Hughes Award, and her novel *Small Days and Nights* was shortlisted for the RSL Ondaatje Award. Her fourth full-length collection of poetry is titled *A God at the Door*. She lives in Tamil Nadu, India.

Lyla FreeChild is a self-taught artist based in Jaipur, India. Her paintings and pottery work revolve around sexuality, pleasure, trauma, social taboos and feminism. To celebrate the beauty of nudity and the sacred feminine power, she often uses her menstrual fluid in her artworks.

Zinthiya Ganeshpanchan is the founder of the Zinthiya Trust, a charity supporting women and girls to be free from violence and poverty. She has over fifteen years of experience advocating against gender-based violence, promoting women's empowerment and campaigning to end period poverty. She was a Clore Social Foundation Experienced Leader Programme fellow in 2018–19 and a Winston Churchill fellow in 2020–21.

Aditi Gupta runs Menstrupedia, the world's most innovative company when it comes to teaching and learning about periods. She has educated more than 50,000 girls about periods, trained 10,000 educators and impacted the lives of 13 million girls worldwide. Aditi was named in the *Forbes India* 30 under 30 list in 2014 for her work towards breaking taboos around menstruation. She is a TED speaker, a UN Goalkeeper and was listed as one of BBC's 100 influential women in 2015. She was also named one of the 'Most Powerful Women in Business' in 2017 by *Businessworld*.

Anshu Gupta is Founder Director, Goonj and responsible for driving its pioneering work on menstrual health and hygiene in India under the aegis of the Not Just A Piece of Cloth (NJPC) initiative. Goonj was one of the first agencies to include cloth pads and women's menstrual needs as part of their disaster relief work and packs. Gupta is a Ramon Magsaysay awardee and an Ashoka and Schwab Fellow.

Prachi Jain is a development professional who worked for Goonj's menstrual health and hygiene initiative Not Just a Piece of Cloth. Prachi has a master's in Sociology from Ambedkar University, Delhi, and her key areas of interest are gender and sexuality.

Anish Kapoor is internationally recognized as one of the world's leading contemporary artists. Since representing Britain at the 44th Venice Biennale in 1990, where he was awarded the Premio Duemila, and winning the Turner Prize in 1991, he has held major solo exhibitions globally. His work is permanently exhibited in some of the most important international collections and museums. Increasingly renowned for artworks that blur the boundary between architecture and sculpture, many of his public works have become iconic landmarks. Kapoor lives and works in London.

Rupi Kaur is a poet, artist and performer. Her poetry collections, *Milk and Honey* and *The Sun and Her Flowers*, have sold millions of copies and have been translated into over forty languages. Her most recent book, *Home Body*, hit #1 on bestseller lists around the world in its first week. Kaur's work explores themes of love, loss, trauma, healing, feminism and migration. She feels most at home when performing on stage and creating art.

Jaydeep Mandal has been working in the menstrual hygiene sector for the last decade as the founder of Aakar Innovations and Aakar Social Ventures. He is also part of India's Prime Minister's Office and NITI Aayog's Champions of Change team as the only member from the menstrual hygiene sector to provide inputs to the Government of India. Aakar won the Bio-based Materials of the Year Award in 2019 and the Global Bioplastics Award in 2018 for their Anandi pads. Mandal is an engineer with an MBA in Innovations and Entrepreneurship from the Graduate School of Business at Stanford University.

K. Madavane is a retired professor who used to teach at the Jawaharlal Nehru University in Delhi. He completed his PhD on the subject of death in the theatre of the absurd from the same institution. Born in Pondicherry, he has directed over fifty plays in many languages which have been staged internationally. Amongst his most acclaimed plays are *Tughlaq* (Girish Karnad), *Tartuffe* (Moliere), *The Mahabharata* *of Women* (Madavane), *Hamlet* and *Macbeth* (Shakespeare). His collection of short stories, *Mourir à Bénarès*, was translated and published by Picador India in 2018 as *To Die in Benares*. His play *1947: The Man from Lahore* was shortlisted for the Hindu Playwright Award in 2017.

Amna Mawaz Khan is a performance artist trained in the Bharatanatyam, Kathak and Uday Shankar dance styles. She is a political organizer aligned with the Pakistani socialist-feminist movement. On Instagram, she is @amnadabbadoo. She tweets @ Anarchistani.

Sarah Naqvi is an Indian artist based in Mumbai/Amsterdam and largely engages with narratives around religious and societal polarization. Their work centres around art as a tool for activism and amplifies the fight against existing realities. Primarily working with textile, embroidery and found objects, they have a keen interest in puppetry. They were a recipient of The Phenomenal She Award in 2019, conferred by the Indian National Bar Association, and the NID Ford Foundation Grant in 2018.

Ayra Indrias Patras is Assistant Professor in the Department of Political Science at Forman Christian College University in Lahore. She is interested in the intersection of gender, peace and minority rights in Pakistan. She writes about women and marginalized communities and lobbies and advocates for the constitutional rights of religious minorities. She has been working to improve menstrual awareness and health in Punjab, Pakistan for fifteen years.

Victoria Patrick has translated more than seventy books from English to Urdu and published several award-winning poetry collections on women's issues. She has won over sixty awards, including the Best Poetess Award, Sitara-e-Pakistan, Adbi Wirsa Award, ID Shahaba Award, Lyricist Award, Fatima Jinnah Gold

Medal, Silver Jubilee Celebration Award, LCC Award and BM Yad Award. She is also a lyricist and her songs have been sung by Nusrat Fateh Ali Khan and Noor Jehan. She is also known for her radio column 'Hamari Duniya'.

Radha Paudel is an anaesthetic nurse turned author and activist. A survivor of menstrual discrimination, she has dedicated her life to changing the narrative around menstruation by calling for a shift from hygiene to dignity and for a restructuring of gender dynamics in the home. As the founder and CEO of Global South Coalition for Dignified Menstruation (www.dignifiedmenstruation.org), she initiated International Dignified Menstruation Day on 8 December 2019, hosted the first international workshop on dignified menstruation in 2020 and launched five books on the same theme.

Radhika Radhakrishnan is a feminist researcher and a PhD student in the Massachusetts Institute of Technology's doctoral programme in History, Anthropology, Science, Technology and Society (HASTS). Her research focuses on understanding the challenges faced by gender-minoritized communities with emerging digital technologies in India and finding entry points to intervene meaningfully. She also writes for media publications, gives public talks and hosts podcasts on digital rights from an intersectional gender lens. You can read more about Radhakrishnan›s work here: https://radhika-radhakrishnan.com/.

Lisa Ray describes herself as a woman of no fixed address who has enjoyed an accidental career in front of the camera despite an innate terror of being the centre of attention. After publishing her memoir *Close to the Bone*, a memoir about surviving blood cancer, Ray is emboldened to go back into her shell and pursue writing and her passion for the visual arts. She is currently working on her next book and has co-founded an online curated arts-oriented platform called the Upside Space, set to launch before the metaverse takes over our daily lives.

BIOGRAPHICAL NOTES

Mariam Siar is from Afghanistan and now lives in Australia. She is a student at Deakin University in Australia, with a BA and MA in International Relations. Her passion lies in gender equality and poverty alleviation, and she hopes she can contribute to these endeavours through her NGO Afghan Women's Support Group.

Pioneering Pakistani-American artist **Shahzia Sikander** is widely celebrated for expanding and subverting pre-modern and classical Central and South-Asian miniature painting traditions and launching the form known today as neo-miniature art. Her innovative work has led to survey exhibitions at the Morgan Library, the Hirshhorn Museum, the Whitney Museum of American Art and the MFA Houston Museum. A member of RISD's Board of Trustees, she has won numerous awards, including a MacArthur "Genius" Fellowship and the National Medal of Arts.

Shashi Tharoor, a third-term Member of Parliament for Thiruvananthapuram, India, is the bestselling author of twenty-three books, both fiction and non-fiction, besides being a former Under Secretary-General of the United Nations and a former Minister of State for Human Resource Development and for External Affairs in the Government of India. He is the recipient of numerous awards, including the Pravasi Bharatiya Samman, a Commonwealth Writers' Prize and the Crossword Lifetime Achievement Award. In 2019, he was also awarded the Sahitya Akademi Award in the category of 'English Non-Fiction' for his book *An Era of Darkness*. He chairs the Parliament's Standing Committee on Information Technology.

Meera Tiwari is an associate professor of Global Development at the University of East London. Her research interests lie in UNICEF's sustainable development goals (SDGs), poverty reduction and exploring social and economic poverties within the framework of the Capability Approach. She has experience of field research in India, Ethiopia, Tanzania, Brazil, Lebanon and East London and has published widely on several dimensions of deprivation that marginalized communities experience.

Tashi Zangmo is a founding director of the Bhutan Nuns Foundation (BNF), a non-profit organization established in 2009 under the patronage of Her Majesty the Queen Mother, Tshering Yangdoen Wangchuck. The foundation is committed to ensuring that all Buddhist nuns in the country and other women and young girls at the grassroots enjoy improved living conditions, quality education and self-reliance, thus enabling women's successful participation in the socio-economic development of Bhutan. In 2012, she was awarded the Mary Lyon Award by Mount Holyoke College. She was listed among BBC's Top 100 Influential Women in 2018.

Copyright Acknowledgements

Photo and Illustration Credits

Notes

The Christian Women Sweepers of Lahore

1. Asif Aqeel, 'Christians required only as sweepers,' *The Friday Times*, 23 October 2015. Available at: https://www.thefridaytimes. com/christians-required-only-as-sweepers/.
2. Asif Aqeel and Mary Gill, 'Shame and Stigma in Sanitation,' *Centre for Law and Justice, Lahore*. Available at: https://docplayer. net/183708047-Shame-and-stigma-in-sanitation.html.
3. "ANI, 'Minority Sentiments Hurt by Ad Carried by Pakistan Daily,' *South Asia Learning Multimedia News Agency*, 31 August 2018. Available at: https://www.aninews.in/news/world/ asia/minority-sentiments-hurt-by-ad-carried-by-pakistan-daily201808312148300001/.
4. John O'Brien, *The Unconquered People: The Liberation Journey of the Oppressed Caste* (Karachi: Oxford University Press, 2012), 260–61.
5. Asif Aqeel and Ayra Indrias Patras, 'Punjabi Christians' Disconnect and Denial of Their History,' *International Conference on the Punjabi History and Culture Vol II*, ed. Sajid Mehmood Awan et al. (Islamabad: Centre for Excellence Quaid-e-Azam University, 2020), 593–4.
6. Aisha Khan et al., 'Analytical Study on Provision of Public Toilet in Lahore City,' *Journal of Research in Architecture and Planning* 26, no. 25 (2019). Available at: https://jrap.neduet.edu.pk/arch-journal/JRAP_2019(FirstIssue)/03.pdf .

7. Khalid Sindhu, 'One Public Toilet for Every 1 Million Lahoris,' *The News International*, 14 October 2018. Available at: https://www.thenews.com.pk/tns/detail/566488-one-public-toilet-every-1-million-lahoris.

8. 'Dispelling Religious Myths around Menstruation in Pakistan,' *UNICEF*, 12 July 2018. Available at: https://www.unicef.org/rosa/stories/dispelling-religious-myths-around-menstruation-pakistan.

9. Joar Svanemyr, Qadeer Baig, and Venkatraman Chandra-Mouli. 'Scaling up of Life Skills Based Education in Pakistan: A Case Study,' *Sex Education* 15, no. 3 (2015): 257. Available at: https://doi.org/10.1080/14681811.2014.1000454.

10. Waqar Ali et al., 'Awareness and Practices regarding menstrual hygiene in Female Patients of Rehman Medical Institute,' *JKCD*, 9 no. 4 (2019): 3. Available at: https://www.researchgate.net/profile/Haider-Sami-2/publication/338411470_awareness_and_practices_regarding_menstrual_hygiene_in_female_patients_of_rehman_medical_institute/links/5e1374d9a6fdcc28375a2bcf/awareness-and-practices-regarding-menstrual-hygiene-in-female-patients-of-rehman-medical-institute.pdf.

11. 'Menstrual Hygiene Management in Pakistan,' *IRSP*, 13 November 2017. Available at: http://irsp.org.pk/menstrual-hygiene-management-pakistan/.

12. Adnan Lodhi, 'Shocking: "Padman" banned in Pakistan,' *Express Tribune*, 10 February 2018. Available at: https://tribune.com.pk/story/1631295/4-shocking-padman-banned-pakistan.

13. Sana Tajuddin in an email to the author dated 29 February 2020.

14. Matt Payton, 'Students Are Covering Their University Walls with Sanitary Pads for an Important Reason," *Independent*, 18 April 2016. Available at: https://www.independent.co.uk/news/world/asia/pakistani-students-university-sanitary-towels-protest-sexism-period-taboo-a6982631.html.

15. Aurat March Lahore (@auratmarchlahore), 'Menstrual Hygiene Camp.' Instagram photo, 5 March 2021. Available at: https://www.instagram.com/p/CMCxxjPHybI/.

Menstrupedia: India's Myth-busting Comic Book Guide

1. 'The Journey of Menstrual Hygiene Management in India | #ThePadEffect,' *Feminism in India*, 19 May 2017. Available at: https://feminisminindia.com/2017/05/19/journey-menstrual-hygiene-management-india/.

Periods Are Never Easy: Coping with Menstruation in Afghanistan

1. *Formative Research on Menstrual Hygiene Management in Afghanistan: Knowledge, Perceptions and Experiences of Adolescent Girls*, UNICEF, August 2016. Available at: http://www.wins4girls.org/resources/2016%20Afghanistan%20Final%20Report%20MHM.pdf.
2. Sahar Fetrat, 'Afghanistan – Menstruation Challenges for Afghan Girls,' *WUNRN*. Available at: https://wunrn.com/2016/07/afghanistan-menstruation-challenges-for-afghan-girls/.
3. Ibid.
4. Zahida Stankezai. 'It Was Almost Surreal,' *UNICEF Afghanistan*, 21 November 2018. Available at: https://www.unicef.org/afghanistan/stories/it-was-almost-surreal.
5. *Formative Research on Menstrual Hygiene Management …*, UNICEF, August 2016
6. 'Let Us Break the Taboos and Silence.' *UNICEF Afghanistan*, 30 October 2018. Available at: https://www.unicef.org/afghanistan/stories/let-us-break-taboos-and-silence.
7. Sahar Fetrat, 'Afghanistan – Menstruation Challenges for Afghan Girl.'
8. Ibid.
9. Ruchi Kumar, 'In Afghanistan, Making Menstruation Mentionable,' *Undark Magazine*, 30 September 2019. Available at: https://undark.org/2019/02/18/afghanistan-menstruation-taboo/.

10. Zahida Stankezai. 'It Was Almost Surreal,' *UNICEF Afghanistan*.
11. Sue Cavill, *Menstrual Hygiene in South Asia: Synthesis Report*, 2021. Available at: https://washmatters.wateraid.org/sites/g/files/jkxoof256/files/menstrual-hygiene-in-south-asia---synthesis-report.pdf.
12. Sahar Fetrat, 'Afghanistan – Menstruation Challenges for Afghan Girl.'

Red Dye on a Pad: Two Transwomen on their Experience of Menstruation

1. Zofeen T Ebrahim, 'Don't We Count? Transgender Pakistanis Feel Sidelined by Census,' *Reuters*, 7 October 2017. Available at: https://www.reuters.com/article/pakistan-transgender-census-idUSL8N1ME398.
2. Jon Boone, 'Pakistan Transgender Leader Calls for End to Culture of "Gurus",' *Guardian*, 25 December 2016. Available at: https://www.theguardian.com/society/2016/dec/25/pakistan-transgender-leader-culture-of-gurus--nadeem-kashish#:~:text=A%20leader%20of%20Pakistan's%20historic,unwanted%20children%20into%20their%20care.
3. Arya Karijo, 'Pakistan's Trans Community Is Still Living with the Violence of Empire,' O*penDemocracy, 30 March 2021*. Available at: https://www.opendemocracy.net/en/5050/pakistans-trans-community-is-still-living-with-the-violence-of-empire/.
4. Asif Mehmood, 'Transgender community: Lahore Embraces Its Pariahs,' Tribune, 23 October 2019. Available at: https://tribune.com.pk/story/2085142/1-transgender-community-lahore-embraces-pariahs/.
5. Kajiro, 'Pakistan's Trans Community,' *OpenDemocracy*.
6. Ibid.

My Menstrual Rights Bill: Awakening a Nation

1. Latika Vashist, 'The Terms of Consent: On the Farooqui Verdict,' *Hindu*, 4 October 2017. Available at: https://www.thehindu.com/opinion/op-ed/the-terms-of-consent/article19797667.ece
2. 'Confusing Consent — On the Farooqui Verdict,' *Hindu*, 28 September 2017. Available at: https://www.thehindu.com/opinion/editorial/confusing-consent/article19764181.ece
3. Iyengar, Kirti, and Kristina Gemzell Danielsson, 'A Need for Overhaul of Policy on Contraception and Abortion in India,' *The Lancet Global Health* 6, no. 1 (2018). Available at: https://doi.org/10.1016/s2214-109x(17)30473-4.
4. Menaka Rao, 'India's Harrowing Legal System Forces Even Rape Victims to Bear Unwanted Babies,' *Quartz India*, 29 July 2016. Available at: https://qz.com/india/745396/indias-harrowing-legal-system-forces-even-rape-victims-to-bear-unwanted-babies/
5. Sailee Dhayalkar, 'Bombay HC Allows Nashik Woman to Terminate 30-week Pregnancy,' *Indian Express*, 22 September 2018. Available at: https://indianexpress.com/article/cities/mumbai/bombay-hc-allows-nashik-woman-to-terminate-30-week-pregnancy-5369236/
'India Media Storm over 10-year-old Pregnant Rape Victim,' *BBC*, 7 August 2017. Available at: https://www.bbc.com/news/world-asia-india-40823438.
'Denied Abortion By Supreme Court, 10-Year-Old Chandigarh Rape Victim Delivers Baby Girl Through C-Section,' *India Times*, 9 January 2018. Available at: https://www.indiatimes.com/news/india/denied-abortion-by-supreme-court-10-year-old-chandigarh-rape-victim-delivers-baby-girl-through-c-section-328019.html.
'Supreme Court Allows Two Minor Rape Victims to Terminate Pregnancies,' *Times of India*, 21 September 2017. Available at: https://timesofindia.indiatimes.com/india/supreme-court-

allows-two-minor-rape-victims-to-terminate-pregnancies/articleshow/60783618.cms.

'Mumbai's Minor Rape Survivor, Battling Cancer, Seeks Termination of 24-week Pregnancy,' *Hindustan Times*, 13 September 2018. Available at: https://www.hindustantimes.com/mumbai-news/mumbai-s-minor-rape-survivor-battling-cancer-seeks-termination-of-24-week-pregnancy/story-AMohtlNUCBXm2031uW1emN.html.

6. Amit Anand Choudhury, 'SC: Raped Minors Should Get Quick Nod for Abortion,' *Times of India*, 27 August 2017. Available at: https://www.pressreader.com/india/the-times-of-india-mumbai-edition/20170827/282278140461713.

7. Rashmi Verma, 'About 23 Per Cent Girls Drop out of School on Reaching Puberty,' *Down to Earth*, 15 January 2018. Available at: https://www.downtoearth.org.in/blog/health/23-girls-drop-out-of-school-on-reaching-puberty-59496.

Right to Bleed at the Workplace

1. Pallavi Latthe, et al., 'Dysmenorrhea,' *American Family Physician*, 15 February 2012. Available at: https://www.aafp.org/afp/2012/0215/p386.html.

2. J. Chawla, 'Mythic Origins of Menstrual Taboo in Rig Veda,' *Economic and Political Weekly* 29, no. 43 (1994): pp. 2817–827.

3. U. Chakravarti, 'Conceptualising Brahmanical Patriarchy in Early India: Gender, Caste, Class and State,' *Economic and Political Weekly* 28, no. 14 (1993): pp. 579–85.

4. B. R. Ambedkar, *Castes in India: Their Mechanism, Genesis and Development. Readings in Indian Government and Politics Class, Caste, Gender*, 2004, pp.131–53.

5. E. M. Whelan, 'Attitudes toward Menstruation,' *Studies in Family Planning* 6, no. 4 (1975): pp. 106–108.

6. E. Westermarck, *Ritual and Belief in Morocco* (New York:Macmillan and Company, 1926).

7. International Institute for Population Sciences (IIPS) and ICF, *National Family Health Survey (NFHS-4), 2015-16*, IIPS Mumbai, 2017, p. 82. Available at: http://rchiips.org/nfhs/NFHS-4Reports/India.pdf.

8. 'One in Five Men Have Erectile DYSFUNCTION. 90% of Women EXPERIENCE PMS. Guess Which ONE Researchers Study More,' *Independent*, 19 August 2016. Available at: https://www.independent.co.uk/news/science/pms-erectile-dysfunction-studies-penis-problems-period-pre-menstrual-pains-science-disparity-a7198681.html

9. *Unveiled Realities: A Study on Women's Experiences with Depo-Provera, an Injectable Contraceptive* (SAMA, 2003).

10. J. Chawla, 'Mythic Origins of Menstrual Taboo in Rig Veda,' (1994).

11. 'Questions and Answers about the Workplace Rights of Muslims, Arabs, South Asians, and Sikhs under the Equal Employment Opportunity Laws,' *US Equal Employment Opportunity Commssion*, 19 January 2017. Available at: https://www.eeoc.gov/facts/backlash-employee.html.

12. Monisha Rajesh, 'We Bleed. Accept it and Deal with It': Breaking India's Taboo on Menstruation,' *Guardian*, 3 December 2015. Available at: https://www.theguardian.com/lifeandstyle/2015/dec/03/we-bleed-accept-it-and-deal-with-it-breaking-indias-taboo-on-menstruation.

Blood on My Chair: The Need for Period-friendly Workplaces in Bangladesh

1. 'Bangladesh BD: Labour Force Participation Rate: Modeled ILO Estimate: Female: % of Female Population Aged 15+,' *CEIC*. Available at: https://www.ceicdata.com/en/bangladesh/labour-force/bd-labour-force-participation-rate-modeled-ilo-estimate-female--of-female-population-aged-15.

'Bangladesh BD: Labour Force Participation Rate: Modeled

ILO Estimate: Male: % of Male Population Aged 15+.' *CEIC*. Available at: https://www.ceicdata.com/en/bangladesh/labour-force/bd-labour-force-participation-rate-modeled-ilo-estimate-male--of-male-population-aged-15.

2. 'Female Unemployment in Bangladesh: Are We on the Right Track?' *LightCastle Partners*, 9 November 2020. Available at: https://www.lightcastlebd.com/insights/2020/10/female-unemployment-in-bangladesh-are-we-on-the-right-track/.

   See also, 'Bangladesh: Female-to-Male Ratio in Work Environment by Type 2016,' *Statista*, 9 November 2021. Available at: https://www.statista.com/statistics/918552/bangladesh-female-to-male-ratio-ratio-in-work-environment-by-type/.

3. 'Female Unemployment in Bangladesh …,' *LightCastle Partners*.

4. 'Bangladesh Can Prosper with More and Better Jobs for Women, Report Says,' *World Bank* , 29 April 2019. Available at: https://www.worldbank.org/en/news/press-release/2019/04/28/bangladesh-more-and-betters-jobs-for-women-needed-for-faster-growth.

5. 'Female Unemployment in Bangladesh …,' *LightCastle Partners*.

6. 'Almost 90% of Men/Women Globally Are Biased Against Women." *UNDP*, 5 March 2020. Available at: https://www.undp.org/press-releases/almost-90-menwomen-globally-are-biased-against-women.

7. Deutsche Welle, 'Bangladesh Garment Workers Face Menstruation Taboos,' *Taiwan News*, 23 October 2019. Available at: https://www.taiwannews.com.tw/en/news/3802055.

8. Ibid.

9. Maiya Falach, 'Period Poverty in Bangladesh,' *The Borgen Project*, 6 October 2020. Available at: https://borgenproject.org/period-poverty-in-bangladesh/.

10. Ibid.

11. 'Bangladesh Can Prosper with More and Better Jobs for Women, Report Says,' *World Bank*.

12. Deutsche Welle, 'Bangladesh Garment Workers Face Menstruation Taboos,' *Taiwan News*.

13. Ibid.

14. 'No Maternity Leave for Workers, Though Mentioned in Law,' *Dhaka Tribune*, 12 May 2018. Available at: https://archive. dhakatribune.com/bangladesh/2018/05/13/no-maternity-leave-for-workers-though-mentioned-in-law.

15. 'Budget FY22: VAT Exemption on Sanitary Napkin Production Proposed,' *Dhaka Tribune*, 3 June 2021. Available at: https:// archive.dhakatribune.com/business/economy/2021/06/03/ budget-fy22-vat-exemption-on-sanitary-napkin-production-proposed.

16. 'Female Unemployment in Bangladesh ...,' *LightCastle Partners*.

17. 'Human Rights,' *United Nations*. Available at: https://www. un.org/en/%E2%80%9Cclose-home%E2%80%9D-universal-declaration-human-rights-0.

Red Nectar of the Sacred Lotus: A Buddhist Persepctive on Menstruation

1. 'Restricted Area for Women in Thailand,' *Wikigender*. Available at: https://www.wikigender.org/wiki/restricted-area-for-women-in-thailand-why/#:~:text=to%20Buddhist%20beliefs.-,Understanding%20Buddhism%20in%20Thailand,which%20 restricts%20women%20from%20entering.

2. 'Culture and Menstruation,' *Wikipedia*, 18 March 2022. Available at: https://en.wikipedia.org/wiki/Culture_and_menstruation.

3. 'The Position of Women in Buddhism,' *Tsemrinpoche*, 4 November 2013. Available at: https://www.tsemrinpoche.com/tsem-tulku-rinpoche/external-article/the-position-of-women-in-buddhism.

4. 'Women in Buddhism,' *Buddhist Studies: Buddha Dharma Education Association and BuddhaNet*. Available at: http://www. buddhanet.net/e-learning/history/wbq21.htm.

5. Sadhguru, 'Sadhguru on Temple Entry for Women and Dalits,'

YouTube video, 27 May 2016. Available at: https://www.youtube.
com/watch

Increased Period Poverty during Covid-19 in Lahore, Pakistan

1. 'Steps Sought to Stop possible Rise in Domestic Violence,' *Dawn*, 6 April 2020. Available at: https://www.dawn.com/news/1546756.
2. S. Ali, 'In Lockdown, Sanitory Napkins Become a Luxury,' *Tribune*, 20 April 2020. Available at: https://tribune.com.pk/story/2205396/lockdown-sanitary-napkins-become-luxury.
3. 'Gendered Voices in Pakistan's COVID-19 Field: Issues and Needed Actions: 28 April 28 2020,' Shirkat Gah Women's Resource Centre, 28 April 2020. Available at: https://www.docdroid.net/RIeF6jT/shirkat-gah-covid-19-brief-issue-1-pdf.
4. S. S. Asim , Samrah Ghani, et al, 'Assessing Mental Health of Women Living in Karachi During the Covid-19 Pandemic,' *Front Glob Women's Health*, 12 January 2021. Available at: https://pubmed.ncbi.nlm.nih.gov/34816167/.
5. C. Wenhem, J. Smith, and R. Morgan, 'Covid-19: The Gendered Impacts of the Outbreak,' *The Lancet*, 395, no. 10227 (2020): 846–8.
6. S.S. Asim, Samrah Ghani, et al, 'Assessing Mental Health of Women Living in Karachi …'

Menstruation in Fiction: The Authorial Gaze

1. Maria Popova, 'Anaïs Nin on Writing, the Future of the Novel,' *Marginalian*, 18 September 2015. Available at: https://www.themarginalian.org/2013/09/20/anais-nin-on-writing-1947/.
2. Raza Naeem, 'Remembering Ismat Chughtai, Urdu's Wicked Woman,' *Wire*, 27 October 2019. Available at: https://thewire.in/books/remembering-ismat-chughtai-urdus-wicked-woman.
3. Umer Nangiana, '"Women Are Still Impure in the Land of the Pure",' *Tribune*, 21 September 2011. Available at: https://tribune.

com.pk/story/256686/women-are-still-impure-in-the-land-of-the-pure.

4. Raza Naeem, 'Fahmida Riaz, Our New Aqleema,' *Wire*, 18 December 2018. Available at: https://thewire.in/books/fahmida-riaz-our-new-aqleema.

5. Theresa C. Dintino, 'Women Writers on Writing: Virginia Woolf's "Angel In The House" and What It Takes to Be a #Nastywoman,' *Nasty Women Writers*, 24 September 2019. Available at: https://www.nastywomenwriters.com/virginia-woolfs-angel-in-the-house-and-what-it-takes-to-be-a-nastywoman/.

6. Maria Popova, 'No Place for Self-Pity, No Room for Fear: Toni Morrison on the Artist's Task in Troubled Times,' *Marginalian*, 9 March 2018. Available at: https://www.themarginalian.org/2016/11/15/toni-morrison-art-despair/.

A Caregiver's Perspective on Managing Menstrual Hygiene

1. 'Pakistan: Cousin Marriages Create High Risk of Genetic Disorders: DW: 07.02.2022.' *Deutsche Welle*. Available at: https://www.dw.com/en/pakistan-cousin-marriages-create-high-risk-of-genetic-disorders/a-60687452.

2. Farooq Azam Rathore and Sahibzada Nasir Mansoor, 'Disability Rights and Management in Pakistan: Time to Face the Bitter Truth,' *Journal of the College of Physicians and Surgeons Pakistan 2019* 29, no. 12 (2019): 1131–32. Available at: https://www.jcpsp.pk/archive/2019/Dec2019/01.pdf.

3. Ibid.

4. Leah Rodriguez and Gaëlle Langué, 'This Pakistani Activist Created an App to Deliver Menstrual Products to People with Disabilities,'" *Global Citizen*, 17 May 2017. Available at: https://www.globalcitizen.org/en/content/girlythings-pakistan-period-products-disabilities/.

308 NOTES

Digitizing Menstruation: Algorithms for Cleansing Bodies

1. M. Douglas, *Purity and Danger: An Analysis of Concepts of Pollution and Taboo*, London: Routledge, 2002.
2. J. Frazer, *The Golden Bough*, New York: Macmillan, 1951.
3. M. L. Søndergaard, 'Sharing the Abject in Digital Culture,' *Excessive Research* (blog), 28 September 2015. Available at: https://transmedialeblog.wordpress.com/2015/09/28/marie-louise-sondergaard-sharing-the-abject-in-digital-culture/.
4. E. Goldberg, 'All the Inconceivable Ways Women Deal with Their Periods Worldwide,' *HuffPost*, 7 December 2017. Available at: https://www.huffpost.com/entry/menstruation-myths_n_7495568.
5. C. M. Røstvik, C. M. (2018) 'Blood in the Shower: A Visual History of Menstruation and Clean Bodies,' *Visual Culture & Gender*, 13 (2018): pp. 54–63. Available at: http://www.vcg.emitto.net/index.php/vcg/article/view/114.
6. S. B. Webster, 'The History of the Curse: A Comparative Look at the Religious and Social Taboos of Menstruation and the Influence They Have on American Society Today,' MA thesis, University of North Carolina, 2017.
7. Uta Ranke Heinemann, 'Female Blood: The Ancient Taboo and its Christian Consequences,' in André Deutsch (Ed.) *Eunuchs for Heaven*, London, 1990, pp. 12–17. Retrieved from: https://web.archive.org/web/20081229154303/http://www.womenpriests.org/body/ranke.asp.
8. Damien AtHope, 'Are You Aware That There Are Religions That Worship Women Gods, Explain Now Religion Tears Women Down?' *Damien Marie AtHope*, 24 October 2017. Available at: https://damienmarieathope.com/2017/10/are-you-aware-that-there-are-religions-that-worship-women-gods-explain-now-religion-tears-women-down/?v=32aec8db952d.

9. J. Chrisler 'Leaks, Lumps, and Lines: Stigma and Women's Bodies,' *Psychology of Women Quarterly* 35 (2011): pp. 202–214.
10. T. Buckley and A. Gottlieb, 'Introduction: A Critical Appraisal of Theories of Menstrual Symbolism,' in *Blood Magic: The Anthropology of Menstruation*. Berkeley: University of California Press, 1988.
11. 'The Dawn of the Femtech Revolution,' *McKinsey & Company*, 15 February 2022. Available at: https://www.mckinsey.com/industries/healthcare-systems-and-services/our-insights/the-dawn-of-the-femtech-revolution.
12. 'Femtech Market to Reach USD 60.01 Billion by 2027: Cagr of 15.6%: Emergen Research,' *Cision PR Newswire*, 14 September 2020. Available at: https://www.prnewswire.co.uk/news-releases/femtech-market-to-reach-usd-60-01-billion-by-2027-cagr-of-15-6-emergen-research-899205870.html.
13. A. French, K. Sharma, F. Regalado and L. Hoang, 'Asia's Femtech Revolution: The Quest for Better Women's Health,' *Financial Times*, 8 March 2022. Available at: https://www.ft.com/content/55459493-cf69-450c-b9c1-0c356347de97.
14. 'Pakistan Ranked Least Internet Inclusive Country in South Asia: Report,' *Asia News Network*, 6 March 2020. Available at: https://asianews.network/pakistan-ranked-least-internet-inclusive-country-in-south-asia-report/.
15. J. Levy and N. Romo-Avilés, 'A Good Little Tool to Get to Know Yourself a Bit Better: A Qualitative Study on Users' Experiences of App-supported Menstrual Tracking in Europe,' *BMC Public Health*, 19 (2019): pp. 2–11.
16. A. Karlsson. 'A Room of One's Own? Using Period Trackers to Escape Menstrual Stigma,' *Nordicom Review*, 40 (Special Issue 1) (2019): pp. 111–23.
17. S. Phade, 'What's a Prosumer and Are You One?' *Future Proof*, 7 May 2018. Available at: https://www.futuresplatform.com/blog/whats-prosumer-and-are-you-one.

18. Elizabeth Bacharach, Ashley Martens and Sarah Bradley, 'The 11 Best Period Tracker Apps to Get to Know Your Cycle According to Ob-Gyns,' *Women's Health*, 20 December 2021. Available at: https://www.womenshealthmag.com/health/g26787041/best-period-tracking-apps/.
19. Ibid.
20. Ibid.
21. H. Nissenbaum, *Privacy in Context: Technology, Policy and the Integrity of Social Life*, California, Stanford University Press, 2010.
22. R. Sanders, 'Self-tracking in the Digital Era: Biopower, Patriarchy, and the New Biometric Body Projects,' *Body and Society*, 23 no. 1 (2017): pp. 36–63.
23. M. Rajagopalan, 'Period Tracker Apps Used by Millions of Women are Sharing Incredibly Sensitive Data with Facebook,' *BuzzFeed News*, 9 September 2019. Available at: https://www.buzzfeednews.com/article/meghara/period-tracker-apps-facebook-maya-mia-fem.
24. S. Brown. 'These Menstrual Tracking Apps Reportedly Shared Sensitive Data with Facebook,' *CNET*, 10 September 2019. Available at: https://www.cnet.com/news/these-menstrual-tracking-apps-reportedly-shared-sensitive-data-with-facebook/.
25. B. Krett 'The Evolution of the Quantified Self: A Conversation with Self-Tracking Pioneer Gary Wolf,' *IFTF*, 1 May 2018. Available at: http://www.iftf.org/future-now/article-detail/the-evolution-of-the-quantified-self/.
26. Sondergaard, 'M. (2016) Sharing the Abject in Digital Culture,' 2015. Available at: https://transmedialeblog.wordpress.com/2015/09/28/marie-louise-sondergaard-sharing-the-abject-in-digital-culture/.
27. J. Delaney, M. J. Lupton and E. Toth, *The Curse: A Cultural History of Menstruation*, New York, Dutton, 1976.
28. L. Dean-Jones, 'Menstrual bleeding according to the Hippocrates and Aristotle,' *Transactions of the American Philosophical Association*, 119 (1989): pp. 177–91.

29. J. Levy and N. Romo-Avilés, "'A Good Little Tool to Get to Know Yourself a Bit Better'": A Qualitative Study on Users' Experiences of App-Supported Menstrual Tracking in Europe,' *BMC Public Health* 19 (2019): p. 1213. Available at: https://doi.org/10.1186/s12889-019-7549-8.

30. 'Why Use a Period Tracker or App?' *Natracare*, 12 August 2021. Available at: https://www.natracare.com/blog/why-use-period-tracker-apps/.

31. L. Worsfold, L. Marriott, S. Johnson and J. Harper, 'Period Tracker Applications: What Menstrual Cycle Information are They Giving Women?' *Womens' Health*, 17 (2021).

32. Dileep Srivastava and S. Gupta 'How to Develop a Women Health Tracking Application?' *Appinventiv*, 27 January 2020. Available at: https://appinventiv.com/blog/women-health-tracking-app-development/.

   D. Lupton, *The Quantified Self: A Sociology of Self-Tracking*, Cambridge, Polity Press, 2016.

33. J. V. Dijck, 'Datafication, Dataism and Dataveillance: Big Data Between Scientific Paradigm and Ideology,' *Surveillance and Society* 12, no. 2 (2014): 197–208.

34. S. Bhattacharya, 'Mending Broken Systems: FemTech Can Radically Change How Medicine Has Neglected Women's Pain Until Now,' *Times of India*, 22 October 2019. Available at: https://timesofindia.indiatimes.com/blogs/toi-edit-page/mending-broken-systems-femtech-can-radically-change-how-medicine-has-neglected-womens-pain-until-now/.

35. B. Kronemyer, 'Female Health Technology Takes Center Stage.,' *Contemporary OB/GYN*, 2018; 63 (2018): 23–24.

36. R. Capurro 'Digitization as an Ethical Challenge,' *AI and Society* 32 (2017): 277–83.

37. J. W. Rettberg, *Seeing Ourselves through Technology: How We Use Selfies, Blogs and Wearable Devices to See and Shape Ourselves*, Basingstoke: Palgrave Macmillan, 2014.

38. Capurro, 'Digitization as an Ethical Challenge,' 2017.

39. Michel Foucault, 'The Ethics of the Concern for Self as a Practice of Freedom,' in P. Rabinow (ed.), *Ethics, Subjectivity and Truth Essential works of Foucault: Volume 1*, New York: New Press, 1997.

40. W. Brown, *Undoing the Demos*, Brooklyn: Zone Books, 2015.

41. Judith Butler, *Bodies that Matter*, New York: Routledge, 1993.

42. K. E. Levy, 'Intimate Surveillance,' *Idaho Law Review* 51, (2015): pp. 679–93.

Bleeding behind Bars: An Account of Menstruation under Incarceration

1. 'Pakistan: Poor Conditions Rife in Women's Prisons,' *Human Rights Watch*, 28 October 2020. Available at: https://www.hrw.org/news/2020/09/07/pakistan-poor-conditions-rife-womens-prisons#.

2. Ibid.

3. Anju Anna John, 'Period Poverty in Prisons: Ensuring Menstrual Hygiene and Dignity in India,' *Penal Reform International*, 23 February 2021. Available at: https://www.penalreform.org/blog/period-poverty-in-prisons-ensuring-menstrual-hygiene-and/.

4. Ibid.

What Has Dignity Got to Do with Menstrual Health?

1. C. Bobel, *The Managed Body*, Switzerland: Palgrave Macmillan, 2019.

2. M. Dickemann, 'A Third Explanation for Female Infanticide,' *Human Ecology*, 9 no. 1 (1981), pp. 97–104.
   J. Dreze and A. Sen, *India: Economic Development and Social Opportunity*, Delhi: Oxford University Press, 1995.
   L. S. Vishwanath, 'Female Infanticide: The Colonial Experience,' *Economic and Political Weekly*, 39 no. 22 (2004), pp. 2313–18.
   T. Patel, *Sex-selective Abortion in India: Gender, Society and Reproductive Technologies.* New Delhi: Sage, 2007.

K. Sen, 'The Lost Girls: Girls Are Still Aborted in States with More Educated Women,' *The Independent*, 14 January 2014. Available at: https://www.independent.co.uk/news/science/the-lost-girls-girls-are-still-aborted-in-states-with-more-educated-women-by-amartya-sen-9059544.html.
3. C. Negash, S. J. Whiting, C. J. Henry, T. Belachew, and T. G. Hailemariam, 'Association between Maternal and Child Nutritional Status in Hula, Rural Southern Ethiopia: A Cross Sectional Study,' *PLoS One*, 10 no. 11 (2015).
P. Y. Goodwin, D. A. Garrett and O. Galal, 'Women and Family Health: The Role of Mothers in PromotingFamily and Child Health,' *International Journal of Global Health and Health Disparities*, 4 no.1 (2005).
4. UNICEF, *Guidance on Menstrual Health and Hygiene*, 2019. Available at: https://www.unicef.org/documents/guidance-menstrual-health-and-hygiene.
5. Plan International, *Break the Barriers: Girls' Experience of Menstruation in the UK*, 2018. Available at: https://plan-uk.org/act-for-girls/girls-rights-in-the-uk/break-the-barriers-our-menstrual-manifesto.
R. Karki and C. Espinosa, 'Breaking Taboos: Menstruation, Female Subordination and Reproductive Health, the Case of India,' *Insights of Anthropology*, 2 no.1 (2018), pp. 111–120.
6. 'The 17 Goals | Sustainable Development,' *United Nations*. Available at: https://sdgs.un.org/goals.
7. NITI Ayog, *SDG India Index Report*, New Delhi, 2018. Available at: https://sdghub.com/project/sdg-india-index-baseline-report-2018/.
8. Ibid.
9. E. Anand, J. Singh and S. Unisa, 'Menstrual Hygiene Practices and its Association with Reproductive Tract Infections and Abnormal Vaginal Discharge among Women in India,' *Sexual and Reproductive Healthcare*, 6 no.4 (2015), pp. 249–54.

10. A. Hutton, 'The Bollywood Film Breaking the Taboo around Periods,' *BBC*, 19 January 2018. Available at: https://www.bbc.co.uk/news/entertainment-arts-42732782. 'Women Empowerment NGO in Munbai,' *Myna Mahila Foundation*, 10 October 2021. Available at: https://mynamahila.com.

11. 'The State of the World's Children 2016 Statistical Tables,' UNICEF, 18 January 2018. Available at: http://data.unicef.org/resources/state-worlds-children-2016-statistical-tables/.

12. *Vocational & Life Skills Training of Out-of-School Adolescent Girls in the Age Group 15-18 Years:National Colloquiam Report*, NCPR, 2017. Available at: https://ncpcr.gov.in/showfile.php?lang=1&devel=1&&sublinkid=1357&lid=1558.

13. Geeta Pandey, 'Period-shaming' Indian College Forces Students to Strip to Underwear,' *BBC*, 16 February 2020. Available at: https://www.bbc.co.uk/news/world-asia-india-51504992.

14. 'Menstrual Hygiene,' *UNICEF*. Available at: https://www.unicef.org/wash/menstrual-hygiene.

15. UNICEF, *Guidance on Menstrual Health and Hygiene*, 2019.

16. R. Sennett, *Respect, in a World of Inequality*, New York: W.W. Norton, 2003.

17. A. Sen, *Development as Freedom*, Oxford: Oxford University Press, 1999.

18. S. Alkire, 'Choosing Dimensions: The Capability Approach and Multidimensional Poverty,' in N. Kakwani and J. Silber (eds.), *The Many Dimensions of Poverty*, New York: Palgrave-MacMillan, 2007.

19. 'Maternal Mortality Rate (MMR)." Press Information Bureau. Available at: https://www.pib.gov.in/PressReleasePage.aspx?PRID=1697441.

20. Balraj Muralidharan Nair and Manicklal Chakraborty, 'Literacy Rate of India 2021 || State Wise Literacy Rate,' *Census of India 2021*, 22 December 2019. Available at: https://censusofindia2021.com/literacy-rate-of-india-2021/.

21. H. Prakash and A. Yadav, 'State Variations in Female Labour Participation in India: A Study of 68th NSS and First Periodic Labour Force Survey,' *Jharkhand Journal of Development and Management Studies XISS, Ranchi* 18, no. 3 and 4 (2020): pp. 8505–19

22. 'Sex Ratio of India 2021 || States & UT Census Data Analysis,' *Census of India 2021*, 14 December 2019. Available at: https://censusofindia2021.com/sex-ratio-of-india-2021/.

23. M. Tiwari, 'Exploring the Role of Capabilities in Social Innovation,' *Journal of Human Development and Capabilities*, 18 no. 2 (2017), pp. 181–96.

24. M. Anderson, 'Making Theatre from Data, Lessons for Performance Ethonography from Verbatim Theatre,' *NJ Drama Australia Journal*, 31 no. 1 (2007), pp. 79–91.

Cloth, Ash and Blood: Conversations with Homeless Women about Menstruation

1. Sumeet Waraich, '7 Realities of Homelessness in Pakistan,' *The Borgen Project*, 3 August 2020. Available at: https://borgenproject.org/wp-content/uploads/The_Borgen_Project_Logo_small.jpg, August 3, 2020. https://borgenproject.org/7-realities-of-homelessness-in-pakistan/.

Sowing the Seeds of a Menstrual Revolution: The First Menstrual Workshop in Balochistan

1. 'Balochistan: Girls Drop out of School at Alarming Rate.' *UNPO*, 10 January 2018. Available at: https://unpo.org/article/20554?id=20554.

2. Mobeen Azhar, 'Gay Pakistan: Where Sex is Available and Relationships Are Difficult.' *BBC*, 27 August 2013. Available at: https://www.bbc.com/news/23811826.

3. 'World Report 2021: Rights Trends in Pakistan' *Human Rights Watch*, 13 January 2021. Available at: https://www.hrw.org/world-report/2021/country-chapters/pakistan#.

4. Meghan Davidson Ladly, 'Gays in Pakistan Move Cautiously to Gain Acceptance,' *New York Times*, 3 November 2012. Available at: https://www.nytimes.com/2012/11/04/world/asia/gays-in-pakistan-move-cautiously-to-gain-acceptance.html.

5. 'Transgender Woman Gul Panra Shot Dead, Friend Wounded in Peshawar,' *TheNews*, 9 September 2020. Available at: https://www.thenews.com.pk/latest/712365-transgender-woman-gul-panra-shot-dead-friend-wounded-in-peshawar.

Memory and Imagination: Reclaiming Menstruation

1. Vandana Shiva, 'Women in the Forest' in *Staying Alive: Ecology, and Development*, London: Zed Books, 1988.

2. Elaine Showalter, 'A Literature of Their Own,' in *Feminist Literary Theory: A Reader*, edited by Mary Eagleton, Oxford: Basil Blackwell, 1986, pp. 11–15.

3. Viviane Forrester, 'What Women's Eyes See, New French Feminisms.' in *Feminist Literary Theory: A Reader*, edited by Mary Eagleton, Oxford: Basil Blackwell, 1986, pp. 34–5.

Acknowledgements

My thanks to all the contributors for agreeing to be part of this book, which is the result of their creative collaboration.

Creativity is a key that opens many doors. It can influence change in a wide range of spheres, spiritual, cultural and political. It is a source of hope, a quest for meaning, an attempt to access the enigma of the self and even the mystery of being. My aim for this anthology was to move away from the conventional to a deeper and more honest cultivation of stories about menstruation. I asked myself: How could the different perspectives be best presented? Who would be the writers and artists to capture the diversity of representations? I found that the answer lay in complete creative liberty. There would be no brief on genre or format, only an invitation to share their individual stories in their own way.

As the book began to take form, a common theme became apparent. At the core of every narrative about menstruation was a call for a greater freedom. This meant the choice to speak openly or remain silent; to stay in a room or leave and go to another; to be admitted to a place of worship and family events. It meant choice relating to education, marriage and what to eat. And symbolic of all basic human needs, the right to a dignified menstrual experience instead of a soiled rag.

For some, writing about menstruation is to trigger a private memory of the earliest onset, which was to influence their future identity and relationships. There is a human impulse to guard and keep private what is intimate to one's body, and it has been my good fortune and sometimes a source of pain, to be the first to read the personal accounts of these contributors. I am privileged to have been allowed glimpses into their pasts, and also their artistic process as they strove to write, paint, dance and tell their stories. For those writers and artists who do not have personal experience, it requires imagination and empathy to tell a story from a different standpoint, which is so essential to the comprehensive nature of this collection.

Some of the contributors had been an influence in my life prior to the conception of the book. Others entered the scene further along its progress. Many were working under constraints of culture, financial and health anxieties, bereavement and domestic pressure. And there were other challenges to overcome such as living in remote locations with power outages and no internet. From small beginnings, my search for them gradually reaped rewards and one avenue I pursued led to another. I am grateful to all for their commitment and generosity. I am equally indebted to the many people I encountered on my travels – amongst them street sellers, cleaners, sex workers, the homeless – who will probably never read this book, but were willing to entrust me with their personal experiences.

The book would not be in its present form without the help and encouragement of my editors Teesta Guha Sarkar, Elizabeth James and the team at Pan Macmillan India. My thanks to them.

I would also like to give a mention to my sisters Neemah and Zarah, and my young nieces Aaliyah and Mischa, whose love and support have sustained me throughout my life and during the gathering together of all the varied elements of this book, and shaping them into a cohesive whole.